CANADIAN LABOUR IN POLITICS

STUDIES IN THE STRUCTURE OF POWER:

DECISION-MAKING IN CANADA

Editor: JOHN MEISEL

1. *In Defence of Canada*: *From the Great War to the Great Depression.* By JAMES EAYRS

2. *The Vertical Mosaic*: *An Analysis of Social Class and Power in Canada.* By JOHN PORTER

3. *In Defence of Canada*: *Appeasement and Rearmament.* By JAMES EAYRS

4. *Canadian Labour in Politics.* By GAD HOROWITZ

5. *Federal-Provincial Diplomacy*: *The Making of Recent Policy in Canada.* By RICHARD SIMEON

6. *In Defence of Canada*: *Peacemaking and Deterrence.* By JAMES EAYRS

7. *The Canadian Public Service*: *A Physiology of Government.* By J. E. HODGETTS

Canadian Labour in Politics

GAD HOROWITZ

UNIVERSITY
OF TORONTO
PRESS

© University of Toronto Press 1968
Toronto and Buffalo

ISBN (casebound) 0-8020-1902-1
ISBN (paperback) 0-8020-6155-9
LC 68-101781

Reprinted 1972, 1977

Printed in the United States of America

T

\00333 8724

STUDIES IN THE STRUCTURE OF POWER

DECISION-MAKING IN CANADA

The series "Studies in the Structure of Power: Decision-Making in Canada" is sponsored by the Social Science Research Council of Canada for the purpose of encouraging and assisting research concerned with the manner and setting in which important decisions are made in fields affecting the general public in Canada. The launching of the series was made possible by a grant from the Canada Council.

Unlike the books in other series supported by the Social Science Research Council, the studies of decision-making are not confined to any one of the disciplines comprising the social sciences. The series explores the ways in which social power is exercised in this country: it will encompass studies done within a number of different conceptual frameworks, utilizing both traditional methods of analysis and those prompted by the social, political, and technological changes following the Second World War.

In establishing the series, the Social Science Research Council has sought to encourage scholars already embarked on relevant studies by providing financial and editorial assistance and similarly to induce others to undertake research in areas of decision-making so far neglected in Canada.

J. M.

For David

Preface

This is a historical study of the relationship between the labour movement and the socialist party in Canada, as that relationship has developed
since the birth of modern industrial unionism. The first chapter is a
theoretical introduction which tries to account for the relative strength
of socialism in Canada as contrasted with the United States.

The main sources were correspondence, minutes, and other materials
in the files of the federal New Democratic party and the Canadian Labour
Congress Political Education Department, and personal interviews with
labour leaders and socialist politicians. Useful material was also discovered in the files of the British Columbia New Democratic party, the
British Columbia Federation of Labour, and the Ontario Federation of
Labour Political Education Department. I should like to express my
gratitude to Michael Oliver, former president of the New Democratic
party, for access to the party files, and to George Home, director of the
CLC Political Education Department, for access to the files of his
department.

I am indebted to Samuel Beer for his patient, helpful supervision of
the doctoral thesis in which this book originated, to Louis Hartz for
reading and commenting on several successive versions of the first
chapter, and to David Lewis and Eugene Forsey for many valuable
comments and suggestions. Of course, I alone am responsible for factual
errors and defective interpretations.

This work has been published with the help of a grant from the Social
Science Research Council, using funds provided by the Canada Council.

G.H.

Contents

CANADIAN LABOUR IN POLITICS

1. *Conservatism, Liberalism, and Socialism in Canada: An Interpretation*

1. INTRODUCTION: THE HARTZIAN APPROACH

In the United States, organized socialism is dead; in Canada socialism, though far from national power, is a significant political force and the official "political arm" of the labour movement. Why these striking differences in the fortunes of socialism in two very similar societies?

Any attempt to account for the differences must be grounded in a general comparative study of the English-Canadian and American societies. It will be shown that the relative strength of socialism in Canada is related to the relative strength of toryism, and to the different position and character of liberalism in the two countries.

In North America, Canada is unique. We cannot understand its uniqueness except by contrasting it with the United States. Yet there is a tendency in Canadian historical and political studies to explain Canadian phenomena not by contrasting them with American phenomena but by identifying them as variations on a basic North American theme. Thus, the Conservative party is seen as the counterpart of Republicanism, the Liberal party is seen as the counterpart of the American Democrats, the party battle before and after Confederation is seen as a Canadian version of the debate between Hamilton and Jefferson, and so on. There is nothing wrong with this approach in itself; I grant that Canada and the United States are similar and that the similarities should be pointed out. But the pan-North American approach, since it searches out and concentrates on similarities, cannot help us to understand Canadian uniqueness. When this approach is applied to the study of English-Canadian socialism, it discovers, first, that like the American variety it is weak, and second, that it is weak for much the same reasons (the fluidity of the class system, the material success of capitalism, and so on).

These discoveries perhaps explain why Canadian socialism is weak in comparison to European socialism; they do not explain why Canadian socialism is so much stronger than American socialism.[1]

The explanatory technique used in this study is that developed by Louis Hartz in *The Liberal Tradition in America*[2] and *The Founding of New Societies*.[3] It is applied to Canada in a mildly pan-North American way by Kenneth McRae in "The Structure of Canadian History," a contribution to the latter book.

The Hartzian approach is to study the new societies founded by Europeans (the United States, English Canada, French Canada, Latin America, Dutch South Africa, Australia) as "fragments" thrown off from Europe. The key to the understanding of ideological development in a new society is its "point of departure" from Europe: the ideologies borne by the founders of the new society are not representative of the historic ideological spectrum of the mother country. The settlers represent only a fragment of that spectrum. The complete ideological spectrum ranges—in chronological order, and from right to left—from feudal or tory through liberal whig to liberal democrat to socialist. French Canada and Latin America are "feudal fragments." They were founded by bearers of the feudal or tory values of the organic, corporate, hierarchical community; their point of departure from Europe is before the liberal revolution. The United States, English Canada, and Dutch South Africa are "bourgeois fragments," founded by bearers of liberal individualism who have left the tory end of the spectrum behind them. Australia is the one "radical fragment," founded by bearers of the working class ideologies of mid-nineteenth-century Britain.

The significance of the fragmentation process is that the new society, having been thrown off from Europe, "loses the stimulus to change that the whole provides."[4] The full ideological spectrum of Europe develops only out of the continued confrontation and interaction of its four elements; they are related to one another, not only as enemies, but as parents and children. A new society which leaves part of the past behind it cannot develop the future ideologies which depend on the continued

---

[1]The 1956 CCF Convention received the following message from the American Social Democratic Federation: "Comradely greetings from the weakest socialist organization in the Western Hemisphere to the strongest one, the CCF of Canada. It is a comfort to have a big strong brother next door to us." CCF Convention Proceedings (1956), p. 8.

[2](New York, 1955), hereafter cited as *Liberal Tradition*.

[3](New York, 1964), hereafter cited as *New Societies*.

[4]*Ibid.*, p. 3.

presence of the past in order to come into being. In escaping the past, the fragment escapes the future, for "the very seeds of the later ideas are contained in the parts of the old world that have been left behind."[5] The ideology of the founders is thus frozen, congealed at the point of origin.[6]

Socialism is an ideology which combines the corporate-organic-collectivist ideas of toryism with the rationalist-egalitarian ideas of liberalism. Both the feudal and the bourgeois fragments escape socialism, but in different ways. A feudal fragment such as French Canada develops no whig (undemocratic) liberalism; therefore it does not develop the democratic liberalism which arises out of and as a reaction against whiggery; therefore it does not develop the socialism which arises out of and as a reaction against liberal democracy. The corporate-organic-collectivist component of socialism is present in the feudal fragment—it is part of the feudal ethos—but the radical rationalist-egalitarian component of socialism is missing. It can be provided only by whiggery and liberal democracy, and these have not come into being.

In the bourgeois fragment, the situation is the reverse: the radical rationalist-egalitarian component of socialism is present, but the corporate-organic-collectivist component is missing, because toryism has been left behind. In the bourgeois fragment socialism withers "because there is no sense of class, no yearning for the corporate past."[7] The absence of socialism is related to the absence of toryism.

Though liberalism and socialism agree that *individuals* ought to be equal, their conceptions of the *society* within which individuals have their being are radically different. Liberalism sees life in society as a competition among individuals; the prize is individual "achievement" or "success"; equality is essentially equality of *opportunity* in the struggle for success. The emphasis is on the individual; there is hardly any perception of the concrete reality of classes, or of the "common good" as something more than the sum of individual goods. The individual is thought of as self-determining or autonomous rather than a *member*

[5]*Ibid.*, p. 25.

[6]Perhaps the simplest example of this is the radical political culture of Australia: a theoretically underdeveloped, non-militant quasi-socialism of Chartists and trade unionists, which does not develop into the more doctrinaire, more militant, more socialist socialism of twentieth-century Britain because this socialism requires for its development a continuing confrontation with the ideologies the Australians left behind: "Without the continuing pressure of the English feudal and bourgeois challenges, the spirit of Harold Laski loses its source. . . . Australian radicalism . . . remains . . . fixed at the point of origin," *Ibid.*

[7]*Ibid.*, p. 7.

determined by the class and community of which he is a member. It is because socialism has a conception of society as more than an agglomeration of individuals pursuing happiness—a conception close to the tory view of society as an organic community—that it finds the liberal idea of equality (equality of opportunity) inadequate. Socialists disagree with liberals about the essential meaning of equality because socialists have a tory conception of society.

In a liberal bourgeois society which conceives of itself as an agglomeration of individuals the demand for equality will express itself as left-wing or democratic liberalism as opposed to whiggery. The left will point out that all are not equal in the competitive pursuit of individual happiness. The government will be required to assure greater equality of opportunity—in the nineteenth century, by destroying monopolistic privileges; in the twentieth century by providing a welfare "floor" so that no one will fall out of the race for success, and by regulating the economy so that the race can continue without periodic crises.

In a society which thinks of itself as a community of classes rather than an aggregation of individuals, the demand for equality will take a socialist form: for equality of condition rather than mere equality of opportunity; for co-operation rather than competition; for a community that does much more than provide a context within which individuals can pursue happiness in a purely self-regarding way. At its most "extreme," socialism is a demand for the abolition of classes so that the good of the community can truly be realized. This is a demand which cannot be made by people who can hardly see class and community: the individual fills their eyes.

2. THE APPLICATION TO CANADA

It is a simple matter to apply the Hartzian approach to English Canada in a pan-North American way. English Canada can be viewed as an offshoot of the American liberal society, lacking a tory heritage and therefore lacking the socialist ideology which grows out of it. Canadian domestic struggles, from this point of view, are a northern version of the American struggle between big-propertied liberals on the right and petit-bourgeois and working-class liberals on the left; the struggle goes on within a broad liberal consensus, and the voice of the tory or the socialist is not heard in the land. This approach, with important qualifications, is adopted by Hartz and McRae in *The Founding of New*

Societies. English Canada, like the United States, is a bourgeois fragment: no toryism in the past, therefore no socialism in the present.

But Hartz notes that the liberal society of English Canada has a "tory touch," that it is "etched with a tory streak coming out of the American revolution."[8] The general process of bourgeois fragmentation is at work in both English Canada and the United States, but there are differences between the two fragments which Hartz describes as "delicate contrasts,"[9] McRae as "subtle" and "minor."[10] Put in the most general way, the difference is that while the United States is the perfect bourgeois fragment, the "archetype" of monolithic liberalism unsullied by tory or socialist deviations, English Canada is a bourgeois fragment marred by non-liberal "imperfections"—a tory "touch" and therefore a socialist "touch." The way Hartz and McRae would put it is that English Canada and the United States are "essentially" alike; differences are to be found but they are not "basic." Surely, however, whether one describes the differences as delicate, subtle, and minor or as basic, significant, and important depends on what one is looking for, on what one wishes to stress. Hartz himself points out that "each of the fragment cultures is 'unique', a special blend of European national tradition, historical timing,"[11] and so on. He is "concerned with both general processes and the individuality of the settings in which they evolve."[12] Nevertheless, his main focus is on the uniformities, the parallel lines of development, discovered in the comparative study of the United States and English Canada. This follows quite naturally from his *world* historical perspective, his emphasis on the three-way contrast of feudal, liberal, and radical fragments. From this perspective, the differences between English Canada and the United States are indeed "subtle" and "minor." But they are not absolutely minor: they are minor only in relation to the much larger differences among feudal, bourgeois, and radical fragments. If one shifts one's perspective, and considers English Canada from within the world of bourgeois fragments, the differences suddenly expand. If one's concern is to understand English-Canadian society in its uniqueness, that is, in contrast to American society, the differences become not "delicate" but of absolutely crucial importance.

Hartz's pan-North Americanism is a matter of perspective: he recognizes the un-American characteristics of English Canada, but considers them minor in relation to the much larger differences between

[8]*Ibid.*, p. 34.   [9]*Ibid.*, p. 71.
[10]"The Structure of Canadian History," in *ibid.*, p. 239.
[11]*Ibid.*, p. 72.   [12]*Ibid.*, p. 34.

bourgeois and other fragments. McRae's pan-North Americanism, however, is not merely a matter of perspective, for he seems to consider
English Canada's un-American characteristics to be absolutely minor.
For McRae, they are minor not only from the world perspective, but
from the narrower perspective which considers the bourgeois fragments
alone.

Take as an example the central concern of this study—the differing
weights of Canadian and American socialism. From the world perspective, the difference is perhaps "insignificant." As Hartz says, "there may
be a tory touch in English Canada, but the fragment, despite the C.C.F.
of recent times, has not yielded a major socialist movement."[13] From the
narrower perspective, however, the presence of a socialist movement in
English Canada is remarkable. The danger of a pan-North American
approach is that it tends either to ignore the relative strength of Canadian
socialism or to dismiss it as a freak. It explains away, rather than
explains, the strength of Canadian socialism. This is the approach
adopted by McRae. Hartz is content to point out that English Canada
does not have a major socialist movement. McRae's stress on English-
Canadian–American similarity is so strong, however, that it is no longer
a question of perspective but of error, for he attempts to boil a minor
socialist movement away into *nothing*, and thence to conclude that there
is no "basic" difference between the two bourgeois fragments.

The first step in his argument is to point out that socialism was
"successful" only among Saskatchewan farmers, that it "failed" in the
industrial areas. The CCF was therefore "basically" a movement of
agrarian protest similar to American farmers' protests; its failure in
urban Canada is parallel with the failure of socialism as a working-class
movement in the United States.[14] But words like "success" and "failure"
are dangerous because they hide degrees of success and failure. The
CCF *failed* to become a major party in urban Canada, but it *succeeded*
in becoming a powerful minor party—a success denied to the American
socialists. This is a difference, not a similarity. Furthermore, McRae
ignores the fact that in one urban Canadian province—British Columbia
—the CCF did succeed in becoming a major party. And he ignores the
ties between the Canadian labour movement and the CCF-NDP by
erroneously identifying the Canadian labour movement "in broad terms"
with the American, as one "not significantly attracted to socialism."[15]

In the second step of the argument, the success of the CCF in Saskat-

[13]*Ibid.*
[14]*Ibid.*, pp. 269–70.
[15]*Ibid.*, p. 269.

chewan is explained away by dismissing Saskatchewan socialism as just another American agrarian protest. This is also an error, because unlike the American movements the Saskatchewan CCF was *socialist*. Confronting this hard fact, McRae attempts to explain it away by noting that the Canadian prairies were "generously sprinkled with British immigrants already familiar with Fabian socialism."[16] But is it not significant that immigrants who brought socialist ideas to the American liberal society had to abandon them in the process of Americanization, while those who brought these ideas to Canada built a major provincial party with them?

McRae's *coup de grâce* to Canadian socialism is the observation that "with the formation of the NDP . . . the last half-realized elements of socialism . . . seem to have been absorbed into the liberal tradition."[17] The error here is to ascribe the moderation or liberalization of "doctrinaire" socialism in Canada to a special *Canadian* circumstance—the (overestimated) power of liberalism—when it is in fact a part of a general process of liberalization of socialism which is going on in every country of the West. The doctrine of the NDP is no more liberal than that of many other Western socialist parties.

The most important un-American characteristics of English Canada, all related to the presence of toryism, are: (*a*) the presence of tory ideology in the founding of English Canada by the Loyalists, and its continuing influence on English Canadian political culture; (*b*) the persistent power of whiggery or right-wing liberalism in Canada (the family compacts) as contrasted with the rapid and easy victory of liberal democracy (Jefferson, Jackson) in the United States; (*c*) the ambivalent centrist character of left-wing liberalism in Canada as contrasted with the unambiguously leftist position of left-wing liberalism in the United States; (*d*) the presence of an influential and legitimate socialist movement in English Canada as contrasted with the illegitimacy and early death of American socialism; (*e*) the failure of English-Canadian liberalism to develop into the one true myth, the nationalist cult, and the parallel failure to exclude toryism and socialism as "un-Canadian"; in other words the legitimacy of ideological diversity in English Canada.

From a world perspective, these imperfections in English Canada's bourgeois character may appear insignificant. From the point of view of one who is interested in understanding English Canada not merely as a bourgeois fragment, but as a unique bourgeois fragment, the imperfections are significant.

[16]*Ibid.*
[17]*Ibid.*, p. 273.

3. THE PRESENCE OF TORYISM AND ITS CONSEQUENCES

Many students have noted that English-Canadian society has been powerfully shaped by tory values that are "alien" to the American mind. The latest of these is Seymour Martin Lipset, who stresses particularly the relative strength in Canada of the tory values of "ascription" and "élitism" (the tendency to defer to authority) and the relative weakness of the liberal values of "achievement" and "egalitarianism."[18] He points to such well-known features of Canadian history as the absence of a lawless, individualistic-egalitarian American frontier, the preference for Britain rather than the United States as a societal model, and generally, the weaker emphasis on social equality, the greater acceptance by individuals of the facts of economic inequality, social stratification, and hierarchy.

One tory touch in English Canada which is not noted by Lipset but has been noted by many others (including McRae) is the far greater willingness of English-Canadian political and business élites to use the power of the state for the purpose of developing and controlling the economy. This willingness is especially notable in the history of Canada's Conservative party, and is one of the primary characteristics differentiating Canadian conservatism (touched with toryism) from purely individualistic, purely liberal American conservatism. As George Grant puts it, conservatism uses "public power to achieve national purposes. The Conservative party . . . after all, created Ontario Hydro, the CNR, the Bank of Canada, and the CBC."[19] American "conservatism" has little to do "with traditional conservatism, which asserts the right of the community to restrain freedom in the name of the common good."[20]

It is interesting to see how McRae explains away *this* Canadian-American difference. Beginning with the pan-North American assumption that any apparent imperfection in English-Canadian liberalism must be less important than it seems to be, McRae must ascribe the participation of the state in the Canadian economy to the smallness of Canada. A small country, he says, "cannot afford the luxury of fixed [liberal] principles" on an issue of this importance. Canadians have therefore decided the issue of private enterprise *versus* state activity on "pragmatic" rather than "ideological" grounds; government interference has for this

18*The First New Nation* (New York, 1963), esp. chap. 7.
19*Lament for a Nation* (Toronto, 1965), p. 14.
20*Ibid.*, p. 64.

reason not seriously incurred "charges of subverting the liberal way of life."[21] What this argument ignores is the presence of positive concepts *legitimizing* government interference. There are no charges of "subversion," not because Canadian liberalism is in some magical way able to transcend its ideology while American liberalism cannot, but because Canadian liberalism is weaker, or "touched with toryism." I am not attempting here to subvert the well-established economic explanation of the role of the state in the Canadian economy; of course, it was "necessary" to make use of the state in Canada. The question is: why did this necessity not produce ideological strain? In the United States there is a feeling that principle is being betrayed when the state interferes. In Canada there is no such feeling, not because the principle is escaped via "pragmatism," but because the Canadian principle is *different*. Here McRae abandons altogether the Hartzian approach, which consists in relating broad societal differences to cultural or ideological differences, not in trying to explain phenomena by relating them to immediate external-environmental pressures such as the "smallness of the country" or the "frontier." McRae has his cake and eats it too: Canada's liberal traits are related to the political culture. Therefore they are "basic." The non-liberal traits are related to extraneous factors such as the smallness of the country or the accidental and unexplained presence of "Fabians" on the prairies. Therefore they are not "basic."

McRae's overestimation of the power of American liberalism in Canada appears to be related to his concern with puncturing the myth of the Loyalists. This is the notion, common among Canadian historians, that the Loyalist émigrés from the American revolution were a genuine tory element; that their expulsion from the United States to Canada accounts for the development of the United States in a liberal direction and of English Canada in a conservative direction. English Canada's "point of departure," in this view, is not liberal but conservative. The idea is that English Canada was founded by British tories whose purpose was to build a society which would be not liberal like the American but conservative like the British. McRae correctly finds this myth to be an exaggeration of the difference between the Loyalists and the revolutionaries, between English Canada and the United States.[22] The picture of English Canada as a feudal fragment rather than a bourgeois fragment (which is what is implied by the Loyalist myth) is indeed a false one.

McRae argues correctly that the Loyalists and the family compacts did not represent British toryism, but pre-revolutionary American

[21]Hartz, *New Societies*, p. 270.
[22]*Ibid.*, p. 234.

whiggery with a "tory touch." But he errs in underestimating the weight of the "touch." He notes a few factors differentiating the Loyalists, and subsequently English Canadians in general, from the revolutionary Americans: belief in monarchy and imperial unity, greater stress on "law and order," revulsion against American populistic excesses, different frontier experiences, and so on. But he notes them only to dismiss them. "Basically," the Loyalist, and therefore the English Canadian, *is* the American liberal.[23] He is not "exactly" like the American, McRae adds,[24] but nevertheless, he is the American. This is going too far. It is legitimate to point out that Canada is not a feudal (tory) fragment but a bourgeois (liberal) fragment touched with toryism. It is not legitimate to boil the tory touch away to nothing. If the tory touch was strong enough to produce all the un-American characteristics we are considering, it becomes misleading to identify the English Canadian as the American liberal.

Possibly McRae is pushed into his pan-North Americanism by his assumption that a *significant* tory presence in English Canada can be derived only from the discovery of a similar presence in pre-revolutionary America, and thus from an interpretation of the American revolution as a genuine social revolution directed against a significant tory presence in the United States[25]—which would indeed be a false interpretation. But no such interpretation is necessary. Let us put it this way: pre-revolutionary America was a liberal fragment with insignificant traces of toryism, extremely weak feudal survivals. But they were insignificant in the *American* setting; they were far overshadowed by the liberalism of that setting. The Revolution did not have to struggle against them, it swept them away easily and painlessly, leaving no trace of them in the American memory. But these traces of toryism were expelled into a *new* setting, and in this setting they are no longer insignificant. In this new setting, where there is no pre-established overpowering liberalism to force them into insignificance, they play a large part in shaping a new political culture, significantly different from the American. As William Nelson writes in *The American Tory*, "the Tories' organic conservatism represented a current of thought that failed to

[23]*Ibid.*, p. 234.
[24]*Ibid.*, p. 238.
[25]"If the United States achieved its present liberal ethos through the expulsion of genuine preliberal or feudal elements at the revolution, then it is logical to look for these elements in Canada. But if . . . the American experience is fundamentally a liberal one from its earliest origins, and if the American revolution was not a social revolution, then it is folly to represent the Loyalists as a genuine Tory . . . privileged class. . . . If the American experience was basically a liberal one, how could the main Loyalist heritage be anything else?" *Ibid.*, p. 235.

reappear in America after the revolution. A substantial part of the whole spectrum of European . . . philosophy seemed to slip outside the American perspective."[26] But it *reappeared* in Canada. Here the sway of liberalism has proved to be not total, but considerably mitigated by a tory presence initially and a socialist presence subsequently. There is no need to return to the discredited interpretation of the American revolution as a social revolution.

One Canadian-American difference strikes both Hartz and McRae with particular force: the persistent power of family-compact whiggery in Canada as contrasted with the rapid and easy victories of Jeffersonian and Jacksonian democracy in the United States. In the United States the Federalist-Whigs are easily defeated, the democratization of political life occurs swiftly and thoroughly. Later the Whigs give up their antipathy to the people, adopt the rhetoric of democracy and egalitarianism, and return to power as Republicans through adroit appeals to the Horatio Alger dream, the "capitalist lust" of the American little man. By contrast, in Canada the family compacts are able to maintain ascendancy and delay the coming of democracy because of the tory touch "inherited in part from American Loyalism, which restrained egalitarian feeling in Canada."[27] McRae notes that even with the defeat of our tory-touched whigs and the coming of responsible government, "there was no complete repudiation of the Compacts and what they stood for. . . . Something of the old order" was preserved even after its disappearance.[28]

Despite the importance which Hartz and McRae ascribe to the persistence of whiggery as one of the factors which differentiate English Canada from the United States, the most significant aspect of the phenomenon from their point of view is that it ultimately disappeared.[29] The American and English-Canadian bourgeois fragments, though separated at the beginning by the power of the Canadian whigs, ultimately move together, close to the point of almost exact similarity. From my point of view, however, the early power of whiggery serves to emphasize the importance of the tory touch in English Canada. After all, whiggery "ultimately" fell not only in the United States and Canada, but everywhere. The significant contrast is not between situations in which it falls and those in which it does not fall, but between situations in which it falls quickly and those in which it persists.

In the United States, the masses could not be swayed by the Federalist-Whig appeals to anti-egalitarian sentiments. In Canada the masses *were* swayed by these appeals: the role of the Compacts was to save "the

[26](New York, 1961), pp. 189–190.   [27]Hartz, *New Societies*, p. 91.
[28]*Ibid.*, p. 37.   [29]*Ibid.*, p. 37.

colonial masses from the spectre of republicanism and democracy."[30]
What accounts for this is the tory presence in English-Canadian political
culture—the "greater acceptance of limitation, of hierarchical patterns."[31]
As McRae admits, this outlook did not disappear with the defeat of the
compacts, and the character of Canadian right-wing liberalism continued
to be distinctive after the coming of democracy. The American Whigs
returned to power as Republicans by encouraging the dream of the little
man to be equal with the big man: the notions of capitalism and democracy had to be thoroughly merged. In Canada there was "greater
acceptance of hierarchical patterns"; the Alger dream was much weaker
in the masses, so there was no need to harness it in order to keep the
right wing in the saddle.

The next step in tracing the development of the English-Canadian
political culture must be to take account of the tremendous waves of
British immigration which soon engulfed the original American Loyalist
fragment. Here McRae's concern is to argue that the liberal ideology
of the Loyalist fragment had already "frozen, congealed at the point of
origin"; that the national ethos had already been fully formed (an
American liberalism not "exactly" like American liberalism); that the
later waves of immigration played no part in the formation of the
English-Canadian political culture; that they found it already given,
established, and were impelled to acclimatize to it.[32] It is important for
McRae to prove this point, for while there is room for the argument
that the Loyalists were American whigs with a tory touch, the later
British immigrants had undoubtedly been heavily infected with non-
liberal ideas, and these ideas were undoubtedly in their heads as they
settled in Canada. The political culture of a new nation is not necessarily
fixed at the point of origin or departure; the founding of a new nation
can go on for generations. If the later waves of immigration arrived
before the *point of congealment* of the political culture, they must have
participated actively in the process of culture formation. If this be so,
the picture of English Canada as an almost-exactly American liberal
society becomes very difficult to defend. For *even if* it is granted that
the Loyalists were (almost exactly) American liberals, it is clear that
later participators in the formation of the culture were not.

Between 1815 and 1850 almost one million Britons emigrated to
Canada. The population of English Canada doubled in twenty years and
quadrupled in forty. The population of Ontario increased tenfold in

[30]*Ibid.*, p. 243.
[31]Lipset, *The First New Nation*, p. 251.
[32]Hartz, *New Societies*, pp. 244–7.

the same period—from about 95,000 in 1814 to about 950,000 in 1851.[33] McRae himself admits that "it would be inaccurate to say that this wave of migration was absorbed into the original fragment: an influx of these proportions does not permit of simple assimilation."[34] Nevertheless, he concludes that "despite the flood tide of immigration . . . the original liberal inheritance of English Canada survived and dominated."[35] According to McRae, the universal urge to own property and the classlessness of North American society had such a powerful impact on the immigrants that they simply "forgot their old notions of social hierarchy" and became American liberals.[36] Surely this argument is an instance of stretching the facts in order to fit a theory! Do people simply "forget" their old notions so quickly and so completely? Is it not possible that the immigrants, while they were no doubt considerably liberalized by their new environment, also brought to it non-liberal ideas which entered into the political culture mix, and which perhaps even reinforced the non-liberal elements present in the original fragment? If the million immigrants had come from the United States rather than Britain, would English Canada not be "significantly" different today?

The difficulty in applying the Hartzian approach to English Canada is that although the point of departure is reasonably clear, it is difficult to put one's finger on the point of congealment. Perhaps it was the Loyalist period; perhaps it was close to the mid-century mark; there are grounds for arguing that it was in the more recent past. But the important point is this; no matter where the point of congealment is located in time, the tory streak is present before the solidification of the political culture, and it is strong *enough* to produce what I consider to be *significant* "imperfections," or non-liberal, un-American attributes of English-Canadian society.

My own opinion about the point of congealment is that it came later than the Loyalists. The United States broke from Britain early, and the break was complete. Adam Smith and Tom Paine are among the last Britons who were spiritual founding fathers of the United States. Anything British, if it is of later than eighteenth-century vintage, is un-American. The American mind long ago cut its ties with Britain and began to develop on its own. When did Canada break from Britain? When did the Canadian mind begin to develop on its own? Not very long ago most Canadians described themselves as followers of the "British way of life," and many railed against egalitarian ideas from south of the border as "alien." Nineteenth-century British ideologists

[33]*Ibid.*, p. 245.   [34]*Ibid.*, p. 246.
[35]*Ibid.*, p. 247.   [36]*Ibid.*, p. 246.

are among the spiritual founding fathers of Canada. In the United States they are alien, though we may make an exception for Herbert Spencer.

The indeterminate location of the point of congealment makes it difficult to account in any precise way for the presence of socialism in the English-Canadian political culture mix, though the presence itself is indisputable. If the point of congealment came *before* the arrival of the first radical or socialist-minded immigrants, the presence of socialism must be ascribed primarily to the earlier presence of toryism. Since toryism is a significant part of the political culture, at least part of the leftist reaction against it will sooner or later be expressed in its own terms, that is in terms of *class* interests and the good of the community as a corporate entity (socialism) rather than in terms of the individual and his vicissitudes in the competitive pursuit of happiness (liberalism). If the point of congealment is very early, socialism appears at a later point not primarily because it is imported by British immigrants, but because it is contained as a potential in the original political culture. (It might even have appeared autonomously, without the immigrants.) The immigrants then find that they do not have to give it up—that it is not un-Canadian—because it "fits" to a certain extent with the tory ideas already present.

If the point of congealment is very late, the presence of socialism must be explained as a result of *both* the presence of toryism and the introduction of socialism into the culture mix before congealment. The immigrant retains his socialism not only because it "fits" but also because nothing really *has* to fit. He finds that his socialism is not un-Canadian partly because "Canadian" has not yet been defined. Certainly both factors—the prior presence of toryism, and the late immigration of radicals—are essential to any adequate explanation of the origins of English-Canadian socialism, but it is impossible at this point to assign relative weights to the two factors.

Canadian liberals cannot be expected to wax enthusiastic about the non-liberal traits of their country. They are likely to condemn the tory touch as anachronistic, stifling, undemocratic, out of tune with the essentially American ("free" and "classless") spirit of English Canada. They dismiss the socialist touch as an "old-fashioned" protest, no longer necessary (if it ever was) in this best (liberal) of all possible worlds in which the "end of ideology" has been achieved. The secret dream of the Canadian liberal is the removal of English Canada's "imperfections" —in other words, the total assimilation of English Canada into the larger North American culture. But there is a flaw in this dream which might give pause even to the liberal. Hartz places special emphasis on one very unappetizing characteristic of the new societies—intolerance—which is strikingly absent in English Canada. Because the new societies, other than Canada, are unfamiliar with legitimate ideological diversity, they are unable to accept it and deal with it in a rational manner, either internally or on the level of international relations.

The European nation has an "identity which transcends any ideologist and a mechanism in which each plays only a part."[37] Neither the tory nor the liberal nor the socialist has a monopoly in the expression of the "spirit" of the nation. But the new societies, the fragments, contain only one of the ideologies of Europe; they are one-myth cultures. In the new setting, freed from its historic enemies past and future, ideology transforms itself into nationalism. It claims to be a moral absolute, "the great spirit of a nation."[38] In the United States, liberalism becomes "Americanism"; a political philosophy becomes a civil religion, a nationalist cult. The American attachment to Locke is "absolutist and irrational."[39] Democratic capitalism is the American way of life; to oppose it is to be un-American.

To be an American is to be a bourgeois liberal. To be a French Canadian is to be a pre-Enlightenment Catholic; to be an Australian is to be a prisoner of the radical myth of "mateship"; to be a Boer is to be a pre-Enlightenment bourgeois Calvinist. The fragments escape the need for philosophy, for thought about values, for "where perspectives shrink to a single value, and that value becomes the universe, how can value itself be considered?"[40] The fragment demands solidarity. Ideologies which diverge from the national myth make no impact; they are not understood, and their proponents are not granted legitimacy. They are denounced as aliens, and treated as aliens, because they *are* aliens.

When the historic enemies of the fragment ideologies confront these ideologies once more—from the outside—in the form of the world revolution of the twentieth century, the fragments are incapable of responding rationally to the challenge. Their response takes one or more of the three forms of isolationism (retreat from the confrontation), messianism (the effort to impose the fragment ideology on the whole world), and anti-alien hysteria, "so that in desperate moments, as under McCarthy and Verwoerd, the fragment rocks with the cry of treason."[41] The fragments cannot understand or deal with the fact that all men are not bourgeois Americans, or radical Australians, or Catholic French

[37]*Ibid.*, p. 15. [38]*Ibid.*, p. 10.
[39]Hartz, *Liberal Tradition*, p. 11.
[40]Hartz, *New Societies*, p. 23.
[41]*Ibid.*, p. 22.

Canadians, or Calvinist South Africans. They cannot make peace with the loss of ideological certainty.

The specific weakness of the United States is its "inability to understand the appeal of socialism" to the third world.[42] Because the United States has "buried" the memory of the organic medieval community "beneath new liberal absolutisms and nationalisms"[43] it cannot understand that the appeal of socialism to nations with a predominantly non-liberal past (including French Canada) consists precisely in the promise of "continuing the corporate ethos in the very process" of modernization.[44] The American reacts with isolationism, messianism, and hysteria.

English Canada, because it is the most "imperfect" of the fragments, is not a one-myth culture. In English Canada ideological diversity has not been buried beneath an absolutist liberal nationalism. Here Locke is not the one true god; he must tolerate lesser tory and socialist deities at his side. The result is that English Canada does not direct an uncomprehending intolerance at heterodoxy, either within its borders or beyond them. In English Canada it has been possible to consider values without arousing the all-silencing cry of treason. Hartz observes that "if history had chosen English Canada for the American role" of directing the Western response to the world revolution, "the international scene would probably have witnessed less McCarthyite hysteria, less Wilsonian messianism."[45]

Americanizing liberals might consider that the Pearsonian rationality and calmness which Canada displays on the world stage—the "mediating" and "peace-keeping" role of which they are so proud—is related to the un-American (tory and socialist) characteristics which they consider to be unnecessary imperfections in English-Canadian wholeness. The tolerance of English-Canadian domestic politics is also linked with the presence of these imperfections. If the price of Americanization is the surrender of legitimate ideological diversity, even the liberal might think twice before paying it.

McRae comes close to qualifying his pan-North Americanism out of existence by admitting at one point that "it would be a mistake to underrate the emotional attachment that many Canadians . . . still feel for British institutions. . . . English Canadians . . . cap the foundations of their North American liberal social ethos with a superstructure embodying elements of the wider British political heritage."[46] But his pan-North Americanism must triumph in the end: the *foundations* of

42*Ibid.*, p. 119.   43*Ibid.*, p. 35.   44*Ibid.*, p. 119.
45*Ibid.*, p. 120.   46*Ibid.*, p. 267.

English Canada are American liberal, only the superstructure is British. My argument is essentially that non-liberal British elements have entered into English-Canadian society *together* with American liberal elements at the foundations. The fact is that Canada has been greatly influenced by both the United States and Britain. This is not to deny that liberalism is the dominant element in the English-Canadian political culture; it is to stress that it is not the sole element, that it is accompanied by vital and legitimate streams of toryism and socialism which have as close a relation to English Canada's "essence" or "foundations" as does liberalism. English Canada's "essence" is both liberal and non-liberal. Neither the British nor the American elements can be explained away as "superstructural" excrescences.

4. UN-AMERICAN ASPECTS OF CANADIAN CONSERVATISM

So far, I have been discussing the presence of toryism in Canada without referring more than once or twice to the Conservative party. This party can be seen as a party of right-wing or business liberalism, but such an interpretation would be far from the whole truth; the Canadian Conservative party, like the British Conservative party and unlike the Republican party, is not monolithically liberal. If there is a touch of toryism in English Canada, its primary carrier has been the Conservative party. It would not be correct to say that toryism is *the* ideology of the party or even that *some* Conservatives are pure tories. These statements would not be true even of the British Conservative party. The primary component of the ideology of business-oriented parties is liberalism; but there are powerful traces of the old pre-liberal outlook in the British Conservative party,[47] and less powerful but still perceptible traces of it in the Canadian party. If we define ideology as a complex of ideas which is used to legitimize behaviour, we may say that Republicans have access only to the liberal ideology in legitimizing their behaviour, while British and, to a lesser extent, Canadian Conservatives have access to both liberal and tory ideologies. A Republican is always a liberal. A Conservative may be at one moment a liberal, at the next moment a tory; he is usually something of both.

If it is true that Canadian Conservatives can be seen from some angles as right-wing liberals, it is also true that figures such as R. B. Bennett,

[47]See Samuel Beer, *British Politics in the Collectivist Age* (New York, 1965), esp. chaps. 3 and 9 to 13.

Arthur Meighen, and George Drew cannot be understood simply as Canadian versions of William McKinley, Herbert Hoover, and Robert Taft. The Canadian Conservatives have something British and non-liberal about them. It is not simply their emphasis on loyalty to the crown and to the British connection but also a touch of the authentic tory aura—traditionalism, élitism, the strong state, and so on. The Canadian Conservatives lack the American aura of rugged individualism. Theirs is not the characteristically American conservatism which conserves only *liberal* values.

The Conservative attachment to the monarchy is not usually interpreted as having any profound ideological meaning; it is not usually considered to indicate a liberal-conservative difference between the Liberal and Conservative parties. But we ought not to forget that the historic identification of toryism with the monarchy, and the antipathy or coolness of liberalism thereto, has been one of the most important distinctions between these two ideologies in Britain and on the Continent. True liberals may be able to accept hereditary monarchy, but they cannot love it. The historic Anglophilia of the Conservatives and the historic Americanophilia of the Liberals are also not devoid of ideological meaning. A true tory cannot be expected to adore the land of liberalism; a true liberal cannot be expected to idealize a country choked by feudal survivals.

Historic toryism finds expression today in the writings of Conservatives like W. L. Morton, who points out among other things that the Declaration of Independence guarantees "life, liberty, and the pursuit of happiness," while the British North America Act guarantees "peace, order and good government."[48] Morton describes the United States as a liberal society integrated from below, by a *covenant* of brothers, and Canada as a monarchical society held together at the top, integrated by *loyalty* to the crown.[49] Neither of these characterizations may be true, but we are dealing with *ideology* here; we are observing the presence of a non-liberal ideology in the Canadian Conservative party.

In another of his writings, Morton stresses the tory belief in loyalty to leaders and in readiness to let them govern.[50] This élitist attitude finds *institutional* expression in the predominance assigned to the leader in both the British and Canadian Conservative parties. But it has also expressed itself, in both parties, in a conception of parliamentary democ-

[48]*The Canadian Identity* (Toronto, 1961), p. 111.
[49]*Ibid.*, pp. 99–114.
[50]"Canadian Conservatism Now," in Paul Fox, ed., *Politics: Canada* (Toronto, 1962), p. 287.

racy not as government by the people but as government by ministers of the crown for the people. In Britain this view has been expounded by L. S. Amery,[51] and in Canada by Morton. Both men reject the "dangerous and improper idea of the electoral mandate":[52] ministers of the crown ought not to see themselves as agents carrying out instructions given to them beforehand by the people, but as governors, acting according to their own conception of what the common good requires. The people should not presume to *instruct* their governors, but *trust* them to govern well. The governors are answerable to the people only in the sense that the people may remove them if they do not govern well. Surely this was the position of Arthur Meighen in his persistent disagreement with Mackenzie King about the nature of democratic leadership.

Canadian and British Conservatives have been able to rationalize their grudging acceptance of the welfare state and the managed economy by recalling their pre-capitalist, collectivist traditions. Morton exhorts Canadian Conservatives to embrace the welfare state on the ground that "laissez-faire and rugged individualism" are foreign to "conservative principles." He accuses liberalism of having "prepared the way" for communism by encouraging "class war in unrestrained competition."[53] Can one conceive of a respected philosopher of Republicanism denouncing "rugged individualism" as foreign to traditional Republican principles?

It is possible to perceive in Canadian Conservatism not only the elements of business liberalism and orthodox élitist-collectivist toryism, but also an element of "tory democracy" or "tory radicalism"— a paternalistic concern for the condition of the working class and a picture of the Conservative party as their champion against unenlightened elements of the bourgeoisie. It is this aspect of the tory tradition which was brilliantly expressed in Britain by Disraeli and Lord Randolph Churchill. Sir John A. Macdonald's approach to the emergent Canadian working class was in some respects similar to Disraeli's. Later Conservatives acquired the image of arch-reactionaries and arch-enemies of the workers; but let us not forget that "Iron Heel" Bennett was also the Bennett of the Canadian New Deal.

The question arises: why is it that in Canada the Conservative leader proposes—in language at least as radical as Roosevelt's[54]—a new deal

[51]L. S. Amery, *Thoughts on the Constitution* (London, 1947).
[52]Morton, "Canadian Conservatism Now," p. 289.
[53]*Ibid.*
[54]"Selfish men . . . men whose mounting bank rolls loom larger than your happiness, corporations without souls and without virtue . . . fearful that this Government might impinge on what they have grown to regard as their immemorial

for the Canadian people? Why is it that the Canadian "counterpart" of Hoover apes *Roosevelt*? This phenomenon is usually interpreted as sheer historical accident, a product of Bennett's desperation and opportunism. But the answer may be that Bennett was not Hoover. Even in his orthodox days Bennett's views on the state's role in the economy were far from similar to Hoover's; Bennett's attitude was that of Canadian, not American, conservatism. Once this is recognized, it is possible to entertain the suggestion that Bennett's sudden radicalism, his sudden concern for the people, may not have been *mere* opportunism. It may have been a manifestation, a sudden activation under pressure, of a latent "tory-democratic" or "tory-radical" streak. Let it be noted also that the depression produced two Conservative splinter parties, both with "radical" welfare state programs and both led by former subordinates of Bennett: H. H. Stevens' Reconstruction party and W. D. Herridge's New Democracy.

The Bennett New Deal is only the most extreme and the best known instance of what is usually considered to be an accident or an aberration —the occasional manifestation of "radicalism" or "leftism" by otherwise orthodox Conservative leaders in the face of opposition from their "followers" in the business community. Meighen, for example, was constantly embroiled with the "Montreal interests" who objected to his railway policy. The *Montreal Star* called it "a . . . ruinous fantasy of the most demented form of socialism."[55] On one occasion Meighen received a note of congratulations from William Irvine: "The man who dares to offend the Montreal interests is the sort of man that the people are going to vote for."[56] This same Meighen expressed on certain occasions, particularly after his retirement, an antagonism to big government and creeping socialism that would have warmed the heart of Robert Taft; but he combined his business liberalism with gloomy musings about the folly of universal suffrage[57]—musings which Taft would have rejected as un-American. Meighen is far easier to understand from a British than from an American perspective, for he combined, in different proportions at different times, attitudes deriving from all three Conservative ideological streams: right-wing liberalism, orthodox toryism, and tory-radicalism.

The Western or agrarian Conservatives of the contemporary period, John Diefenbaker and Alvin Hamilton, are usually dismissed as "prairie

right of exploitation, will whisper against us. They will call us radicals. They will say that this is the first step on the road to socialism. We fear them not." The Fourth Address, Jan. 9, 1935.

[55]Roger Graham, *Arthur Meighen*, II (Toronto, 1963), p. 152.
[56]*Ibid.*, p. 269.
[57]*Ibid.*, III (Toronto, 1965), pp. 71–4.

radicals" of the American type, and considered to be absolutely foreign bodies—"renegades"—in Canadian Conservatism. But they cannot be dealt with so simply. Their views on the crown, the British connection, and the danger of American domination are derived from the orthodox tory tradition. Their stress on the Conservative party as champion of the people and their advocacy of welfare state policies might represent not only anti-Bay Street agrarianism but *also* the same type of tory-radicalism which was expressed before their time by orthodox business-sponsored Conservatives like Meighen and Bennett. The peculiarly prairie or agrarian-populist aspect of Diefenbaker and Hamilton is perhaps a genuinely foreign body in Canadian Conservatism, since it derives neither from business liberalism nor from pre-capitalist toryism. But prairie radicalism is not *all* there is to them. Diefenbaker Conservatism is therefore to be understood not simply as a Western populist phenomenon, but as an odd *combination* of traditional Conservative views with attitudes absorbed from the Western Progressive tradition.

Another "aberration" which is not really an aberration is the contemporary phenomenon of the red tory. At the simplest level, he is a Conservative who prefers the Co-operative Commonwealth Federation/New Democratic party to the Liberals, or a socialist who prefers the Conservatives to the Liberals, without really knowing why. At a higher level, he is a conscious ideological Conservative with some "odd" socialist notions (W. L. Morton) or a conscious ideological socialist with some "odd" tory notions (Eugene Forsey). The very suggestion that such affinities might exist between Republicans and socialists in the United States is ludicrous enough to make some kind of a point.

Red toryism is, of course, one of the results of the relationship between toryism and socialism which has already been elucidated. The tory and socialist minds have *some* crucial assumptions, orientations, and values in common, so that *from a certain angle* they may appear not as enemies but as two different expressions of the same basic ideological outlook. Thus, at the very highest level, the red tory is a philosopher who combines elements of toryism and socialism so thoroughly in a single integrated *Weltanschauung* that it is impossible to say that he is a proponent of either one as *against* the other. Such a red tory is George Grant, who has associations with both the Conservative party and the NDP, defends Diefenbaker, laments the death of "true" British conservatism in Canada, attacks the Liberals as individualists and Americanizers, and defines socialism as a variant of conservatism (each "protects the public good against private freedom").[58]

[58]*Lament for a Nation*, p. 71. See "Tories, Socialists and the Demise of Canada," *Canadian Dimension*, May–June 1965, pp. 12–15.

5. THE CHARACTER OF CANADIAN SOCIALISM

Canadian socialism is un-American in two distinct ways. It is un-American in the sense that it is a significant and legitimate political force in Canada, insignificant and alien in the United States. But Canadian socialism is also un-American in the sense that it does not speak the same language as American socialism. In Canada, socialism is British, non-Marxist, and worldly; in the United States it is German, Marxist, and otherworldly.

I have argued that the socialist ideas of British immigrants to Canada were not sloughed off because they "fitted" with a political culture which already contained non-liberal components, and probably also because they were introduced into the political culture mix before the point of congealment. Thus socialism was not alien here. But it was not alien in yet another way; it was not borne by foreigners. The personnel and the ideology of the Canadian labour and socialist movements have been primarily British. Many of those who built these movements were British immigrants with past experience in the British labour movement; many others were Canadian-born children of such immigrants.[59] And in British North America, Britons could not be treated as foreigners.

When socialism was brought to the United States, it found itself in an ideological environment in which it could not survive because Lockean individualism had long since achieved the status of a national religion; the political culture had already congealed, and socialism did not fit. American socialism was alien not only in this ideological sense, but in the ethnic sense as well; it was borne by foreigners from Germany and

[59]The Canadian socialist movement has been so heavily British and Protestant that the CCF found it extremely difficult, in most places, to appeal to any non-"WASP" group except the Jews. Jerry Caplan writes: "Foreign groups that wanted to protest the effects of the depression voted Liberal because they could not identify with the CCF. . . . Not only was its membership drawn largely from the United Church, the CCF's character was molded in the image of that body. The party leaders were eminently respectable Anglo-Saxon Protestants, and quite often, members of the Orange Lodge." (G. Caplan, "The CCF in Ontario, 1932–45" [unpublished MA thesis, University of Toronto, 1961], p. 162.) A recent study of the CCF in Ontario shows that the proportion of those of British birth or descent is higher in the party than in the total population.

Ethnic group	1951 population	1951 CCF membership
British	67%	77%
French	10	3
Other	2	5
Jewish	21	16

Leo Zakuta, *A Becalmed Protest Movement*
(Toronto, 1964), 31.

other continental European countries.[60] These foreigners sloughed off their socialist ideas not simply because such ideas did not fit ideologically, but because as foreigners they were going through a general process of Americanization; socialism was only one of many *ethnically* alien characteristics which had to be abandoned. The immigrant's ideological change was only one incident among many others in the general process of changing his entire way of life. According to David Saposs, "the factor that contributed most tellingly to the decline of the socialist movement was that its chief following, the immigrant workers, . . . had become Americanized."[61]

A British socialist immigrant to Canada had a far different experience. The British immigrant was not an "alien." Canada was British North America, under the British crown and the British flag. The English-Canadian culture not only granted legitimacy to his political ideas and absorbed them into its wholeness; it absorbed him as a person into the English-Canadian community, with relatively little strain, without demanding that he change his entire way of life before being granted full citizenship. He was acceptable to begin with, by virtue of being British. It is impossible to understand the differences between American and Canadian socialism without taking into account this immense difference between the ethnic contexts of socialism in the two countries.

The ethnic handicap of American socialism does not consist merely in the fact that its personnel was heavily European. Equally important is the fact that the socialism borne by these Europeans was a *brand* of socialism—Marxism—which found survival difficult not only in the United States but in all English-speaking countries. Hartz recognizes that "Marxism . . . was the one manifestation of the European viewpoint which had followers in America."[62] Marx has not found the going easy

---

[60]Until the turn of the century American socialists were primarily Europeans. In the first decade of the century there was an influx of native Americans; in 1908, 71 per cent of the membership of the Socialist party were American-born. But after 1912 the situation reverted to normal. (M. Seidler, *Norman Thomas* [Syracuse, 1961], p. 41.) From 1912 to 1919 the percentage of the membership which belonged to foreign language federations increased from 12 to 53 per cent. From 1920 to 1932 the *Jewish Daily Forward*, a Yiddish language newspaper, was "the most powerful influence in the Socialist Party." (Daniel Bell, "The Background and Development of Marxian Socialism in the United States," *Socialism in American Life*, ed. D. Egbert and S. Persons [Princeton, 1952], p. 310). During the depression, there was again an influx of natives; these were mostly quasi-Communists, the young "militants" with whom Norman Thomas was identified at the time. They were well to the left of the older European group, who were orthodox Marxist social-democrats.

[61]*Communism in American Unions* (New York, 1959), p. 7.

[62]*Liberal Tradition*, p. 254.

in the United States; but neither has he found the going easy in Britain, Canada, Australia, or New Zealand. The socialism of the United States, the socialism of De Leon, Berger, Hillquit, and Debs, is predominantly Marxist and doctrinaire, because it is European. The socialism of English Canada, the socialism of Simpson, Woodsworth, and Coldwell is predominantly Protestant, labourist, and Fabian, because it is British.

Contrast the American and Canadian socialist parties in the thirties. At the American party's convention of 1936 "giant pictures of Marx . . . decorated the hall." The Internationale was sung. The convention was split between the "militants," proponents of the Detroit Declaration of 1934, and the "old guard." The militants used phrases like "the bogus democracy of capitalist parliamentarians" and "the dictatorship of the revolutionary masses."[63] The old guard, orthodox reformist Marxists, denounced the militants for flirting with communism. In 1936 Norman Thomas and Earl Browder were discussing a common ticket for the 1936 elections and actually agreed on certain forms of united front activity. During the same period, the Socialist party opened its doors to the Trotskyites.[64]

At about the same time, the Reverend J. S. Woodsworth, MP, was denouncing the ideas of revolution and proletarian dictatorship and expelling the Communist-infiltrated Labour Section from the Ontario CCF. No portraits of Marx hung in CCF convention halls. "Onward Christian Soldiers" was more likely to be sung than the Internationale.

Marxist influence on Canadian socialism there has been, of course, especially in British Columbia. But the main source of whatever strength Marxism has had in Canada has been the proximity of the United States! The strength of the extreme left varieties of socialism in British Columbia can be traced back to the strong influence of American radical unionism —from the Western Federation of Miners to the Industrial Workers of the World—on the British Columbia labour movement.

The prevalence of doctrinaire Marxism helps to explain the sectarianism of the American Socialist party. The distinctive quality of a sect is its "otherworldliness." It rejects the existing scheme of things entirely; its energies are directed not to devising stratagems with which to lure the electorate, but to elaborating its utopian theory. Daniel Bell describes the American Socialist party as one "whose main preoccupation has been the refinement of 'theory' at the cost, even, of interminable factional divisions."[65] "It has never, even for a single year, been without

63Seidler, *Norman Thomas*, pp. 126–8.
64Bell, "Marxian Socialism in the US," p. 382.
65*Ibid.*, p. 401.

some issue which threatend to split the party."[66] For Bell, the failure of American socialism is its failure to make the transition from sect to party, to concern itself with popular issues and votes rather than theoretical disputes. The unfortunate decisions made by the party—especially the decisions to oppose the two world wars—were a result of this sectarianism, this refusal to compromise with the world.

The CCF has not been without its otherworldly tendencies; there have been doctrinal disagreements; the party has always had a left wing which has seemed to be concerned primarily with "socialist education" rather than practical political work. But this left wing has been a constantly declining minority. The party has expelled individuals and small groups —mostly Communists and Trotskyites—but it has never split. Its life has never been threatened by disagreement over doctrinal matters. It is no more preoccupied with theory than the British Labour party. Its orientation is not otherworldly; it has made compromises with the world no less significant than those made by democratic socialism in Europe. It sees itself, and is seen by the public, not as a coterie of ideologists but as a party like the others, and second to none in its avidity for office. If it has been attacked from the right for socialist "utopianism" and "impracticality," it has been attacked even more, and again from the right, for abandoning the "true" socialist faith in an unprincipled drive for power.[67]

Its doctrinaire Marxist bent was not the only factor which prevented the American socialist party from compromising with the world. Equally important was the party's continual remoteness from power. European socialist parties, despite their taste for Marxist theorizing, were true political parties rather than sects because they were important forces in

---

[66]*Ibid.*, p. 221.

[67]The CCF has been quite conscious of this difference between itself and its less fortunate brother in the land of Locke. A CCF pamphlet describes the "socialist party led by Norman Thomas" as incapable of capturing "the imagination of the American worker. Its doctrinaire attitude to social questions, its pacifist approach to the menace of totalitarianism, and its complete failure to be a political party accepting political opportunities without being opportunistic have practically annihilated its influence." (Doris Archer, "Political Action in the CIO and CCL," *Talking about Unions* [Toronto: Ontario CCF Women's Committee on Organized Labour, December, 1949], p. 12). During the war years the CCF had been careful to avoid identification with the "Thomas group." In David Lewis' words, "no socialist party could be supported which took the United States Socialist Party's position on the war. . . . It is politically very dangerous for us to be identified in any way with any force in the United States that could be interpreted as being anti-war." The CCF preferred to identify itself with "the vast majority of socialists and progressives . . . rightly or wrongly behind the Roosevelt forces." David Lewis to Carlyle King, Oct. 18, 1944, NDP files.

political life. As Bell points out, the American party was *more* doctrinaire than the European parties: "With none of the strings of responsibility which held the European socialists, the party reacted by formulas. . . . "[68] The CCF, though never so close to power as the European socialists, was much closer than the Americans, close enough early enough in its life to make power more important to it than doctrinal purity.

The contrast between American Marxist socialism and Canadian non-Marxist socialism, and the weakness of Marxism not only in America but in all other English-speaking countries, at first led me to conclude that Hartz's "single factor" explanation of the illegitimacy of American socialism might be overdone. This question arose: was it socialism *per se* that could not live in the United States, or only Marxist socialism? What if American socialism had looked to Britain rather than Germany, if it had been "empirical" rather than doctrinaire Marxist? The first answer that suggested itself was that if American socialism had not been handicapped by its Marxian character—if it had been handicapped only by the fact that America had not known toryism and therefore would not listen to socialism—it might have been able to live a little longer and might not have died such a horrible death.

What this line of reasoning ignored was the fact that there *was* an impact in America of British socialist thought which was, however, even weaker than the Marxist impact. Why, in America, an English-speaking country, should the British influence on socialism have been so much weaker than the German? Precisely because the "single factor" explanation is *not* overdone. Socialism could not attain any degree of strength in America, for the Hartzian reason, *except* for a short while as a socialism *in* America but not *of* America, that is to say, except among unassimilated foreign groups. There was an unassimilated continental European group; there was never an unassimilated British group. The British influence was therefore much weaker than the Marxist.

At first I thought that since Marxism fails not only in the United States but in all English-speaking countries, *peculiarly American* characteristics cannot be the explanation of its failure in the United States. This is true; the peculiarly American characteristics account for the failure of *all* socialisms, *even* English-speaking socialism, in the United States. The failure of Marxian socialism is less complete and less rapid than the failure of the others—Marxism becomes "the one manifestation of the European viewpoint which had followers in America"—precisely because of the peculiar American cultural characteristics which mean doom

[68]"Marxian Socialism in the US," p. 314.

for all socialisms *except* those sustained by immigrants prior to their Americanization. The strength of Marx relative to other socialisms in America is a confirmation of the Hartzian hypothesis.

6. CANADIAN LIBERALISM: THE TRIUMPHANT CENTRE

Canadian Conservatives are not American Republicans; Canadian socialists are not American socialists; Canadian Liberals are not American liberal Democrats.

The un-American elements in English Canada's political culture are most evident in Canadian Conservatism and socialism. But Canadian liberalism has a British colour too. The liberalism of Canada's Liberal party should not be identified with the liberalism of the American Democratic party. In many respects they stand in sharp contrast to one another.

The three components of the English-Canadian political culture have not developed in isolation from one another; each has developed in interaction with the others. Our toryism and our socialism have been moderated by liberalism. But by the same token, our liberalism has been rendered "impure," in American terms, through its contacts with toryism and socialism. If English-Canadian liberalism is less individualistic, less ardently populistic-democratic, more inclined to state intervention in the economy, and more tolerant of "feudal survivals" such as monarchy, this is due to the uninterrupted influence of toryism upon liberalism, an influence wielded in and through the conflict between the two. If English-Canadian liberalism has tended since the depression to merge at its leftist edge with the democratic socialism of the CCF-NDP, this is due to the influence which socialism has exerted upon liberalism, in and through the conflict between them. The key to understanding of the Liberal party in Canada is to see it as a *centre* party, with *influential* enemies on both right and left.

Hartz's comparison of the Liberal Reform movements of the United States and Europe casts light on the differences between American and English-Canadian liberalism. Hartz defines Liberal Reform as the movement "which emerged toward the end of the nineteenth century to adapt classical liberalism to the purposes of small propertied interests and the laboring class and at the same time which rejected socialism."[69] The fact that European Liberal Reform was confronted with a significant socialist challenge meant (*a*) that liberals, influenced by socialist theory, tried to

[69]Hartz, *Liberal Tradition*, p. 228.

"transcend the earlier individualism" and recognized "the need for collective action to solve the class problem,"[70] and (*b*) that liberals, faced with powerful enemies on both the left and the right, presented an ambivalent conservative-radical image; they attacked the tories and the *status quo*, but they also defended the *status quo* from its socialist enemies.

American liberals, impervious to the socialist challenge and therefore unaffected by socialist ideas, remained "enslaved" to individualism. "Even in its midnight dreams," American Liberal Reform "ruled out the concepts of socialism."[71] Its goal was not to reform modern capitalism by abandoning Lockean individualism and moving in the direction of socialism, but, by smashing or controlling trusts and bosses, to restore the old individualistic way of life. It struggled to retain individualism and still to recognize the new problems of a modern industrial society: "An agonized reluctance . . . characterized the outlook of Progressivism toward the positive legislation advanced everywhere by Western Liberal Reform."[72] Yet American Liberal Reform had an unambiguous radical image; its only enemies were the big-propertied liberals of the right. American Liberal Reformers were thus "saved from a defensive appearance, were able to emerge as pure crusaders."[73] If they had had to answer socialist attacks, they would have appeared much less radical.

The relevance of this analysis for the English-Canadian situation is apparent. In English Canada, Liberal Reform, represented by King's Liberal party, has had to face the socialist challenge. Under socialist influence, it abandoned its early devotion to "the lofty principles of Gladstone, the sound economics of Adam Smith, and the glories of laissez faire."[74] King's *Industry and Humanity* and the Liberal platform of 1919 mark the transition of English Canadian Liberalism from the old individualism to the new Liberal Reform.[75]

[70]*Ibid.*, p. 231.   [71]*Ibid.*, p. 234.
[72]*Ibid.*, p. 243.   [73]*Ibid.*, p. 229.
[74]Bruce Hutchison, *The Incredible Canadian* (Toronto, 1952), p. 6. Hutchison writes of *Industry and Humanity*: "In almost every respect this book repudiates the historic Liberalism of Canada, denounces the economic system which Liberal politics have nurtured, proposes a society of an entirely different sort, edges uncomfortably close to the theories of the Socialist CCF." *Ibid.*, p. 39. See also F. A. McGregor, *The Fall and Rise of Mackenzie King: 1911–1919* (Toronto, 1962), pp. 230–47.
[75]Before the thirties there was no *strong* socialist party in Canada. I would therefore be on safer ground if I were to locate the socialist challenge and liberal response in the thirties rather than at the time of the First World War. Nevertheless, the King of *Industry and Humanity* and the platform of 1919 does manifest the kind of transition from classical individualism to socialized Liberal Reform that occurred in Europe. The socialist challenge was there, not in the form of a menace at the polls, but "in the air," in the political culture as a *legitimate* ideology

King's Liberal Reform, since it had to answer attacks from the left as well as from the right, projected a notoriously ambivalent conservative-radical image:

> Truly he will be remembered
> Wherever men honor ingenuity
> Ambiguity, inactivity, and political longevity.

When he faced Bennett and Meighen, King was the radical warrior, the champion of the little people against the interests. When he turned to face Woodsworth and Coldwell, King was the cautious conservative, the protector of the *status quo*. He

> . . . never let his on the one hand
> Know what his on the other hand was doing.[76]

Roosevelt's New Deal involved "departures from the liberal faith of a very substantive kind."[77] Unlike the earlier Progressivism it did not shun state action. But neither did it consciously abandon Locke. Since Roosevelt did not have to face the socialist challenge, he did not have to "spell out his liberal premises. He did not have to spell out any real philosophy at all. His 'radicalism' could consist of what he called 'bold and persistent experimentation' which of course meant nothing in terms of large social faiths and was indeed perfectly compatible with Americanism."[78] The Republican opposition tried to alert the American people to the fact that Roosevelt's experiments were indeed socialistic and un-American, but the American people did not listen. They were convinced by Roosevelt's plea that his legislative schemes were "mere technical gadgetry,"[79] that questions of political philosophy were not relevant. Roosevelt and the American people, by closing their eyes to the philosophical implications of the New Deal, had their cake and ate it too: they subverted Lockean individualism in fact, but they held on to their Americanism, their Lockean individualist faith. "Alger could

---

which evoked response—rejection and incorporation—from other ideologies even though it was not yet a power at the polls. And from 1921—the time of Woodsworth's election to the Commons—the *direct* political influence of Woodsworth on King comes into the picture, even though Woodsworth in the twenties did not represent a significant electoral danger to King. American liberalism did not have to answer socialist attacks not primarily because of the weakness of socialism at the polls but because of its weakness in the political *culture*—its alien, illegitimate, un-American character. I might also mention that British Liberalism began to revise itself in response to the socialist challenge long before socialism became a significant electoral menace.

[76]F. R. Scott, "W.L.M.K.," *The Blasted Pine*, ed. F. R. Scott and A. J. M. Smith (Toronto, 1962), p. 28.

[77]Hartz, *Liberal Tradition*, p. 263.   [78]*Ibid.*

[79]*Ibid.*, p. 260.

remain intact, and a succession of ideologically dehydrated 'problems' could be solved."[80]

Hartz points out that this "pragmatism" of the New Deal enabled it to go farther, to get more things done, than European Liberal Reform. "The freewheeling inventiveness typified by the TVA, the NRA, the WPA, the SEC"[81] was nowhere to be found in Europe. Defending itself against socialism, European Liberal Reform could not submerge questions of theory; it had to justify innovations on the basis of a revised liberal ideology; it had to stop short of socialism openly. The New Deal, since it was not threatened by socialism, could ignore theory; it "did not need to stop short of Marx openly"; hence it could accomplish more than European Liberal Reform.

King had to face the socialist challenge. He did so in the manner of European Liberal Reform. No need to worry about abandoning individualism; Locke was not Canada's national god; like European liberalism, Canadian liberalism had been revised. The similarity of socialism and Liberal Reform could be acknowledged; indeed, it could be emphasized, made into political capital for the purpose of attracting the socialist vote. Is this not the meaning of King's celebrated remark that the socialists were "Liberals in a hurry" and of his consistently conciliatory attitude to the socialist group in Parliament? At the same time, King had to answer to the arguments of socialism, and in doing so he had to spell out his liberalism. He had to stop short of socialism openly.[82] Social reform, yes; extension of public ownership, yes; the welfare state, yes; increased state control of the economy, yes; but not too much. Not socialism. The result was that King, like the European liberals, could not go as far as Roosevelt.

Hartz emphasizes the striking "contrast between the 'radical' aggressive mood of Liberal Reform in the American New Deal and the 'conservative' defensive mood of Liberal Reform in Western Europe";[83] the type of young radical who became a socialist in Europe became a New Dealer in America. Bring Canada into this picture, and the European rather than the American character of Canadian Liberal Reform becomes crystal clear. Substitute the word "Canada" for "Europe" in Hartz's description of the contrast between European and

[80]Hartz, *New Societies*, p. 111.

[81]Hartz, *Liberal Tradition*, p. 271.

[82]Speaking in the Commons on February 27, 1933, King assured the socialists that their objectives were not alien to the spirit of Liberalism. His objection was to their "implied method of reform through dictatorship." Norman McL. Rogers, *Mackenzie King* (Toronto, 1935), p. 186.

[83]Hartz, *Liberal Tradition*, p. 260.

American Liberal Reform,[84] and the description will still ring true. The mood of King Liberalism was conservative and defensive. There was no "feeling of high adventure, sense of iconoclasm, genuine 'radicalism' "[85] about it; the young men who became New Dealers in the United States became CCFers in Canada.

"What makes the New Deal 'radical,' " says Hartz, "is the smothering by the American Lockean faith of the socialist challenge to it." Roosevelt did not need to reply to Norman Thomas as the European liberals had to reply to their socialists. Roosevelt therefore did not have to "spell out his liberal premises and hence create the atmosphere of indecision which this necessarily involved."[86] Atmosphere of indecision: is this not the characteristic atmosphere of King Liberalism?

Hartz asks: "What would Roosevelt have said had he . . . been compelled to take Thomas . . . seriously?"[87] and shows that Roosevelt would have been forced to defend private property against nationalization, to attack "bureaucracy" and the all-powerful state, to criticize "utopianism" and "impracticability" in politics. He would have had to qualify his radicalism by an attack on the larger radicalism which faced him to the left. "In other words, instead of being 'radical,' he would be half radical and half conservative, which is precisely the position that the Liberal Reformers of Europe were compelled to occupy. Instead of enlisting the vigorous passions of youth, he might easily be described as a tired man who could not make up his mind; a liberal who tried to break with Adam Smith but could not really do so."[88] What Roosevelt *would* have said if he had answered Norman Thomas is what King *did* say in answering Woodsworth and Coldwell. Like the Europeans, and unlike Roosevelt, he had to defend private property, he had to attack excessive reliance on the state, he had to criticize socialism as "impracticality" and "utopianism." "Half radical and half conservative . . . a tired man who could not make up his mind": is this not the living image of Mackenzie King?

"In America, instead of being a champion of property, Roosevelt became the big antagonist of it: his liberalism was blocked by his radicalism."[89] In Canada, since King had to worry not only about Bennett and Meighen and Drew, but also about Woodsworth and Coldwell and Douglas, King had to embark upon a defence of private property. *He* was no traitor to his class. Instead of becoming the antagonist of property, he became its champion: his radicalism was blocked by his liberalism.

[84]*Ibid.*, pp. 259–72. [85]*Ibid.*, p. 260. [86]*Ibid.*, p. 261
[87]*Ibid.*, p. 262. [88]*Ibid.*. [89]*Ibid.*, p. 267.

An emphasis on the solidarity of the nation as against divisive "class parties" of right and left was "of the very essence of the Reformist Liberal position in Europe." "Who," asks Hartz, "would think of Roosevelt as a philosopher of class solidarity?"[90] Yet that is precisely what Roosevelt would have been if he had had to respond to a socialist presence in the American political culture. And that is precisely what King was in fact in Canada. His party was "the party of national unity." One of his most repeated charges against the CCF was that it was a divisive "class party"; the purpose of the Liberal party, on the other hand, was to preserve the solidarity of the Canadian people—the solidarity of its classes as well as the solidarity of French and English.

Hartz sums up Roosevelt in these words: "What emerges then . . . is a liberal self that is lost from sight: a faith in property, a belief in class unity, a suspicion of too much state power, a hostility to the utopian mood, all of which were blacked out by the weakness of the socialist challenge."[91] King's liberal self was not lost from sight, for the socialist challenge was stronger in Canada than in the United States.

The Liberal party has continued to speak the language of King: ambiguous and ambivalent, presenting first its radical face and then its conservative face, urging reform and warning against hasty, ill-considered change, calling for increased state responsibility but stopping short of socialism openly, speaking for the common people but preaching the solidarity of classes:

The Canadian voter is in favour of progress AND against social experimentation.[92]

The Liberal party believes in the minimum of interference and control by the state . . . and is opposed to any scheme of overall control of the economy; BUT it is in favour of intervention by the government when required to meet the needs of the people.[93]

Liberalism accepts social security but rejects socialism; it accepts free enterprise but rejects economic anarchy; it accepts humanitarianism but rejects paternalism.[94]

Liberalism . . . while insisting on equality of opportunity rejects any imposed equality which would discourage and destroy a man's initiative and enterprise. It sees no value in equality . . . which comes from lopping off the

---

[90]*Ibid.*   [91]*Ibid.*, p. 270.

[92]National Liberal Federation, *The Liberal Party of Canada* (Ottawa: National Liberal Federation, 1957), p. 15. My emphasis.

[93]*Ibid.*, p. 72. My emphasis.

[94]L. B. Pearson, Introduction to J. W. Pickersgill, *The Liberal Party* (Toronto, 1962), p. x.

tallest ears of corn. It maintains . . . that initiative and enterprise should be encouraged, and that reward should be the result of effort.[95]

Liberalism insists that the government must not stand by helpless in the face of . . . human suffering. . . . Liberals, however, do not believe in socialism, with its veneration of the powerful state; with its emphasis on bureaucracy; with its class consciousness. . . . It is the responsibility of government to bring about conditions in which free enterprise can operate more productively and vigorously.[96]

The Liberal view is that true political progress is marked by . . . the reconciliation of classes, and the promotion of the general interest above all particular interests, whether of class or creed or occupation.[97]

In the United States, the liberal Democrats are on the left; there is no doubt about that. In Canada, the Liberals are a party of the centre, appearing at times leftist and at times rightist. As such, they are much closer to European, especially British, Liberal Reform than to the American New Deal type of liberalism.

In the United States, the liberal Democrats have absorbed the socialists. If anything remains of socialism in the United States (outside of the infinitesimal Socialist Party–Social Democratic Federation) it remains as a kind of repressed or sublimated socialism, the socialism of avowed *ex*-socialists who are now merely the most liberal of liberal Democrats. The American socialists of the thirties have been *aufgehoben* in the Democratic party. In Canada, liberalism and socialism are still opposing forces.

In the United States, the liberal Democrats are the party of organized labour. The new men of power, the labour leaders, have arrived politically; their vehicle is the Democratic party. In English Canada, if the labour leaders have arrived politically, they have done so in the CCF-NDP. They are nowhere to be found in the Liberal party. The rank and file, in the United States, are predominantly Democrats; in Canada at least a quarter are New Democrats, and the remainder show only a relatively slight and by no means consistent preference for the Liberals as against the Conservatives.[98]

In the United States, left-wing "liberalism," as opposed to right-wing "liberalism," has always meant opposition to the domination of American life by big business and has expressed itself in and through the Democratic party; the party of business is the Republican party. In Canada, business is close to both the Conservatives and the Liberals.

[95]*Ibid.*
[97]*Ibid.*, p. 68.

[96]*Ibid.*, p. 115.
[98]See below, pp. 41–4.

The business community donates to the campaign funds of both[99] and is represented in the leadership circles of both.

A comparison of two election broadsides, one by an American liberal Democrat and one by a Canadian Liberal, is most instructive. *Kennedy or Nixon*, by Arthur Schlesinger Jr., is suffused with the spirit of the New Deal. Liberalism is defined as "opposition to control of the government by the most powerful group in the community." The Democratic party is described as the party which unites all other groups, including individual "nonconformist businessmen" who have transcended their class interests, for the struggle against the forces of business orthodoxy, against the *status quo*. The Republican party is labelled as the party of the orthodox business "establishment." It "has characteristically identified the general welfare with the welfare of the most powerful group in our society—the business community. . . . It represents the organized wealth of the country." The book closes with an attack on bankers, owners of television stations, Wall Street brokers, General Motors, Du Pont, and the American Medical Association.[100]

The Liberal Party by J. W. Pickersgill, is suffused with the ambivalent, centrist, radical-conservative spirit of Mackenzie King. The Liberal Party is for judicious reform, against unreasoning attachment to the *status quo*, but of course it is also opposed to headstrong and irreverent socialism. Schlesinger does not hesitate to relate liberalism to the conflicting interests of specific social forces. Pickersgill defines liberalism in vague, inoffensive generalities: "The first principle of Liberalism is that the state . . . exist(s) to serve man, and not man to serve the state. The second principle of Liberalism is that the family is the foundation of human society and that it is the duty of all governments to promote the welfare of the family and the sanctity of the home."[101] The Liberal party does not represent the opposition of society to domination by organized business. It claims to be based on no particular groups, but on *all*. It is not against any particular group; it is for *all*. The idea that there is any real conflict between the interests of various groups—the notion of the class struggle, democratic or otherwise—the very terms "right" and "left," are explicitly rejected: "The terms 'right' and 'left' belong to

[99]"Opinions on the motivation behind this political giving to the two old parties are not difficult to gather from the collectors of these contributions and from the officials of the parties. These reasons have included, in the relative frequency with which they are expressed: 1. Preservation of private enterprise. 2. Preservation of the two-party system." Nine other reasons follow. E. E. Harrill, "Money in Canadian Politics," in H. Thorburn, ed., *Party Politics in Canada* (Toronto, 1963), p. 68.

[100](New York, 1960), pp. 43, 46, 50.

[101]*The Liberal Party*, p. 64.

those who regard politics as a class struggle. . . . The Liberal view is that true political progress is marked by . . . the reconciliation of classes, and the promotion of the general interest above all particular interests."[102]

A party of the left can be distinguished from parties of the centre and right according to two interrelated criteria: its policy approach, and its electoral support.

Policy approach

The broad policy approach of left parties is to introduce innovations on behalf of the deprived, underprivileged, or "lower" strata of society. Right parties tend first to resist the innovations on behalf of the threatened privileged or "upper" strata, then to absorb or incorporate the innovations in modified form. Centre parties play an ambivalent role, striving to act on behalf of both broad class groupings. They tend to take on a leftist colour in periods of innovation and a rightist colour in periods of consolidation.

The Liberals, unlike the liberal Democrats, have not been a party of innovation. As a centre party, they have allowed the CCF-NDP to introduce innovations; they have then waited for signs of substantial acceptance by all strata of the population and for signs of reassurance against possible electoral reprisals before actually proceeding to implement the innovations. By this time, of course, they are, strictly speaking, no longer innovations. The centre party recoils from the fight for controversial measures; it loves to implement a consensus. Roosevelt was the innovator *par excellence*. King, though he was in his own mind in favour of reform, stalled until public demand for innovation was so great and so clear that he could respond to it without antagonizing his business-sponsored right wing. He rationalized his caution into a theory of democratic leadership far different from Roosevelt's conception of the strong presidency: "Mackenzie King's conception of political leadership, which he often expressed, was that a leader should make his objectives clear, but that leadership was neither liberal nor democratic which tried to force new policies . . . on a public that did not consent to them."[103] "He believed that nothing was so likely to set back a good cause as

[102]*Ibid.*, p. 68. David Marquand notes that the British Liberal party's "proudest boast is that they are not tied to the great power blocs of modern society, that they are a party of individuals and not of interests. . . . Their ideology . . . is characterized by a pervasive disdain for the unpleasant realities of social and political conflict and a refusal to admit that society is made up of opposing groups." "Has 'Lib-Lab' a Future?" *Encounter*, April 1962, p. 64.

[103]Pickersgill, *The Liberal Party*, pp. 26–7.

premature action."[104] This was the official Liberal explanation of King's
failure to embark on any far-reaching program of reform until 1943.
King himself undoubtedly believed that his caution was based at least
in part on a "democratic" theory of leadership.

But his diaries suggest that the reforms came when they did because
CCF pressure became so threatening that it could no longer be ignored
by King's right-wing colleagues, so threatening that King felt able to
surrender to it without jeopardizing the unity of his party. The bare facts
are these: In August 1943 the CCF became the official opposition in
Ontario. In September 1943 the CCF overtook the Liberals in the
Gallop poll.[105] King's reaction is summed up in the following quotation
from his diary: "In my heart, I am not sorry to see the mass of the
people coming a little more into their own, but I do regret that it is not
the Liberal party that is winning that position for them. . . . It can still
be that our people will learn their lesson in time. What I fear is we will
begin to have defections from our own ranks in the House to the
CCF."[106] Almost immediately after the release of the September Gallup
poll, the Advisory Council of the National Liberal Federation, meeting
at King's request, adopted fourteen resolutions "constituting a program
of reform . . . of far reaching consequences."[107] King wrote in his diary:
"I have succeeded in making declarations which will improve the lot of
. . . farmers and working people. . . . I think I have cut the ground in
large part from under the CCF. . . ."[108] "The great numbers of people
will see that I have been true to them."[109]

The Liberal slogan in the campaign of 1945 was "A New Social Order
for Canada." The election of June 11 returned King to power with a
drastically reduced majority. The CCF vote rose from 8.5 per cent to
15.6 per cent, and its representation in the Commons from 8 to 29. But
King's swing to the left had defeated the CCF's bid for major party
status. The CCF success was much smaller than it had expected. The
success was actually a defeat, a disappointing shock from which socialism
in Canada has not yet recovered.

The Liberal-CCF relationship in 1943–45 is only the sharpest and
clearest instance of the permanent interdependence forced upon each by

[104]J. W. Pickersgill, *The Mackenzie King Record*, I, *1939–1944* (Toronto,
1960), p. 10.
[105]Canada: CCF 29%, Liberals 28%; Ontario: CCF 32%, Liberals 26%; the
West: CCF 41%, Liberals 23%. *Globe and Mail*, Toronto, Sept. 29, 1943.
[106]Pickersgill, *Record*, p. 571.
[107]NLF, *The Liberal Party of Canada*, p. 53.
[108]Pickersgill, *Record*, p. 601.
[109]*Ibid.*, p. 623.

the presence of the other, a relationship which one student describes as "antagonistic symbiosis." The Liberals depend on the CCF-NDP for innovations; the CCF-NDP depends upon the Liberals for implementation of the innovations. When the left is weak, as before and after the Second World War, the centre party moves right to deal with the Conservative challenge; when the left is strengthened, as during the war and after the formation of the NDP, the centre moves left to deal with that challenge.

In a conversation between King and Coldwell shortly before King's death, King expressed his regrets that Coldwell had not joined him. With Coldwell at his side, he would have been able to implement reforms which were close to his heart; reforms which had either been postponed until the end of the war or not introduced at all. He said the CCF had performed the valuable function of popularizing reforms so that he could introduce them when public opinion was ripe. Coldwell replied that it was impossible for him to join King, especially in view of the people by whom King was surrounded.[110] There, in a nutshell, is the story of the relationship between the Liberal party and the CCF-NDP. The Liberals, says King, are too conservative because the left has not joined them. The left has not joined them, replies Coldwell, because they are too conservative.

King wanted to show the people that he was "true to them." He was saddened that the CCF and not the Liberals were fighting the peoples' battles. But he could not move from dead centre until CCF power became so great that the necessity of moving was clear, not only to himself, but to all realistic politicians. King's best self wanted to innovate; yet he saw the Liberal party not as a great innovating force but as the party which would implement reforms once they had been popularized by the CCF. Yet he wanted to absorb the CCF. The lot of the centrist politician is not a happy one.

Norman Thomas explains his party's failure to make a significant impact on politics during the depression with a phrase: "It was Roosevelt in a word."[111] The explanation of the impact made by the CCF on Canadian politics during the depression and especially the Second World War has been presented just as simply by Eugene Forsey: "Canada has had no Roosevelt and no New Deal."[112]

The absence of Lockean monotheism strengthened socialism in Canada. Socialism was present in the political culture when liberalism

[110]Interview with M. J. Coldwell, March 28, 1962.
[111]Seidler, *Norman Thomas*, p. 313.
[112]Untitled manuscript, n.d., NDP files.

began to concern itself with the problems of the industrial age; liberalism was therefore forced to react to the socialist challenge. In doing so, it was cast in the mould of European Liberal Reform (centre) parties— ambivalent, radical and conservative, alternating attacks on the *status quo* with defence of the *status quo*. Socialism had sufficient initial strength in English Canada to force liberalism into the European rather than the American position—centre rather than left. King Liberalism was therefore not capable of reacting to the depression in a Rooseveltian manner. As a result, socialist power grew.

Socialism was not powerless, so there was no New Deal. There was no New Deal, so socialism grew more powerful. Socialism grew more powerful, so King reacted with "A New Social Order for Canada." The centre and the left dance around one another, frustrating one another and living off the frustration; each is locked into the dance by the existence of the other.

I have been stressing the strength of Canadian socialism in order to make clear the differences between the Canadian and the American situations. Of course, this does not mean that the differences between Canada and Europe can be ignored. Canadian socialism has been strong enough to challenge liberalism, to force liberalism to explain itself, and thus to evoke from it the same sort of centrist response as was evoked in Europe. But socialism in Canada has not been strong enough to match or overshadow liberalism. The CCF became a significant political force, but except for the years 1942–45 it never knocked on the gates of national power.

In Europe, the workingman could not be appeased by the concessions of Liberal Reform. The centre was squeezed out of existence between its enemies on the right and on the left. In Canada, the centre party's concessions were sufficient to keep the lower strata from flocking *en masse* to the left. The concessions were not sufficient to *dispose* of the socialist threat, but they were sufficient to draw the socialists' sharpest teeth. In Canada the centre party emerged triumphant over its enemies on the right and on the left. Here, then, is another aspect of English Canada's uniqueness: it is the only society in which Liberal Reform faces the challenge of socialism *and* emerges victorious. The English Canadian fragment *is* bourgeois. The toryism and the socialism, though significant, are "*touches.*"

Electoral support
The higher occupational and status groups of a society tend to give relatively more of their electoral support to parties of the right than do

the lower occupational and status groups, which tend to favour parties of the left. Parties of the centre are generally supported by roughly equal percentages of each of the two broad groupings of voters.

There is a dearth of information about the influence of class on voting behaviour in Canada, but there are strong indications that the higher strata are more likely than the lower to vote Conservative, the lower strata are more likely than the higher to vote CCF-NDP, and that both groups are *equally* attracted to the Liberals. This would of course confirm the picture of Conservatives as the right, NDP as the left, and Liberals as the "classless" centre. This is in sharp contrast to the situation in the United States where the lower strata prefer the Democrats, the higher prefer the Republicans, and there is no centre party.

The left-centre-right character of NDP, Liberals, and Conservatives appears very clearly in the distribution of the trade union vote among the three parties in the federal election of 1962 (Table I).

TABLE I

TRADE UNION VOTING, FEDERAL ELECTION 1962

	Union families	Non-union families
Conservative	26%	40%
Liberal	38	38
NDP	22	8

The appeal of the Conservatives is substantially greater in the non-union group; the appeal of the NDP is much greater in the union group; the Liberal appeal is exactly the same for both groups.[113] The centre party appeals to no particular class: it appeals to none in particular, to all in generalities.

[113]R. Alford, "The Social Bases of Political Cleavage in 1962," in J. Meisel, ed., *Papers on the 1962 Election* (Toronto, 1964), p. 211. These figures are for Canada as a whole. The picture becomes more complicated when one looks at the distribution of the federal vote in each province. In British Columbia, Ontario, and Manitoba, the picture of Conservatives (together with Social Credit in British Columbia) on the right, Liberals in the centre, NDP on the left is repeated:

	Ontario		Manitoba		British Columbia	
	Union	Non-union	Union	Non-union	Union	Non-union
Conservative	29%	49%	18%	49%	11 ⎫ 30	27 ⎫ 58
Social Credit	—	—	—	—	19 ⎰	31 ⎰
Liberal	39	33	39	33	35	29
NDP	27	11	39	6	35	13

But in Alberta, Saskatchewan, and Nova Scotia the great popularity of Diefenbaker

Although this picture of the relationship between class and voting is broadly true, it is also true that class voting in Canada is, generally speaking, overshadowed by regional and religious-ethnic voting. In some parts of Canada, e.g. Ontario, class voting is as high as in the United States or higher. Nevertheless, in Canada *considered as a whole* class voting is lower than in the United States; non-class motivations appear

pushes the Conservatives to the left of the Liberals. This is particularly striking in Alberta.

	Alberta		Saskatchewan		Nova Scotia	
	Union	Non-union	Union	Non-union	Union	Non-union
Conservative	72%	38%	33%	49%	46%	46%
Social Credit	17	36	—	—	—	—
Liberal	11	20	10	25	29	46
NDP	—	—	57	17	25	8

In Alberta, the *Conservatives* appear as the left party, Social Credit and the Liberals share the right-wing position, and no party has anything like an equal appeal to unionists and non-unionists. In Saskatchewan, the NDP is clearly on the left, the Liberals on the right, and the Conservatives in a position which might be described as centre-left (receiving a higher percentage of the non-union vote, but clearly more appealing to the unionists than the Liberals). In Nova Scotia, the NDP retains the left position, the Liberals are on the right, and the Conservatives are the centre party.

In Quebec, the Liberals are back in the normal central position and the Conservatives are back on the right, but Caouette's Créditistes take the place of the NDP on the left:

	Union	Non-union
Conservative	15%	28%
Liberal	41	46
Créditiste	41	24

New Brunswick is the only province in which the *Liberals* appear on the left:

	Union	Non-Union
Conservative	33%	55%
Liberal	56	36

This is probably a result of the Acadian orientation of the Liberals in New Brunswick. Alford provides no data for Prince Edward Island and Newfoundland.

In no province except New Brunswick are the Liberals in a position comparable to that of the liberal Democrats in the United States. On the contrary, in three provinces the Diefenbaker appeal pushes the Liberals into a position well to the right of Canada's traditional right-wing party, the Conservatives. It is also noteworthy that in the five provinces in which the NDP exists as a significant political force, at least 25 per cent (Nova Scotia) and as many as 57 per cent (Saskatchewan) of members of union *families* vote for it. This does not support McRae's view of the Canadian labour movement as one which is, like the American, "not significantly attracted to socialism."

When the manual–non-manual distinction rather than the unionist–non-unionist to be very strong.[114] Alford points out that although particular localities or provinces may associate a particular party with particular classes, the associations are not the same throughout the country: there is no single solid class basis for politics from coast to coast. He attributes this to the lack of integration of Canada as a nation: there are few *national* experiences affecting the same social group in exactly the same way all across the country.[115] The same social group therefore reacts in different ways in different parts of the country: Alberta unionists greatly prefer the Conservatives, New Brunswick unionists greatly prefer the Liberals.

Regenstreif observes that "a significant feature of Canadian political behaviour is the seeming instability of voter commitment to party over time."[116] Social groups veer from party to party, e.g. prairie farmers from the Liberals, Social Credit, and the CCF to the Conservatives, Quebec workers from the Liberals to Social Credit, Eastern professional and business men from the Conservatives to the Liberals. This shifting is made possible by the relative *weakness* of the images which tie particular groups to particular parties; a group can shift the weight of its support radically and rapidly from one party to another with relatively little feeling of strain. Regenstrief suggests that one factor accounting for this weakness of the images linking parties to social groups is the persistent cultivation by the Liberal party of its classless image, its "abhorrence of anything remotely associated with class politics,"[117] its refusal to appeal to any class *against* any other class. The result for the political system is that there are few groups upon which any party can rely for the same consistent degree of support over time.

---

distinction is applied to the voting data, essentially the same distribution is found: Conservatives on the right, Liberals at the centre, and NDP on the left, with similar deviations on the provincial level.

	Canada		Ontario		Alberta		New Brunswick	
	Manual	Non-manual	Manual	Non-manual	Manual	Non-manual	Manual	Non-manual
Conservative	30%	41%	29%	50%	47%	32%	40%	61%
Liberal	39	39	42	39	13	39	46	33
NDP	15	8	24	9	—	—	—	—
Social Credit	—	—	—	—	35	29	—	—

Alford, "Social Bases", pp. 218–22.

[114]R. Alford, *Party and Society* (Chicago, 1963), chap. 9.
[115]Alford, "Social Bases," pp. 203–4.
[116]Peter Regenstreif, "Group Perceptions and the Vote," in Meisel, ed., *Papers*, p. 249.
[117]*Ibid.*

What this points to again is the unique character of English Canada as the only society in which the centre triumphs over left and right. In Europe the classless appeal of Liberal Reform doesn't work: the centre is decimated by the defection of high-status adherents to the right and of low-status adherents to the left. In Canada, the classless appeal of King centrism is the winning strategy, drawing lower-class support to the Liberals away from the left parties, and higher-class support away from the right parties. This forces the left and right parties themselves to emulate (to a certain extent) the Liberals' classless strategy. The Conservatives transform themselves into Progressive Conservatives. The CCF transforms itself from a "farmer-labour" party into an NDP calling for the support of "all liberally minded Canadians." The Liberal refusal to appear as a class party forces both right and left to mitigate their class appeals and to become themselves, in a sense, centre parties.

Class voting in Canada may be lower than in the United States not entirely because regional-religious-ethnic factors are "objectively" stronger here (Canada's lack of integration as a nation) but also because King Liberalism, by resolutely avoiding class symbols, has *made* other symbols more important.

> He blunted us.
> We had no shape
> Because he never took sides,
> And no sides,
> Because he never allowed them to take shape.[118]

7. THE PARTY SYSTEM

A socialism imported from Britain could play a significant role in British North America, where Locke had to share his power with other deities. A socialism imported from Europe could not become an important force in the United States, where Lockean monotheism reigned supreme. But this is not by any means the whole story.

American socialism was twice cursed: by the supremacy of Locke, and by a party system which discourages the formation of third parties and dispenses with them soon after they are formed. Canadian socialism was twice blessed: by the inability of Locke to become the one god, and by a party system which encourages the formation of third parties and enables them to remain in existence once they are formed.

One view of the Canadian party system pictures it as the American

[118]Scott, *The Blasted Pine*, p. 27.

party system in little. Of course, Canadian parties have to operate in a parliamentary rather than a congressional-presidential framework, but from the pan-North American point of view the main thing about Canadian parties is that they operate in a social context which resembles the American in its great diversity and heterogeneity. The Canadian major parties are therefore seen as "in essence" American: broad coalitions which are capable of encompassing all politically significant groups in the country.

It is true that the function of all North American parties is to weld divergent groups by the arts of compromise and conciliation into a single political machine capable of electing an American president or forming a Canadian government. Canadian like American parties act as "brokers" for the many sectional, ethnic, and economic interests of a continental federation. No North American party can succeed unless it draws support from all or most of the major regions. The great North American party leaders—and the Canadian, I dare say, even more than the American—have excelled in the art of group diplomacy. Macdonald, Laurier, and King were men who knew how to unite bickering sectional groups for the "common good."

The trouble with the pan-North American approach is again that it sees the similarities, but either ignores the differences or explains them away as "exceptions." From this point of view, third parties in Canada are like third parties in the United States—evanescent protest movements whose function is to air some ignored grievance or popularize some new idea, and whose fate is to be absorbed by the major parties as soon as the latter wake up to the necessity of making concessions to the dissenters: "In Canada the appearance of a third party . . . means that the two traditional parties have failed in their efforts satisfactorily to emulate the Republicans and the Democrats, that they have fallen down on their job of catering for all major interest groups and that they have left the . . . public unconvinced that between them they span the political spectrum."[119] This approach assumes that the major parties are capable of catering to all major interest groups and of spanning the entire political spectrum. That is their "job." Since they are capable of doing the job, the fact that they are not doing it at any particular moment means that they have "fallen down on their job" just as the American parties occasionally do.

How, then, are we to explain the persistent strength of third parties in Canada? How are we to account for the fact that Canada has had since

[119]Anthony Howard, "Left Wing Party for Canada," *Manchester Guardian Weekly*, March 16, 1961.

the depression two minor parties—the CCF-NDP and Social Credit—which have perversely refused to be absorbed into the major parties?

A system which has been operating for over thirty years in such a manner as to produce and sustain minor parties cannot reasonably be identified with a system which just as consistently discourages and destroys minor parties. We have here not a single system which functions "well" south of the border and "poorly" north of the border, but two different systems, one of which operates in one way, and the other in a different way. A "job" which has not been done for thirty years is no longer a "job." The major parties in Canada are *not* capable of spanning the entire political spectrum.

Canadian political parties, since they operate in a parliamentary system of government, are far more cohesive and disciplined than American parties. Compromise in an American party usualy involves merely agreement to disagree, since policy differences will not result in the loss of office. In Canada the price of disagreement, when it finds expression in parliament or even if it is expressed publicly at all, is likely to be the loss of office.

The constituent elements of a Canadian party are under great pressure to arrive at a common policy and to stick to it; they must therefore accept a far greater degree of direction from the official party leadership than their American counterparts need accept from their leaders. Once policy is formed, the only alternatives for dissident groups are submission or secession. They cannot, like their American counterparts, maintain their autonomy and still remain within the party.

Viewing the situation from the front benches of the Commons rather than the back benches, the Canadian party leader is far more dependent on his followers in the Commons and their sponsors in the country than the American president. He has no independent base of power. If he is to remain the leader, he must keep his party solidly behind him and his policies.

The Canadian party strives mightily to build a facade of unity on all contentious issues and to avoid public disagreement like the plague. The party will try to carry on the process of compromise in secret and to arrive at a decision which will antagonize as few of its members as possible. Once the decision is reached it satisfies no one, but everyone must support it enthusiastically in public. Compromise must produce unity. Those who are antagonized beyond endurance have no recourse except resignation.

The process of compromise in the American party is qualitatively different. It need not produce unity. Everyone knows that Southern

Democrats are opposed to integration, that Northern Democrats are for it, and that the party platform will be a compromise. But the compromise does not need to masquerade as the general will. The Southerners can go on opposing integration in Congress and in public debate; the Northerners can continue to press for it. *The party* as such has no policy. It can be tarred with no particular brush.

The American dissident can follow his own line just as well inside a major party as outside. The Canadian dissident—the Western farmer, say, or the socialistically inclined industrial worker, or the French-Canadian nationalist—if he is inside a major party, must accept the yoke of the leader and the binding decisions of the caucus. For the American dissident the incentive to get out and stay out of the major party is weak; for the Canadian dissident it is strong.

In a word, the relations of dependence and control are much stronger in the Canadian party than in the American. Consequently, the major parties in Canada are handicapped in the performance of their "broker" function. The degree of unity which they must achieve is so great that they have not between them been able to accommodate all the significant interests of the country. The result is that the incentive to form third parties and to preserve their existence is much greater in Canada than in the United States.

The Progressive revolt of the twenties was a revolt against the strict discipline of the Liberal caucus; its purpose was to free representatives of agrarian constituencies from the Liberal whip, to allow representatives of farmers to speak and vote as representatives of farmers. A Democrat or a Republican representing an agrarian area in Congress need not fear that his party allegiance would restrict his freedom to act in the interests of his constituents, and a Populist or Progressive could for this reason return to the old party without qualms.

The Progressive revolt itself, though spectacular, was short-lived. Most of its leaders were reabsorbed into the Liberal party, partly due to the internal weaknesses of their movement, partly in response to the blandishments of King. But the Progressive movement, a movement of Liberal dissidents, was succeeded by two *new* parties which refused to be absorbed—the CCF and Social Credit.

One of the primary functions of a third party in Parliament is to wrest "concessions" from the government and to a lesser extent from the official opposition as well. The ultimate goal may be to achieve major party status—but the immediate goal is to influence legislation and if possible to hold the balance of power. In Congress these tasks are performed by a bloc within one or both parties. The Southern Democrats have held the balance of power in Congress for a generation. A similar group in Canada must operate as a third party.

The CCF's "prevailing self-justification" throughout the fifties was its utility as an instrument for wresting legislative concessions from the government:

At meeting after meeting, in every federal campaign of the 1950's, its speakers . . . revived a tale of thirty years earlier—how J. S. Woodsworth had wrested old age pensions from Mackenzie King . . . when he and a colleague had held the balance of power in the House of Commons in 1926. . . . It took every opportunity to inform the public and remind its followers of its indispensable role in securing welfare legislation . . . its *raison d'être* increasingly became to force its rivals to adopt welfare measures.[120]

The greater utility of third parties in Canada can be seen from yet another angle. There is only one political arena in Canada and in each of its provinces—the legislature. Politics in the United States goes on in two distinct arenas, the legislative and the executive. The contests for the presidency and the governorship overshadow the contests for Congress and the state legislatures. Third parties can play very little part in executive politics (except as adjuncts of the major parties, like the Liberal party of New York) because only one party can win. The presidency and the governorship cannot be controlled by more than one party.[121] As Norman Thomas says,[122] in parliamentary systems "it was only necessary for a socialist or labor party to elect a few representatives and make a good record. Their representation could rapidly snowball. In the United States every four years the election of all members of Congress is subordinate to the election of the president," an all-or-nothing contest from which a minor party can wrest no small gains which might serve as a foundation for future growth.

The differing structures and procedures of Congress and Parliament are also important. In Canada, once a third party elects even a handful of MPs, it is in the national limelight. The rules of the House of Commons, which give all parties the opportunity to state their position on all issues under consideration, make this possible. In the House of Representatives, Norman Thomas would have been just another Representative. In the House of Commons, Woodsworth—even as the leader of a group consisting only of himself and William Irvine—was a party leader;

120Zakuta, *A Protest Party Becalmed*, 88–9.
121In the national legislative arena, the election of Senators overshadows the election of Representatives. Each state has only two Senators; a third party is much less likely to elect a Senator than a Representative, so is handicapped in this arena as well.
122*A Socialist's Faith* (New York, 1951), p. 92.

as such he shared the limelight with the prime minister and the leader of the opposition. A third party in the Canadian parliament, just because it is a separate party, often has an influence greater than its numerical strength might warrant on the content and tone of debate and on legislation, on the shaping of the issues which receive national attention, and on the way in which the issues are resolved.

Once again Hartz's "single factor" explanation seems to be challenged.[123] What if American socialism had not been handicapped by forces *other* than the supremacy of Locke? What if the institutional structure of American politics had helped socialists instead of hindering them? Hartz suggests that there is a connection between cultural and institutional factors: "The issue of third party frustrations in the United States as contrasted with Canada roots back to the peculiar sense of community we have."[124] It is true that the peculiar sense of community of unanimously liberal America expresses itself in the view that an American must be either a Republican or a Democrat—the very thought of a third party is tinged with un-Americanism. But I am not convinced that this would be the case if institutional factors did not frustrate the rise of third parties. Surely it is not the American sense of community that prevents a *legitimate* variant of the American Lockean faith from finding expression in a third party. Still, I would not put any great stress on the party system as an explanation of the weakness of American socialism. The Hartzian cultural analysis shows why socialism as an ideology must die in the United States. If cultural forces kill socialism as an ideology, it will die—regardless of the party system; the American party system only handicaps a socialism which is doomed anyway. The Hartzian analysis applied to Canadian conditions shows why socialism *as an ideology* could become a significant force in Canada. Institutional analysis can show why permanent, significant *third parties* arise, but it cannot explain why one of these parties should be *socialist*. The cultural analysis is necessary to explain the relative strength of a socialist ideology in Canada; the institutional analysis is necessary to explain why this ideology can easily find expression in a permanent separate party.

8. LABOUR AND THE PARTY SYSTEM

This study began with two questions: Why has socialism persisted as a significant political force in Canada while dying in the United States?

[123]See above, p. 28.
[124]In a letter to G.H., July 1, 1963.

Why does the Canadian branch of the North American labour movement support a socialist party as its "political arm" while the American branch supports a liberal "capitalist" party? I have argued that certain characteristics of Canadian political culture and institutions made it possible for a socialist party to exist as a significant political force. The question, "why does the Canadian labour movement support that party?" remains to be answered. The focus now is on the determinants of the official policy of the labour movement.

The Canadian Congress of Labour (CCL) and the Canadian Labour Congress (CLC), in the "political education" literature which they have turned out for the benefit of the rank and file, explain their policy of support for the socialist party in terms of a calculation of indulgences and deprivations: labour has more to gain from support of the CCF-NDP than from any alternative political policy—support of the Liberals, say, or support of "friends of labour" irrespective of party. Most Canadian trade unionists belong to "international" unions which advise their members to vote for "friends of labour" irrespective of party. The Canadian naturally wants to know why he cannot do the same thing. If a Liberal or Conservative or Social Credit candidate claims that he is "friendly," why not vote for him? Why must the CCF-NDP candidate be supported everywhere and under all circumstances? The Canadian Political Action or Political Education Committee (PAC or PEC) tries to answer these questions by giving elementary instruction in political institutions.[125] It explains that the tight discipline required by cabinet government makes it impossible for a "friend of labour" in a party unfriendly to labour to follow his own line:

The U.S. system permits much greater independence on the part of elected members of the Congress. They may vote according to their individual views without endangering the tenure of the Administration. Individual Congressmen and Senators may therefore compile . . . "good" or "bad" voting records and may be supported on the basis of their *records* rather than their party membership. "Rewarding labor's friends and punishing labor's enemies" makes some sense in the U.S. because labour's "friends" and "enemies" are readily identifiable by their voting records in Congress.

In Canada, members of Parliament do not vote . . . according to their individual views. They vote with their party. They do not have "good" or

---

125Ken Bryden to Stanley Knowles, Jan. 27, 1954, NDP files. "It is necessary to emphasize the difference between American and British political institutions because the average guy in the plant knows practically nothing about . . . either. . . . American principles are completely out of place in the Canadian system, because Canada operates under the British and not the American system of government. Our main task is . . . to get this point across to Canadian trade unionists." *Ibid.*

"bad" voting records of their own. It is the Party which has the "good" or "bad" record. If labour wishes to "support its friends and defeat its enemies" in Canada it must do so by electing a "friendly" party and defeating an "unfriendly" party.[126]

AND YOU THOUGHT HE WAS A GOOD GUY?

He had that reputation around town. . . . Sure, he believed in unions. . . . He thought unions were a swell idea. . . . This "good guy" was elected to Ottawa. He was given a seat on one of the back benches and for quite a while he just sat and listened. It was all new and different. . . . Before any major issue came up there was a meeting of the party he represented—a caucus. At that caucus the party line was laid down. And finally some issues came up that . . . vitally affected the families of the people who worked in the home town plants. He remembered what the people back home had said, but it was different now. If he wanted to stay in the party and hope to be a cabinet minister some day then he had to go along. That sympathetic nod that everyone back home had seen so often changed. He was shaking his head now—"No," "No," "No." Because the boys who controlled the old party, who put up the hundreds of thousands for elections had different ideas to the people back home. . . . So, whether he was a so called "good guy" or "bad guy" really didn't make so much difference after all. You couldn't tell a "good guy" from a "bad guy" by their votes![127]

In Canada, then, the only way to "reward your friends" is to reward a *party*; the party most favourable to labour is the CCF-NDP. Gompers' formula realistically applied in Canada means support of the socialist party.

The impression one gets from all this is that the labour leader is an impersonal calculating machine, concerned only with finding the most efficient method of making legislative gains for labour. He supports the CCF simply because the other parties are so tightly disciplined that they are not susceptible to union influence.

But this picture which emerges from the PAC's political science texts exaggerates the effects of party discipline. It is true that in Canada "you can't tell a good guy from a bad guy by his vote." Once a party has decided on its policies, all its MPs must support those policies. But the party line is *set* by a process of compromise; it is a resultant of competing pressures.

Labour men are so few in numbers in the old party caucuses that they are swamped by the business-oriented majorities. But if labour devoted all its political energies to permeating, say, the Liberal party, the number of Liberal "friends" could conceivably be increased to the point where labour would become a powerful force within the Liberal party.

[126]CLC-PEC *Political Education Information Bulletin*, Feb. 1962.
[127]*CCL-PAC Newsletter*, Oct. 1951.

Douglas Fisher has suggested[128] that "the reason for the little speculation on a Liberal-Labour alliance lies . . . in established structures with a built-in survival instinct and a pat attitude to rivals. Personally I believe a dozen determined men could take over the Liberal party. . . ." Fisher probably exaggerates the permeability of the Liberal party. But what emerges here is a different rationale for the political policy of organized labour: not that labour cannot permeate the Liberal party and therefore supports the CCF-NDP, but that labour supports the CCF-NDP and therefore does not try to permeate the Liberal party.

Of course, even if there were a powerful labour bloc within the Liberal party, it would still be operating under the British, not the American, system of government. It could influence party policy, but it would have to do so quietly; and if the policy were unsatisfactory, the labourites would still have to support it in parliament and in public. Labour might reasonably feel that it has more to gain from, say, fifty NDP MPs than fifty Liberal "friends," for these reasons:

1. Labour would have more control over the NDP MPs. The Liberal MPs would be dependent not only on their labour support but also on the Liberal party leadership.

2. The NDP MPs could fight labour's battles vigorously and publicly. The Liberal MPs would have to do the job more cautiously and secretly.

3. The effectiveness of the Liberal MPs would be reduced by their shared responsibility for the behaviour of the Liberal party as a whole. A Democrat can be a labourite pure and simple: he is not committed to any party line, and shares no responsibility for the behaviour of other Democrats. The situation of the Liberal is different: the existence of Liberal anti-labour elements must affect his own behaviour and his own political prospects. Another side of this same coin is that Labour itself might be embarrassed by its association with a Liberal party in which it was not the dominant force. If the Liberal party failed to "deliver the goods" the labour leaders, being Liberals, would have to take part of the blame. This would reduce the effectiveness of labour leaders *as labour leaders*. It would restrict both their responsiveness to rank and file pressures and their ability to play on rank and file sentiments.

4. In terms of sheer legislative gains, fifty NDP MPs *might* be more useful than fifty Liberals, especially if the Liberals were in office. A powerful opposition group is often, and not *only* in the balance-of-power situation, in a better position to wrest concessions from the government than a group within the government party's caucus.

But the point is that this speculation about the relative merits, as

[128]In a letter to the author, March 13, 1961.

techniques for producing legislative gains, of support for the Liberals as against support for the NDP is unrealistic. No labour leader has ever sat down and made such calculations before deciding his union's political policy. Labour supports the socialist party because it is *there*. Of course, labour could make an impact within the Liberal party if it decided to make the effort, or if it had no other choice. American labour *could* become a powerful force in the Republican party; British labour *could* become a powerful force in the Conservative party. They do not make the effort because their attentions are directed elsewhere, because of "established structures" which exist for very good reasons.

Political parties are not impregnable monoliths, but in some, business is a very powerful element. Labour's natural inclination, once it becomes politically active, is not to infiltrate such parties but to oppose them.

Once the structure of labour support for the CCF is established, the question "why this labour support?" cannot be answered simply in terms of a calculation of the legislative advantages of such support at any particular moment. Once the structure is established, labour's support of the CCF-NDP is in large part simply a matter of inertia. Of course, it is also a matter of immediate indulgences and deprivations, in the sense that labour support of the CCF-NDP would be meaningless if the CCF-NDP did not exert a certain minimum of influence in Canadian politics. If the CCF-NDP became insignificant in Canadian politics, labour support would fall away. But *given* a significant party, and given an established structure of labour involvement in and support of that party, the "indulgences" which maintain the structure come not only from outside the structure, in the form of influence on Canadian politics, but also from *within* the structure. Support of the CCF-NDP becomes an established policy. It becomes one of the leadership traits which would-be leaders must adopt in order to be co-opted into leadership positions. The party world and the labour world begin to merge, or at least to interlock, so that the prestige, power, and success of a unionist in one of these worlds becomes a base from which power, prestige, and success can be sought in the other.

Union interests become vested in the party. Effort, loyalty, and enthusiasm are invested in the party over a period of years to such a degree that harm to the party is perceived as harm to the union. The union has an investment in the party which it will not lightly withdraw. The question "why does labour support the CCF-NDP?" becomes misleading because the interlocking, the vesting of interest has reached the point where labour, in a sense, *is* the CCF-NDP.

The question "why does labour support the NDP?" is therefore more adequately dealt with by a historical analysis (how and why did this support become an established structure in the first place?) than by trying to measure the utility of support for the socialist party against the utility of support for the Liberal party at some later period during which it is in fact the socialist party which is being supported. The second type of enquiry is based on a false image of the labour leader as calculating machine; it assumes that labour leaders are free from established patterns of involvement, loyalty, and ideology; and it underestimates the indulgences they get from party involvement over and above the indulgence entailed by the party's impact on government policies.

The Canadian labour élite supports the socialist party today because in the late thirties and early forties, socialists assumed powerful positions in some CIO-CCL unions, and were able to lead the industrial union movement as a whole into a close alliance with the socialist party.[129] The socialists in the American CIO movement, far from leading labour into an alliance with their party, were themselves led into the liberal wing of the Democratic party. Why the difference?

In the United States, in the 1930s, the socialist party was dying, and Roosevelt's New Deal was beckoning. Labour, and the socialists in labour, had no place to go but the New Deal. In Canada the socialist party was, to begin with, a significant political force and had by the early forties grown so strong that it seemed on the point of becoming the official opposition. Labour had an alternative to King Liberalism.

When David Dubinsky and Sidney Hillman resigned from the American Socialist party in 1936, they justified their resignation on two grounds. The first was Roosevelt: his radicalism and his role as virtual founding father of the CIO. Dubinsky said: "Roosevelt is the first truly progressive president we have had in this generation. . . . An FDR defeat must be avoided at all cost."[130] Hillman said: "The CIO is the beginning of a real labour movement. That would have been impossible without the NRA."[131] The second was the virtual non-existence of the socialist party. "There is no labour party," said Hillman, "let us not fool ourselves about that. And since there is no labour party, are we just going to sit down and admit that we cannot do anything?"[132]

Howe and Widick describe what must have been the state of Walter

[129]The AFL-TLC unions abstained from any kind of political action, but when the merger of TLC and CCL took place in 1956 the TLC leaders allowed the policy of the united labour movement to be determined by the CCL socialists. See below, chap. 5.

[130]M. Danish, *The World of David Dubinsky* (New York: 1957), pp. 94–5.

[131]H. Josephson, *Sidney Hillman* (New York, 1952), p. 397.

[132]*Ibid.*, p. 398.

Reuther's mind "between 1936 and 1938": "An acute awareness that . . . the socialist movement showed no signs of growth. . . . He felt that those socialists who wished to exert an immediate, substantial influence on American life would have to abandon the party and its doctrines and join the New Deal parade."[133] Canadian socialist labour leaders did not have to make such agonizing calculations. Not only was the CCF making great progress, but King's labour policies were far less friendly than those of Roosevelt.

Many of the delegates to the 1943 CCL convention which endorsed the CCF probably had two things in mind: the astonishing success of the CCF in the Ontario provincial election a few weeks before, and the labour record of the King government: the wage stabilization policy, the failure to make collective bargaining compulsory even in government-controlled industry, and the failure to give labour adequate representation on government bodies directing the war effort. The convention which endorsed the CCF also demanded the resignation of Humphrey Mitchell, King's minister of labour.

In the United States the CIO had Roosevelt's backing. In Canada the policy of the government was not to encourage labour organization, but to hold the balance between labour and management. Collective bargaining was approved in principle in 1939, but not made compulsory until 1944.

CIO organizers in the United States could tell the workers that Roosevelt wanted them in the union. When the CIO entered Canada in 1937, it was met head-on by the Liberal premier of Ontario, Mitchell Hepburn, who promised to drive it from the province. CIO and CCL organizers received no encouragement from King; industrial unionism in Canada was built without the help of King. Those who built it felt that they were doing so in spite of King, "the father of company unionism on this continent."[134] At the same time, the CCF and its supporters in the labour movement were beckoning. The CCF looked strong. The CCL endorsed the CCF.

In the United States the weakness of organized socialism and the attractiveness of Roosevelt's New Deal led the CIO and its socialists into the Democratic party. In Canada the strength of organized socialism and the unattractiveness of King's ambivalent Liberal Reform allowed the CCL socialists not only to remain themselves loyal to the CCF, but to persuade their "brothers" to endorse it.

[133]I. Howe and B. J. Widick, *The UAW and Walter Reuther* (New York, 1949), p. 194.
[134]Forsey, untitled manuscript, n.d., NDP files.

In a word, American labour had no alternative. If an alternative had existed, there is little doubt that labour's alliance with the Democratic party would have been at least less enthusiastic and less complete. The AFL's League for Nonpartisan Action, the CIO's PAC, and the AFL-CIO's Committee on Political Education (COPE) actually represent a compromise between labour's yearning for a party of its own and labour's realization that if it wishes to exert "an immediate substantial influence" on American politics it must do so through the Democratic party. The compromise consists in building "independent" labour political power which is placed at the service of the Democratic party. In principle, labour's support is conditional and revocable. In practice, there is nowhere else to go.

Where labour feels that its independent political power can take the form of a separate political party, one sees phenomena like the Liberal party of New York and the Michigan Commonwealth Federation. The latter, "obviously modelled after the CCF," was organized by secondary leaders of the UAW in 1944: "For a time it appeared as if the MCF might become a powerful factor in Michigan political life, but it ultimately dissolved or was pressured back into the safe ranks of the CIO's PAC."[135]

After Roosevelt's death "progressives" in the American labour movement, believing that the conditions which made the Democratic alliance necessary no longer existed,[136] began searching for alternatives. Some found their way into the Henry Wallace movement. Others were attracted by plans inspired by the socialist party for conferences "on a new political alignment after the 1948 election."[137] The UAW Executive Board was among the groups which were to participate in these conferences. In 1948 C. Wright Mills found that 23 per cent of labour leaders in the AFL and 52 per cent of labour leaders in the CIO were in favour of a new labour party "within the next ten years."[138] Truman's victory in 1948 put an end to resurgent labour partyism. Labour leaders like Reuther "swung back to the view that labor should function within,

[135]Howe and Widick, *The UAW and Walter Reuther*, p. 273. The CCF's David Lewis played a part in the organization of the Michigan party. Lewis to Reuther, Feb. 25, 1944; Lewis to Jolliffe, March 9, 1944, NDP files.

[136]ACWA's statement on Roosevelt's death: "Roosevelt was one of us. He was the friend and guide of labor. He saved us in 1933. . . . We have been running to him with our problems ever since. Now we are on our own." Josephson, *Sidney Hillman*, p. 634.

[137]Thomas, *A Socialist's Faith*, p. 251.

[138]*The New Men of Power: America's Labor Leaders* (New York, 1948), p. 212.

while not identifying itself with the Democratic party."[139] This policy has not been seriously challenged since 1948.

F. H. Underhill and many other pan-North Americans simply assume that the Liberal party is a party of the left like the liberal Democrats of the United States. They admit that it has not *behaved* as a left party, but they consider that this is merely an accident—a matter of personalities perhaps; perhaps King's personality. Any day now, a magic word will be spoken, a great Rooseveltian leader will appear, the Liberal party will shed its misleading centrist image, its "essentially" leftist nature will be clear for all to see, and organized labour and other elements of the left will return from their NDP exile to their "natural" Liberal home.[140] What these people fail to realize is that important political phenomena are seldom accidents. The Liberal party behaves as a centre party because it *is* a centre party. It is a centre party because cultural factors (the presence of non-liberal ideologies) and institutional factors (the tendency to a multiplicity of parties in Canada) have combined to produce a socialist party on its left. It will cease to behave as a centre party when its enemy on the left disappears. But the NDP, although it may not be "going anywhere," is not about to disappear.

Underhill believes that *if* the Liberal party becomes a left party, organized labour and other leftist elements will join it. But the Liberal party will not become a left party unless these elements join it. What makes this vicious circle possible is the existence in Canada of an alternative which does not exist in the United States—a socialist party which is strong enough to play an important role in national politics. As long as labour has this alternative to a Liberal party interlocked with the business community, the Liberal party will continue to be centrist in the European way rather than "truly liberal" (leftist) in the American way; and as long as it continues to be centrist, organized labour will continue to support the socialist party. The "antagonistic symbiosis" of Canadian liberalism and socialism probably cannot be ended even by the magic of a charismatic leader.

[139]Howe and Widick, *The UAW and Walter Reuther*, p. 277.

[140]"It is just possible that the so-called Liberal party under Mr. Pearson will become at last a Rooseveltian party of the left. . . . If that happens, I predict that our trade unions will follow the Reuther example." In a letter to the author, Feb. 18, 1962.

2. *The First Steps*

1. THE TLC AND SOCIALISM

In the United States socialism was alien; in English Canada socialism was "at home." There is no need to look any further for an explanation of the differing attitudes of the American Federation of Labor (AFL) and the Trades and Labor Congress (TLC) to socialism and to political action by labour. The TLC, though it consisted almost entirely of Canadian locals of AFL unions and was greatly influenced by Gompers, never adopted the Gompers approach *in toto.*

Gompers' rejection of socialism and independent political action (that is, a labour party) was complete and unequivocal. His relationship with the socialists in the labour movement was one of personal, political, and ideological enmity. The TLC never embraced socialism; the socialists within it were always a minority. But it never took a stand *against* socialism. Unlike the AFL, it never adopted the phraseology of *laissez-faire* and Lockean individualism. A socialist, James Watters, was president of the TLC from 1911 to 1918. Socialists like James Simpson (vice-president, 1904–09, 1916–17, 1924–36), John W. Buckley (vice-president, 1943–46, and secretary treasurer, 1947–49), and John Bruce were always to be found in its top councils.

The TLC's fraternal delegate to the AFL convention of 1911 was R. Pettipiece, a prominent British Columbia socialist. He complained on his return to Canada that he had been received very coolly, and "it was most difficult to start a thaw." Happily, he was able to find *some* delegates who were "big enough to realize that it was no crime to the trade unions" to belong to a socialist party.[1]

The TLC's 1933 convention, the first of many which were to refuse to endorse the CCF, nevertheless adopted a resolution "in favour of the co-operative ownership of the machinery of production and distribution. . . . By a system of planned economy and progressive absorption of industrial enterprises etc. this can be peacefully accomplished."[2]

During the 1945 federal election campaign, the TLC vice-president,

[1]Quoted by Martin Robin, "Radical Politics and Organized Labour in Canada, 1880–1930," PhD thesis, Queen's University.
[2]TLC Convention Proceedings (1933), p. 189.

John Buckley, wrote a letter to the editor of the *Toronto Daily Star* (May 23) commenting on a "Charter for Management and Labor" which had recently been issued in the United States by William Green, Philip Murray, and Eric Johnston. The "charter" declared that "the rights of private property and free choice of action under a system of private competitive capitalism must continue to be the foundation of our . . . economy." Buckley noted that this declaration was "being continually quoted during the present election by the heads of the old line parties." The vice-president of the TLC therefore begged leave to point out that labour's endorsement of free enterprise applied only in the United States, not in Canada: "In the platform of principles of the TLC I find the following in contradistinction to this pronouncement. . . . Public ownership and democratic management of . . . public utilities, nationalization of banking and credit, government control of natural resources. . . . "

The TLC's statement of post-war policy, *Victory—What Then?*, unanimously adopted by the 1943 convention, was so socialistic that it read like a CCF election manifesto and was, indeed, endorsed by the CCF's 1944 convention. The statement called for "a system of planned economy" and the "sacrifice of free enterprise" to "a new controlled system that will guarantee the organization of all our resources to provide . . . a new social and economic structure." It denounced "capitalistic methods of production" as inefficient and called for the restriction of "private enterprise to those industries that have no part in the national well being or can cause economic disaster." It also included this astounding statement: "We will have to meet the challenge that we are advocating socialism but public control over public enterprise in the interests of the mass of the people cannot in any way be construed as socialism as it is propounded."

One is not surprised to find that two of the five members of the committee which drafted *Victory—What Then?* were prominent CCF supporters: John Bruce, and Bernard Shane of the International Ladies Garment Workers' Union (ILGWU). This is the point: the TLC was not socialist, but neither was it anti-socialist. Socialists have since the turn of the century been influential members of its top councils, and socialist ideas have affected its policies. Socialism in the AFL was not only a minority movement, it was something of a pariah. In the TLC, socialism was a minority movement, but it was in the mainstream.

The area in which the influence of British working class thought on the TLC is most obvious is that of independent political action. In 1883, at its first convention, the TLC declared that workers should be represented in parliament by "men of their own class," and in 1886 it advised its affiliates to "bring out" candidates "wherever practicable."[3] Two presidents of the TLC, Ralph Smith and Alphonse Verville, were elected to the House of Commons as independent labour members, in 1900 and 1906 respectively.

In 1900 the TLC called for the formation of a labour *party* "separate and distinct from the trade union organization."[4] No action was taken until 1906, when the Congress instructed its provincial executives to set up provincial labour parties whose programs would be based on the TLC Platform of Principles; the executives would then stand aside and the parties would function with no formal connection with the union movement. Provincial parties were formed in British Columbia, Alberta, Manitoba, and Ontario. The Ontario Independent Labor Party (ILP) participated in the Ontario farm-labour coalition government of 1919–23.

In 1917 the TLC sponsored the formation of a Canadian Labour party modelled on the British Labour party, "on a basis which would permit united action on the part of trade unionists, socialists, Fabians, cooperators, and farmers."[5] The party was officially founded in 1921, and "for a few years . . . endeavoured to coordinate the various" labour and socialist provincial parties.[6] Its platform called for "a complete change in our present economic and social systems."[7] Its leader from 1921 to 1927 was the socialist John Bruce. In 1927 it was captured by the Communists and ceased to function as a national party, but a number of local branches (e.g., Quebec, Montreal, Toronto, Hamilton, Alberta) remained in existence for some years after 1927.

Although the TLC-sponsored labour parties were, like the British Labour party before 1918, formally non-socialist, their platforms were at least heavily influenced by socialist thought, and individual socialists were very active and influential in them. James Simpson, for example, was the foremost member of the Ontario party.

In the United States socialists called for an independent labour party and Gompers' AFL rejected them. In Canada socialists like Simpson and Bruce collaborated with "conservative" leaders like Paddy Draper and Tom Moore—Canadian counterparts of Gompers—in the movement for independent political action. The little labour parties of those

[3]*Ibid.* (1883), p. 30; (1886), pp. 12–13, 20.
[4]Canada, Department of Labour, *Report on Labour Organization in Canada* (1931), p. 188.
[5]*Ibid.*
[6]*Ibid.* (1929), p. 171.
[7]J. F. Cahan, "A Survey of Political Activities of the Ontario Labour Movement," MA thesis, University of Toronto, 1945, p. 59.

days often squabbled with the even smaller socialist parties[8] which sprang up here and there, but just as often they co-operated with them. The Ontario ILP joined with the Ontario Social Democratic party in a federated labour party which called itself the Ontario Section of the Canadian Labour party. Federated labour parties in other provinces brought together labour and socialist groups.

Except in Nova Scotia, Ontario, and Manitoba after the First World War, labour political action never succeeded in electing more than two or three individuals here and there. In the twenties the TLC's enthusiasm for political action rapidly cooled and for the last four decades of its life it was rigidly non-political. People like Draper and Moore became exponents of pure Gompersism. But the TLC continued to be formally committed to the idea of a labour party. As late as 1931 the Department of Labour's Annual Report was still pointing out that "contrary to the policy of the TLC of Canada, which believes in a labour political party for the Dominion . . . the AFL . . . is opposed to the formation of a labour political party in the United States. . . ." The TLC justified its refusal to take any further political initiative by reference to its 1923 resolution "that labor political autonomy be left in the hands of [the] established labor political party, [that] the Congress again urge all labor organizations to affiliate and . . . that this Congress continue to act as the legislative mouthpiece for organized labor in Canada independent of any political organization engaged in the effort to send representatives . . . to Parliament. . . ."[9]

The AFL rejected the idea of an independent labour party. For the TLC, labour parties were fine things, but it would have nothing *more* to do with them. Frustrated socialists in the TLC might not see any difference between these two approaches, and there was little *practical* difference. But it is a mistake to identify the AFL and TLC approaches to political action. The AFL was opposed to independent political action. The TLC was in favour of it, tried it, failed, and lost faith in it. A purely formal commitment to the idea of a labour party was all that remained.

2. THE TLC AND THE CCF

In 1929 the labour and socialist parties of the West established a Western Conference of Labor Political Parties "to unify the activities

[8]In British Columbia, the socialist party was always stronger than the independent labour parties.
[9]*Report on Labour Organization* (1931), p. 189.

of the affiliated parties . . . and to bring about the entire unification of
the Labor and Socialist Movement throughout Western Canada."[10] The
CCF was founded at the 1932 meeting of the Western Conference by
delegates from Western labour and socialist parties, Western farmers'
parties, and the Fabian "League for Social Reconstruction."

The CCF's electoral performance was from the start a great deal more
impressive than that of its precursors. Soon after its formation, it became
the alternative-government party in two Canadian provinces. In the
British Columbia provincial election of 1933, the CCF polled 31.5 per
cent of the vote and became the official opposition. In 1934, with 24
per cent of the vote, it became the official opposition in the agricultural
province of Saskatchewan.[11]

The leaders of the TLC may have been impressed, but they saw no
reason to reverse the policy upon which they had determined after the
failure of their own post-war experiments with political action. Throughout the thirties TLC conventions rejected suggestions that the Congress
support the CCF, adopting resolutions identical in wording with the
resolution of 1923.[12] Year after year the same arguments were reiterated
by the leadership: the Congress serves a membership consisting of
supporters of *all* political parties; the Congress must deal with governments controlled by various political parties; the Congress must therefore
avoid all partisan entanglements. Any other course would divide the
membership on political lines and impair the usefulness of the Congress
as the "legislative mouthpiece of organized labor."

The approach was not, strictly speaking, Gompersian: the idea of
political action is a fine idea; the British labour party is a wonderful
thing; but political action has failed in Canada. As the secretary treasurer,
Paddy Draper, put it, "if we, as workers, have failed to elect sufficient
labour representatives . . . it is not the fault of the Congress, rather it
is due to . . . our membership who have failed to rally to the support
of labor candidates."[13] In any case, the political and trade union wings

[10]*Ibid.* (1929), p. 172.
[11]H. A. Scarrow, *Canada Votes* (New Orleans, 1962), pp. 224 and 218. The
picture was different in Ontario, Canada's metropolitan province, where the great
bulk of the English-speaking working class was located. Socialism had never been
nearly so strong in Ontario as in the West, and the CCF remained a weak third
party in that province throughout the thirties, polling 4 to 8 per cent of the vote
in provincial and federal elections.
[12]This resolution was reconfirmed in 1924, 1929, 1930, 1931, 1932, 1933 (the
first time that support of the CCF was in question), 1935, 1936, 1937, 1938,
and 1939.
[13]TLC Convention Proceedings (1932), p. 133.

of the labour movement must be kept strictly separate, as in Britain; it is not the function of unions or of labour congresses to take political action. Those who want to do so should go out and build a labour party instead of trying "to load the job on the Congress."[14]

The TLC had, after the tumultuous post-war period, developed into a conservative, respectable organization, contented with its insignificant but solidly established status in Canadian society. The inclination of its leaders was to preserve the hard-won status of their unions, not to take aggressive or unorthodox actions which might disturb their established relationships with Liberal and Conservative politicians and employers. The TLC position can perhaps be better understood by contrasting the TLC with the CCL. What were the factors making for an alliance with the CCF which were present in the CCL and absent in the TLC? First, a young, aggressive leadership, concerned not with preserving an existing structure but with building a new one. Second, a situation, not of established relationships with the Canadian business and politcal élites, but of struggle with those élites. Third, the influence, not of AFL political quietism, but of CIO political activism. Fourth, the greater tendency to political activism of industrial as opposed to craft unionism, a phenomenon not restricted to North America. And last but not least, the leading role played by CCFers in the organization of the new movement, and the assumption by many of them of dominant positions from which they were able to lead the movement as a whole into an alliance with their party.

The disinclination of the TLC to align itself with the CCF was reinforced from the outset by the CCF's association with the TLC's bitter enemy in the trade union field, the All-Canadian Congress of Labour (ACCL). The ACCL was formed in 1927 as a labour centre for national as opposed to international unionism. Its leader was A. R. Mosher, president of the Canadian Brotherhood of Railway Employees (CBRE), the only important union in the Congress. The CBRE and ACCL were, in principle, in favour of independent political action by trade unions and critical of the political inactivity of the TLC. The CBRE Monthly gave prominence to the activities of Woodsworth's labour group in parliament, and the union's printing press published several of Woodsworth's

[14]Delegate Arthur Martel, ibid., p. 134. Some important socialists in the TLC agreed with the policy of the leadership: "Delegate J. W. Bruce maintained that it was not the duty of the Congress to interfere in politics, and to turn it into a political movement would destroy it." Ibid. Labour men were needed in parliament, but the workers "do not vote for them, that's all." Ibid. (1942), pp. 208–9. This was Bruce's position right down to the last TLC convention in 1955.

speeches and pamphlets. At the 1929 Convention of the CBRE, Mosher called for the establishment of a labour party allied to the ACCL and CBRE.[15]

When the CCF was formed at the Calgary Conference of 1932, Mosher was the only labour representative from east of Manitoba. He became a member of the CCF national executive. Plans were made for the affiliation of the CBRE to the national CCF, but when the constitution of the CCF was drawn up at Regina in 1933 no provision was made for union affiliations on a national basis: the CBRE would have to affiliate to the provincial parties. The CBRE convention of 1933 approved provincial affiliation—but such action was never taken.

The reasons are not clear, but two factors seem to have played a part. First of all, there were within the CBRE powerful elements which did not share Mosher's enthusiasm for the CCF. According to Woodsworth, "there was a good deal of opposition within the ranks of the CBRE. So we . . . have never had . . . affiliation."[16] Secondly, Mosher's association with the CCF aroused strong anti-CCF feeling among Mosher's TLC enemies: "The presence of Mosher at the inaugural meeting in Calgary resulted in a vicious blast a few days later directed at us by Carl Berg," a member of the TLC executive.[17]

Mosher and his friends in the CCF, after observing the reaction of the TLC leadership, evidently decided that public identification of Mosher or his organizations with the CCF would harm rather than help the CCF: "It became apparent that his further official association with us was causing resentment among members of the unions affiliated with the AFL."[18] Mosher therefore resigned from the CCF national executive, stopped pressing for affiliation of the CBRE, and terminated his active public association with the party.

The CBRE and ACCL continued their friendly relationship with the CCF, but they did not permit friendliness to develop into actual support. During the 1935 federal election campaign the ACCL's *Canadian Unionist* (Sept.) refrained from endorsing any party: "More than one party's statement of policy contains much we agree with, none goes to our conclusions." Although Mosher and his organizations never officially aligned themselves with the CCF, the damage was done as far as CCF-TLC relations were concerned. The CCF was tainted with

[15]W. E. Greening and M. M. MacLean, *It Was Never Easy* (Ottawa, 1961), pp. 93, 97, 100. This work is a history of the CBRE.
[16]J. S. Woodsworth to Herbert Orliffe, Feb. 1, 1938, NDP files.
[17]E. J. Garland to Lewis, June 27, 1936, *ibid.*
[18]*Ibid.*

opposition to international craft unionism and as such could not be enthusiastically supported—even by socialists within the TLC.

In January 1938 the secretary of the Ontario CCF arranged a conference of CCF leaders and prominent CCFers in the TLC to discuss the possibility of union local affiliations to the CCF in Ontario. The Ontario CCF's secretary wrote: "I . . . feel . . . that even if actual affiliation . . . did not result from such a conference . . . at the very least there would be a clearing away of the feeling of distrust on the part of the international trade unions. . . . This alone would make such a conference worthwhile."[19] Present at the conference were J. S. Woodsworth, M. J. Coldwell, David Lewis, Angus MacInnis, John Mitchell, E. B. Jolliffe, and B. Leavens for the CCF, and J. Bruce, J. W. Buckley, H. D. Langer, Art Schultz, and Charles Millard for the CCF unionists.

The unionists, though all were CCFers, were vehement in their condemnation of the CCF-ACCL relationship. Buckley declared that TLC unions could not "associate with any organization with which the CBRE is connected." Langer said that the chief obstacle to friendly relations between the TLC and the CCF was the TLC's "feeling . . . that the CCF favour the ACCL as against the international unions." Bruce criticized the CCF not only for supporting "dual unions," but for the middle-class composition of much of its leadership and membership. It was not "really a labour party."[20] He had complained as early as 1933 that "the new party was composed of many elements besides workers." Now he advocated the formation of a *labour* party which would affiliate with the CCF. Sentiment favouring a purely labour party distinct from the CCF continued to trouble the CCF leadership throughout the forties and fifties.

No plan for union affiliations resulted from the conference. "General opinion of trade unionists present was that no, or very few unions are now ready to affiliate." The conference did result in a CCF National Council statement "clarifying" the party's attitude to international unionism: "The CCF has always condemned the attacks that . . . are being made on the international trade union movement. . . . The CCF believes that the workers must . . . decide for themselves on the best form of trade union organization."[21]

The CCF had indeed always remained officially neutral in the

[19]Orliffe to Woodsworth, Jan. 31, 1938, *ibid.*
[20]Minutes of informal conference on CCF-Trade Union Co-operation, n.d. [1938], *ibid.*
[21]*Ibid.*

struggle between the TLC and the ACCL, and it continued to profess neutrality in the later contest between the TLC and the CCL. That is, the CCF *as such* did not interfere, in word or deed, in the jurisdictional strife between CCL and TLC unions. But this was not sufficient to overcome the antipathy of the TLC people, for the CCF and CCL were in fact interlocking organizations. Support of the CCF meant support of a party in which CCL leaders were prominent. The TLC was naturally disinclined to support such a party.

3. THE CCF AND THE CCL

Until 1937, the CCF was trapped in a situation in which the labour movement was dominated by conservative TLC unionists lacking any motivation not only for support of the struggling new socialist party but for political activity of any sort. The small contingent of ACCL unionists was friendly, but this very friendliness served only to transform the TLC's apathy into positive antagonism; the CCF reacted to the antagonism defensively, by loosening its ties with the ACCL. The crucial factor in this situation was the overwhelmingly dominant position of the TLC in the labour movement. So long as the non-TLC elements friendly to the CCF were small and weak, their support would do more harm than good, because it could only serve to antagonize the TLC giant.

This vicious circle could be broken only by the creation of another giant side by side with the TLC. This giant began to emerge in 1937, within the TLC itself—as the Canadian branch of the new Committee for Industrial Organization. The next step, in 1939, was the expulsion of the CIO unions from the TLC and their merger with the ACCL to form the Canadian Congress of Labour. The CCL became within a few years the near equal of the TLC in numbers and in power. The advantages of its support for the CCF now far outweighed the negative consequences, in terms of TLC antagonism, of that support.

The first important manifestation of the new unionism in Canada was the bitter strike of the CIO's first Canadian local, United Automobile Workers UAW-22 (Oshawa), against General Motors in 1937. The intervention of Ontario's Liberal premier, Hepburn, on the side of General Motors and his violent opposition to the CIO and all its works made the CIO an important national political issue.[22]

22"Premier Hepburn's stand against the CIO seems to have gained him a place among the tourist attractions of the province. 'Where does Premier Hepburn live? Where is his office?' were the first questions asked yesterday by tourists from New York and St. Louis arriving on the SS Cayuga." *Globe and Mail*, July 13, 1937.

On April 30, 1937, a confidential directive was sent to all CCF units in Ontario: "The CCF must not lose this opportunity to back the trade unions fully . . . by providing union organizers . . . and by organizing groups of workers interested in forming unions. . . . In every community there is the opportunity for the CCF to develop the trade union movement and to build up closer relations between the unions and the political labor movement."[23] Many CCFers, especially members of the Co-operative Commonwealth Youth Movement (CCYM), became CIO organizers. CCF units assisted striking workers by providing pickets and meeting places. CCF MPs addressed meetings of striking workers: "There are dozens of CIO organizers in the province. We have a group of our own people in such work . . . I am doing all I can . . . to see that our people are into this drive. . . . There will be [more] strikes, our men should turn up at them, speak to the workers, spur them on. . . . It is a magnificent opportunity. We must not mess it. Must not."[24]

CCF support for the new CIO unions' organizing drive paid dividends, not immediately in the form of increased support at the polls, but in the form of support from the leadership of the new unions. A key personality in this development and in the entire future history of CCF-union relations in Canada was the president of the UAW local in Oshawa, Charles Millard. Millard had been an active CCFer since 1933. After the Oshawa strike he was appointed director of the UAW in Canada.[25] In 1939 he was replaced by George Burt, who ruled the union with Communist support until the Reuther purge of 1946–47.

Immediately after his defeat in the UAW, Millard was appointed CIO representative for Canada, and in 1940 he was appointed secretary of the Steelworkers' and Packinghouse Workers' Organizing Committees (SWOC and PWOC) in Canada. As the most important CIO leader in Canada, Millard was able to accomplish two things. The first was to purge the Steel Union of the Communists who had entrenched themselves in its Toronto headquarters, and to exclude Communists from positions of importance in other unions which he controlled or influenced. The second was to place the young CCFers who were streaming into the CIO in positions of leadership in their unions. As head of PWOC, he appointed Fred Dowling, former CCYM organizer and labour editor of the Ontario

[23]"Confidential: To All CCF Units: April 30, 1937," NDP files.
[24]Graham Spry to Lewis, March 13, 1937, *ibid.*
[25]While he was director of the UAW Millard was able to persuade the CIO leadership in the United States that "in Canada there is no need for a 'Non-Partisan League,' because the CCF is here." Ted Jolliffe to Lewis, Aug. 24, 1938, *ibid.*

CCF's *New Commonwealth*, to the position of head organizer. Dowling has led the Packinghouse union ever since.

The head office staff of SWOC under Millard consisted of ten active CCFers. Among them were John Mitchell, later president of the Ontario CCF, Murray Cotterill, later director of the CCL-PAC, Eamon Park, later the federal president of the NDP, and Howard Conquergood, later director of the CLC's Political Education Department. As CIO secretary in Canada, Millard also influenced the composition of the staff of the Rubber, Textile, and Shoe and Leather unions. "To claim that . . . staffs of the new industrial unions at this time were hired solely on the basis of their political affiliations would not be an exaggeration."[26]

CCFers were also strong in other CIO unions—the United Mine Workers (UMW), Amalgamated Clothing Workers (ACWA), Mine, Mill and Smelter Workers, and the UAW. The head of ACWA, Sol Spivak, was a CCFer. The head of Mine Mill, Robert Carlin, was a CCFer, but Communists were a strong force in that union. In the UAW the Communists had the upper hand, but CCFers were an important faction. The result of the CIO's invasion of Canada was the creation of a new, young, aggressive industrial union movement in which enthusiastic CCFers held important leadership positions.

Immediately after the TLC expelled the CIO unions in 1939, negotiations began between the CIO unions and the ACCL, and the two organizations merged in 1940 to form the Canadian Congress of Labour. David Lewis, the CCF national secretary, was involved in the negotiations from the beginning. Lewis wrote:

From the CCF point of view [the] merger may prove of very great value. Barrett [of the CIO] continues to be friendly and loyal. . . . Mosher, McLean, and Dowd [of the ACCL] have always been friendly to us. The result, it seems to me, will be that the new organization is likely to become a staunch supporter of the CCF. I realize that there are dangers. Firstly, it will be important to walk warily so as not to provoke the enmity of the AFL unions. . . . Secondly, there is the question of Communists holding important positions in the CIO. . . .[27]

In September 1940, Lewis was present at the founding convention of the new Congress: "The ACCL people . . . asked me to come . . . to assist them . . . in getting the thing properly launched. . . . It shows that their side . . . appreciates our help and the need for working together with the CCF."[28]

[26]Myrtle M. Armstrong, "The Development of Trade Union Political Activity in the CCF," MA thesis, University of Toronto, 1959, p. 40.
[27]To Angus MacInnis, Dec. 21, 1939, NDP files.
[28]Lewis to Jolliffe, Sept. 5, 1940, *ibid.*

The leaders of the new Congress "walked warily" in the political field for the first two years of its life, not only for the reason mentioned by Lewis—the danger of exciting the TLC's antagonism to the CCF—but because the CCL was a new and insecure organization. Its leaders did not feel sure enough of themselves to make support of the CCF an official policy of the Congress.[29] While Millard and others were anxious for immediate action, the consensus of opinion in the CCL and CCF leadership was that caution was necessary until the position of the new organization became consolidated. Hasty action might give the rival TLC an advantage over the CCL in two fields: relations with federal and provincial governments, and jurisdictional competition with the TLC unions. Some CCL leaders even feared that a public alignment of their organization with the CCF might invite raiding by rival TLC unions, with "keep politics out of your union" as the raiders' slogan. Furthermore, from the CCF's point of view, there was little to be gained from trying to push the new Congress into an *immediate* public alignment with the CCF. The purpose of a labour-CCF alliance, was, after all, to convert the unconverted, not to "force the CCF down their throats." The CCF would gain nothing from action which might divide the membership of the new organization on political lines while it was still in its early organizational stage. Labour political action would have to wait until the "necessary educational work" had been done. CCF policy was therefore to maintain close contact and friendly relations with the CCL and its affiliated unions, but to refrain from pressing for political action until the "time was ripe."[30]

Both the CCL and CCF leaders were cautious in this early period, but the CCL leaders were a little more cautious. In August 1941 Lewis came to the CCL leadership with a request that an officer of the Congress run as a CCF candidate in the British Columbia provincial election. "I argued for almost an hour but I am afraid without avail. . . . While they are ready to give the CCF support when they can do so without any publicity they are not yet ready to take even one definite step in the direction of independent political action."[31]

In the federal election of 1940, the CCF, still strong in Saskatchewan and British Columbia, elected eight MPs with 8.5 per cent of the vote.[32]

---

[29]The first CCL convention defeated a Communist resolution which sought to bind affiliates to "non-partisan" political action, and adopted a resolution which left affiliates completely unfettered "while making it clear that the Congress itself was and would remain nonpartisan." *Federationist*, Sept. 19, 1940.

[30]Interview with Lewis, Jan. 15, 1963.

[31]Lewis to Herbert Gargrave, Aug. 30, 1941, NDP files.

[32]Scarrow, *Canada Votes*, p. 104.

But in Ontario the CCF was at its nadir: it ran only twenty-four candidates and got only 3.8 per cent of the vote.[33] By the end of 1941, however, the tide turned; the CCF's period of great expansion began.

The first important CCF victory in the forties was the British Columbia provincial election of October 1941. The CCF won a plurality of the votes (CCF 33.4 per cent, Liberals 32.9 per cent, Conservatives 30.9 per cent) and the second largest number of seats in the legislature (Liberals 21, CCF 14, Conservatives 12).[34] Since no single party had a majority in the legislature, the Liberals and Conservatives formed a coalition government, leaving the CCF in the position of sole opposition party.

The second CCF victory was the York South (Ontario) by-election of February 1942, in which a CCF schoolteacher defeated the mighty Conservative Arthur Meighen and entered the House of Commons as the first CCF MP from Ontario and the second from Eastern Canada. The York South by-election was the signal for a veritable eruption of popular support for the CCF. Between February 1942 and June 1944—when the CCF became the government party in Saskatchewan—the party went from success to success, its coffers filling, its membership lists growing. For the first and last time in its life its dream of becoming a major national party appeared to be on the point of fulfilment.

At the same time, the number of organized workers in Canada almost doubled. The lion's share of the newly organized workers were in CCL unions. The CCL began with 77,000 workers in 1940; by the end of 1942 there were 200,000, an increase of 160 per cent. This new labour movement was one of the main sources of the CCF's increased popular support. The CCL was now solidly established; pro-CCF sentiment among its members had risen dramatically, and the national political atmosphere had changed radically. The time for caution was passing. In 1942 the CCF decided to launch a campaign for local union affiliations in Ontario.

The CCF began as a federation of farmers' organizations, labour and socialist parties, and CCF clubs. It was expected that labour unions would also join the federation—hence the abortive affiliation of the CBRE in 1933. But in the first years of its life the CCF gradually abandoned its federated structure and became a party of individual members organized in constituency associations.[35] By 1937 the CCF

[33]Caplan, "The CCF in Ontario," p. 226.
[34]Scarrow, *Canada Votes*, p. 224.
[35]For the first two years of its life the Ontario CCF was a federation of three groups, the CCF clubs, the United Farmers of Ontario (UFO), and a Labour

leadership, frustrated with its failure in Ontario, resurrected the idea of union affiliation. The 1937 National Convention passed a resolution instructing the National Council to make "every effort to facilitate the affiliation of economic groups such as co-operatives, farm organizations, and trade unions."[36] In 1938 the Ontario CCF amended its constitution to permit the affiliation of "cultural and economic groups."[37]

No action was taken, however, until the affiliation of the UMW District 26 (Nova Scotia) in August 1938. This affiliation was not sought by the CCF. Although it had resurrected the *idea* of union affiliation, neither the party nor the labour movement were thought to be "ready" for it; an affiliated union wing was an *ultimate* goal, to be achieved slowly, cautiously, and in stages, as the idea of affiliation was made acceptable to both the unions and the CCF rank and file.

When the CCF national office was informed that the convention of the UMW District 26 had decided to affiliate to the national CCF, its first reaction was to seek assurances that the decision represented a genuine desire on the part of the union to affiliate with the CCF and that it was not a Communist trick. David Lewis sent a telegram[38] to D. W. Morrison, head of the union:

Have read in morning press decision Truro conference to affiliate CCF. Wish to greet your decision on behalf of National Council. Am anxious to have immediately as full report as possible of conference decision and background. Particularly interested in knowing whether decisions supported by rank and file and whether move sponsored by Communists.

Satisfactory assurances were received from Morrison and others, and Angus MacInnis and David Lewis went to Nova Scotia to set up local CCF organizations "by the side of and independent of the UMW locals" and to work out the details of union affiliation to the CCF. The affiliation was formally completed on October 15, 1938. In drawing up the terms of affiliation, MacInnis and Lewis "followed . . . the constitution of the British Labour Party": The affiliated organization must accept the program and constitution of the CCF; delegates from the affiliated

---

Conference consisting of small labour parties that had survived the early period of political action. These groups had equal representation on the Provincial Council. In 1933 the UFO disaffiliated, leaving the CCF clubs and the Labour Conference deadlocked. The CCF clubs accused the Labour Conference of being infested with Communists and demanded that it be expelled. In 1934 the National Council suspended the Provincial Council, expelled the Labour Conference, and reorganized the provincial party on an individual membership basis. Caplan, "The CCF in Ontario," p. 127.

[36]CCF Convention Proceedings (1937), p. 33.
[37]*New Commonwealth*, April 23, 1938.
[38]Aug. 16, 1938, NDP files.

organization to any CCF body must individually accept and conform to
the party's program and constitution and must not be members or supporters of any party other than the CCF; each affiliated local must pay
per capita dues to the CCF of two cents per member per month. One
important matter was not decided in Nova Scotia—the basis of representation of affiliated unions in CCF bodies and conventions. Lewis and
MacInnis felt that "more satisfactory results will follow if [these] . . .
provisions are made as the need arises than if they were laid down
immediately."[39]

The 1940 national convention of the CCF adopted a constitutional
amendment permitting affiliation of "economic organizations" to the
national as well as the provincial parties. The affiliation of the UMW was
thus legalized *ex post facto*. From 1938 to 1942 there were no further
union affiliations to the CCF; apparently none were sought. But the
York South by-election of February 1942 and the ensuing explosion
of CCF sentiment across the country convinced the Ontario CCF-union
leaders that the time had come to begin a vigorous campaign for local
union affiliation in that province.

On July 25, 1942, the Trade Union Committee of the Ontario CCF
(CCF-TUC) convened a Trade Union Conference. Sixty-nine locals of
forty-three TLC and CCL unions were represented. The Conference
passed the following resolution:

Be it resolved that we believe and affirm that organized labor will be doing
itself a great service and hastening the realization of its aims by entering into
affiliation with the CCF . . . and that until such affiliation is an accomplished fact, this conference calls upon all unions to endorse the CCF as the
official political arm of the trade union movement in Canada.[40]

Charles Millard hailed the resolution as a "stepping stone to full and
complete co-operation between the labour movement and the CCF."[41]

Even before the Trade Union Conference, the CCF-TUC had secured
the affiliation of an Upholsterers local and the Shoe and Leather
Workers' Organizing Committee. Charles Millard was chairman of the
latter and its decision to affiliate was a result of his suggestion.[42] In
September 1942, the TUC imported Clairie Gillis, MP, to act as director
of its work, and launched a campaign for local union affiliations. During

[39]Report of Organizing Tour through Nova Scotia and New Brunswick made
by Angus MacInnis, MP, and David Lewis, National Secretary, n.d., *ibid*. In 1940
the mineworkers of Cape Breton South elected Clairie Gillis to the House of
Commons—the first CCF MP from east of Manitoba.
[40]Proceedings of Trade Union Conference, July 25, 1942, *ibid*.
[41]*Ibid*.
[42]Millard to Lewis, May 7, 1942, NDP files.

Gillis' four-months tenure as director he spoke at numerous local meetings and obtained twenty-seven additional affiliations, fourteen from
CCL unions, twelve from TLC unions, and one from a CCCL union.
(Of the twelve TLC affiliations, five were from ILGWU unions. One of
the CCL affiliations was secured from the Textile Workers' Organizing
Committee, probably with the aid of Millard.) The total membership
of the affiliated unions was about 12,000.[43]

The decision to seek local union affiliations in Ontario made it necessary to complete the work on terms of affiliation that had begun four
years before in Nova Scotia. The relationship between the party and
its projected affiliated-union wing had to be spelled out more clearly.

From the outset one thing was apparent. The CCF was not to be a
labour party pure and simple:

On every possible occasion I have explained to the trade unionists the basic
organizational principle of the CCF as being that of uniting all the three
major classes of Canada into one political instrument—namely, the industrial
workers, the farmers, and the middle class people. . . . In Canada the farmers
and the middle class people combined actually outnumber the industrial
workers, and . . . since the proportion of workers organized in trade unions
still remains relatively small, the rest of the Canadian people far outnumber
those in the ranks of organized labor.[44]

The CCF could not be successful if it were based on organized labour
alone. Furthermore, the bulk of the individual membership of the CCF
consisted of farmers and middle-class people; any scheme of union affiliation must be acceptable to the non-working class individual membership
of the CCF. They would not tolerate being swamped by affiliated-union
delegates at CCF conventions: "At the same time that our CCF becomes
based more and more on the organized working class—the only permanent and solid basis in capitalist society—[we must]—make sure that
there is not any trade union domination of the party so that the farmers
and middle class people know that they can come in on equal footing and
have an equal voice with organized labour.[45]

The CCF therefore made two basic decisions: (1) There was not to
be any British-style bloc voting at conventions or British-style bloc
representation on party executives. The labour organizations which
would affiliate and be represented at conventions would be *locals* voting
separately rather than entire unions voting as blocs; and there was to
be no provision for representation of labour organizations as such on
party executives; all executive members would be elected by the entire

[43]TUC Report to the Ontario CCF Provincial Convention, 1943, *ibid.*
[44]Lewis to Harold Winch, Oct. 7, 1943, *ibid.*
[45]*Ibid.*

convention. (2) The representation of unions at conventions was to be adjusted so that there would be no danger of affiliated-union representatives outnumbering individual-membership representatives.

The first discussions of the specific terms of affiliation took place a few weeks after the York South by-election. At a special meeting of the Ontario CCF executive, Fred Dowling for the TUC proposed that affiliated unions be represented at conventions on the same basis as constituency organizations, and that members of affiliated unions be considered members of the CCF organizations in their constituencies, with all the rights and privileges of individual members.[46] These suggestions, if implemented, would have obliterated the distinction between individual and affiliate membership and were therefore unacceptable to the non-trade unionists in the CCF.

Discussions within the CCF, and between CCF and CCL leaders, continued for about half a year. On September 19 and 20 the CCF National Executive approved a basis of affiliation for recommendation to the provincial sections. The final decision on the various points fell within the jurisdiction of the provincial sections, but the executive urged "as much uniformity across the country as possible."

The main points of the National Executive's recommendation were:

1. The per capita dues of a union to the CCF shall be two cents per member per month, of which one cent shall be paid to the National Office and one cent to the provincial office.
2. The basis of representation at provincial delegate conventions shall be one delegate for each 100 members or major portion thereof, with a minimum of one delegate. [This ratio compares to a ratio ranging from 1:15 to 1:50 for constituency organizations.]
3. An affiliated local shall be entitled to representation at all constituency meetings and conventions in accordance with the number of its members residing in the constituency on the same basis as at provincial conventions.[47]

On a fourth point—the qualifications of delegates from affiliated unions—the executive was not able to reach agreement. Some were of the opinion that delegates should themselves be individual members of the CCF. Others thought that the less stringent requirement of the Nova Scotia terms, that delegates must not be supporters of any other political party, was sufficient. David Lewis favoured the second method, since the first

narrows the field of choice of the delegate by the union very considerably. Out of a union membership of hundreds or thousands it is very likely that only as few as twenty or thirty might be individual members of the CCF.

---

[46]Ontario CCF Provincial Executive Minutes, Feb. 25, 1942, *ibid.*
[47]CCF National Executive Minutes, Sept. 19–20, 1942, *ibid.*

This therefore would mean that only union members who comprise this twenty or thirty could be chosen as delegates. The likelihood is that such a provision would be considered too undemocratic by the unions. . . . We know . . . that there are many thousands of genuine and loyal CCF supporters who are not members of the CCF, and they would by this provision be debarred from representing their unions. . . . I should add that the officers of the Canadian Congress of Labour are much more in favour of the other alternative.[48]

All provinces except Saskatchewan eventually decided on the less stringent requirement.

The 1942 convention of the Ontario CCF passed a constitutional amendment incorporating substantially the same terms as had been recommended by the National Executive. Other provinces adopted the terms of affiliation in 1943 and 1944, adjusting various details to suit their particular situations. The main variations were in the basis of representation at conventions. Alberta, a rural province, allowed one delegate for every twenty-five union members. Nova Scotia, where the membership of the affiliated UMW far outnumbered the individual membership, allowed one delegate for every 500 members. In the other provinces, the basis of representation was 1:100.

The basis of representation of unions at *national* conventions was not settled until 1946. The 1944 national convention allotted affiliated unions forty delegates as an *ad hoc* measure. At that time about 100 locals with a membership of about 50,000 were affiliated to the CCF; the basis of representation was thus tentatively set at 1:500.[49]

The 1946 National Convention amended the constitution to provide the following basis of representation for constituency associations and affiliated unions:

1. For federal constituency associations: One delegate for each constituency with not less than 50 and not more than 500 members. One additional delegate for each additional 500 members or major portion thereof, with a maximum of 10 delegates per constituency.

2. For affiliated local unions: One delegate for the first 500 members and 1 additional delegate for every additional 500 members or major portion thereof, with a maximum of 10 delegates from all the locals of any one union in a province. Locals with less than 500 members shall be entitled to pool their memberships for purposes of convention representation. All delegates must individually accept the constitution and program of the CCF and must not be supporters of any other political party.[50]

---

[48]Lewis to Winch, Oct. 7, 1943, *ibid.*

[49]CCF National Council Minutes, Aug. 29–31, 1944, *ibid.* Only nineteen union delegates participated in this convention. The total number of delegates was 208. This was the first national convention attended by delegates from affiliated unions.

[50]CCF Convention Proceedings (1946), p. 18.

Since the bulk of federal constituency associations had 50 to 500 members, while few local unions had as many as 500 members, these provisions were heavily weighted in favour of the constituency organizations.

The union and party leaders reached agreement very early on one important point: the affiliation of locals whose membership was sharply divided on the issue of affiliation would harm both the labour movement and the party. Affiliation of a local to the CCF was to be avoided if it might result in dissension within the local. Such dissension would impair the effectiveness of the union as a union; it would harm the CCF by antagonizing the unconverted within the union and by putting a weapon in the hands of the propagandists of other parties outside the union. Affiliation was therefore regarded, at least in theory, not as a *preliminary* step in the relationship between the CCF and a particular local, but as the *culmination* of a process of "political education" during which the great majority of the local's membership would be converted into genuine supporters of the CCF. The local was to be allowed to "ripen" before its affiliation was sought.[51]

The CCF's approach to labour was, for the moment, restricted to local unions only. It was still too early to press entire unions or labour congresses to commit themselves. The TLC especially had to be handled with kid gloves.

One of the things that should not be allowed . . . is for any resolution favoring affiliation to the CCF coming before the [TLC] Convention, since such a resolution would present an opportunity for our opponents to have their innings and I doubt very much whether it would stand the slightest chance of passing. . . . Our position would be served best at the present time by silence on the part of the Congress, which would enable us to follow up with the local unions.[52]

The Resolutions Committee of the TLC convention of September 1942 obliged by bringing in a resolution reaffirming the Congress' policy of neutrality: "A special article in the [Winnipeg] Free Press referred to the curious fact that the supporters of the CCF spoke against affiliation. The Free Press did not know that that was no accident."[53]

At the CBRE convention in the same month David Lewis was busy preventing resolutions too favourable to the CCF from reaching the floor. A number of resolutions recommending affiliation had been submitted

[51]Interview with Lewis, Jan. 15, 1963.
[52]Lewis to Knowles, Aug. 7, 1942, NDP files.
[53]MacInnis to Lewis, Sept. 8, 1942, *ibid.*

by CBRE locals. Lewis worked with the resolutions committee and drafted a substitute resolution "simply recommending to the local unions . . . to study the question" of political action. The substitute resolution passed "unanimously after speeches very favourable to the CCF were made from the floor."[54]

The CCF leadership evidently thought that caution was necessary even at the CCL convention of September 1942, where CCFers would be much more numerous than at the TLC or CBRE conventions. Lewis "succeeded in keeping all such resolutions off the agenda, which is really the simplest solution."[55] The CCL convention, with only one dissenting vote, passed a resolution which showered glory on the CCF and recommended that affiliated unions "study . . . its program," but did not formally endorse it or recommend affiliation.[56]

During the six months between April and October 1943 the membership of the Ontario CCF more than doubled. In Ontario and across Canada resentment at the King government's labour policies approached its zenith—as did the popularity of the CCF. In the Ontario provincial election of August 17, 1943, the CCF polled 32.4 per cent of the vote, the Liberals 30.9 per cent, and the Conservatives 36.7 per cent. In the legislature the CCF increased its representation from zero to thirty-four and became the official opposition, with more than twice as many seats as the Liberals and only four less than the Conservatives.[57] The CCF had swept urban Ontario. Among the CCF's thirty-four elected candidates were nineteen trade unionists (ten TLC and nine CCL), including Charles Millard, head of the Steelworkers, and Robert Carlin, head of the Mine, Mill and Smelter workers.

[54]Lewis to MacInnis, Sept. 10, 1942, *ibid.*
[55]*Ibid.*
[56]*CCL Convention Proceedings* (1942), p. 35: "Whereas events have demonstrated beyond any possibility of doubt that political power has been used throughout the years to the detriment of organized labour, and Whereas it is essential that organized labour organize for political action, and Whereas representatives of the CCF in parliament and other legislative bodies have fought ardently and consistently for the objects of and to protect the rights of organized labour, and Whereas the CCF now has a nation-wide political organization and is uniting for common purposes the farmers and the industrial workers of this country, Be it resolved that this Convention expresses its appreciation of the work done on behalf of labour by the CCF members in parliament and that it recommends to its chartered and affiliated unions that they study the program of the CCF." The "whereases" of this resolution were identical word for word, with the "whereases" of the resolution passed by the CCF Trade Union Conference in July that year. Only the "resolve" was changed, in order to preserve the harmony of the convention.
[57]Scarrow, *Canada Votes*, p. 211.

A few weeks later, the CCL convention was presented with this resolution:

Whereas in the opinion of this Congress, the policy and program of the CCF more adequately expresses the viewpoint of organized labour than any other party. Be it therefore resolved that this Convention . . . endorse the CCF as the political arm of labour in Canada, and recommend to all affiliated . . . unions that they affiliate with the CCF.[58]

Evidently the leadership of both the CCF and the CCL felt that the time for action had finally arrived. The circumstances could not be more favourable; the delegates were being asked to back a winner. The resolution was passed by a "tremendous" majority, after having been opposed only by the strong Communist "opposition," which tried, as David Lewis put it, "to confuse the issue by . . . claiming that they had no objection to CCF affiliation" but that the terms of affiliation did not give the unions "adequate and direct representation" as in the " 'grand old Labour Party of Great Britain.' "[59]

The first speaker on the resolution was George Harris, of the Communist-dominated United Electrical Workers (UE). He did not object to political action through the CCF, he said, but to "the method and form of affiliation which unions were required to adopt."[60] Harris was echoed by Harvey Murphy of the Communist-dominated Mine Mill union in British Columbia, and George Burt, Communist-supported head of the UAW. Burt said: "We are not basically opposed to the resolution, except with regard to the basis of affiliation. In spite of the sentiment in Canada and Ontario for the CCF, we . . . are going to make sure we are not . . . buying a pig in a poke."[61]

Charles Millard, head of the Steel union, member of the executive committee of the CCL, member of the CCF National Council, and newly elected Ontario MPP, rose to assure the convention that the resolution was not "precipitate"—it had been under consideration for two years. The terms of affiliation were not laid down for all time; there was no set formula that could not be changed. In each province, an arrangement could be worked out which would satisfy both the party and the unions.

The secretary treasurer, Pat Conroy, closing the debate, said he was not a member of the CCF, but supported the resolution because the CCF was the party that came closest to representing the wishes of the common people. Labour was not getting satisfaction from the King govern-

58CCL Convention Proceedings (1943), p. 55.
59Lewis to MacInnis, Sept. 21, 1943, NDP files.
60CCL Convention Proceedings (1943), p. 55.
61Ibid.

ment: "I can tell you frankly that I am sick and tired of going cap in hand to Mackenzie King to get Labour policies adopted." Conroy appealed to the convention to ignore the Communists' "quibbles" about terms of affiliation. Unions should affiliate to the CCF and then try to change the terms of affiliation if they were not satisfactory.

The Communist attitude to the CCF at this time was that it could and should be transformed into a "true labour party," that is, that the Communist party should be permitted to affiliate to it. The affiliation of Communist-dominated unions would be a step in the right direction; therefore the Communists did not oppose the principle of affiliation *per se*. The CCF, however, was anxious to prevent union affiliation from being used as a technique of Communist infiltration. The terms of affiliation therefore provided that union delegates to CCF conventions must either be themselves individual members of the CCF or not be supporters of any other political party.

The terms of affiliation were, however, designed not only to exclude Communist unionists but to prevent the swamping of constituency delegates by union delegates at party conventions. Affiliated unions were allotted far fewer delegates per member than CCF constituency organizations. The Communists could therefore exploit, as they did at the 1943 convention, the natural suspicion of unionists that the CCF was not prepared to give affiliated unions a fair share of power on the party's policy-making bodies.

The 1943 convention of the Labor-Progressive [Communist] party (LPP) called upon the CCF to transform itself into "a truly federated organization to which trade unions, farm organizations, and the Labor Progressive Party could affiliate."[62] On September 5 the CCF National Council rejected a Labor-Progressive request for affiliation by a vote of twenty-three to four.[63]

The Communist reaction to the CCL's recommendation that unions affiliate to the CCF was to try to discourage affiliations by demonstrating that the CCF was not prepared to give unions adequate and democratic representation on party councils. J. B. Salsberg, the LPP's labour expert, declared that the CCL resolution could not be interpreted as an "unreserved endorsation of the present structure of the CCF." Conroy and Millard had been forced to "apologize" to the convention for the requirement that delegates of affiliated locals must not be supporters of other parties (Salsberg put it this way: the CCF "denies local unions . . . the right to elect any good standing member . . . as its representative to

[62]*Canadian Tribune*, Sept. 4, 1943.
[63]CCF National Council Minutes, Sept. 5–6, 1943, NDP files.

CCF bodies") and for the failure to give equal "representation by population" to affiliated unions.[64] The CCF, according to Salsberg, feared
trade union influence and therefore desired "to keep trade union affiliations to a minimum." Instead of creating the necessary conditions for
genuine affiliation, "the CCF leaders prefer to dominate the trade unions
politically from without."[65]

In order to prove that the CCF was not really interested in "genuine"
trade union affiliation, the Communists arranged that three unions, the
UAW, the International Woodworkers of America (IWA), and the UE
approach the CCF "with a view to canvassing the possibilities of arrang-
ing affiliation . . . on the basis of a guarantee of satisfactory representation." The CCF responded by offering these unions the terms of
affiliation drawn up in September 1942. The three unions then "rejected"
the CCF "proposal" on the grounds that they were discriminatory (did
not permit supporters of parties other than the CCF to act as delegates
of their unions) and undemocratic (did not give affiliated locals the
same number of delegates per member as was given constituency associations). The UE declared that the CCF's terms called for "virtual taxation
without representation."[66]

4. THE COLLAPSE OF THE AFFILIATION PROGRAM

Whatever the intentions of the CCF in the early forties may have been,
a strong affiliated-union wing did not come into being. In no province
outside of Ontario did the CCF at any time actively solicit affiliations.
The number of affiliated locals reached 100, with about 50,000 members, in 1944.[67] The great majority of these were in Ontario and Nova
Scotia.

Sometime in 1944 or 1945 the Ontario CCF's drive for affiliations
ground to a halt. By December 1947 the number of affiliated locals
across the country had fallen to seventy-one.[68] In 1952 only forty-four
locals were affiliated: thirty-seven were CCL locals and seven were TLC
locals.[69] Their total membership was 16,397—about 10,117 in Nova

[64]*Canadian Tribune*, Oct. 16, 1943.
[65]*Ibid.*, Aug. 19, 1944.   [66]*Ibid.*, Nov. 6, 1943.
[67]CCF Convention Proceedings (1944), p. 41.
[68]List of Affiliated Locals, Dec. 1947, NDP files. Thirty-one of these were in
Nova Scotia, twenty-three in Ontario, two in British Columbia, one in Alberta, and
fourteen in Saskatchewan.
[69]CCF Convention Proceedings (1952), p. 19. The distribution by province
was as follows: Nova Scotia, seventeen; Ontario, twenty-three; Saskatchewan,
three; British Columbia, one. The total membership of the affiliated locals
amounted to about half of the individual membership of the CCF.

Scotia, 5,759 in Ontario, 251 in Saskatchewan, and 270 in British Columbia. The number of locals affiliated and their total membership remained approximately the same until the formation of the New Democratic party in 1961.

Even the locals that did affiliate did not really become vital parts of the CCF organization. Contact between affiliated locals and CCF organizations was so slight as to be non-existent. Occasionally a provincial CCF organization would mourn the lack of contact between the CCF and its handful of affiliated locals and consider ways of making affiliation "meaningful," but very little was done anywhere.[70]

In some cases locals were affiliated without assurance that they were "ripe," that is, that they were securely controlled by CCFers. The lack of contact between affiliated locals and the party virtually guaranteed that the affiliations of such locals would be completely meaningless; in at least one case an unripe affiliated local actually opposed the party to which it was affiliated.[71] For most affiliated locals, the real meaning of affiliation consisted in three things: the psychological significance of the formal act in itself; the small monthly per capita fee; and the opportunity to send delegates to CCF conventions.

Participation in conventions was the minimum that could reasonably be expected from affiliated locals. But most of them did not even provide this minimum. Delegates from affiliated locals were always a small minority at CCF conventions. At the 1944 national convention there were 19 out of 208; in 1946, 1948, and 1950 there were none; in 1952, 19 out of 169; in 1954, 4 out of 154, and in 1956, 3 out of 169. Affiliated locals played a similarly insignificant role in Ontario CCF conventions. At the 1945 convention only 14 out of 203 delegates were from affiliated unions; in 1948, 14 out of 255. There was, of course, a great deal of labour participation and labour influence in the CCF—but it did not express itself through formal affiliation of local unions. The CCF remained throughout its life a party based primarily on individual members organized in clubs and constituency associations.

[70]"It has been felt for some time that such affiliation as has been achieved in B.C. has been largely ineffectual. Some time ago . . . this was discussed in the TUC which made recommendations to the Executive to develop interest in CCF affairs within affiliated unions." Jessie Mendels to M. Lebrun, Jan. 4, 1950, BC NDP files.

[71]"The only union in Grey North directly affiliated with the CCF, a [CCL] Furniture Workers' local . . . would not . . . support [the CCF in the Grey North by-election]. The Executive . . . supported the Liberal party. Two of the executive members have been paid by the Liberal party before and probably were this time. One of the executive members is the only LPP member in town so naturally followed the party line. This situation might be a good example of a union that has been affiliated to the CCF and then left in a vacuum." Larry Sefton, Report on the Grey North By-election, Feb. 20, 1945, NDP files.

It seems clear that in the early forties the CCF had decided to build up a large trade-union section. All the preparations were made: CCF constitutions were amended and terms of affiliation were carefully worked out; a campaign for affiliations was actually begun in Ontario; the CCL advised its locals to affiliate. Why then did the CCF not become in actuality a party with a massive trade union section?

In the first place, there was in a significant number of locals an organized Communist opposition to affiliation. In March 1945 the Ontario TUC reported that "affiliation of unions has not proven to be a successful endeavour of recent months" because of Communist opposition.[72]

In the second place, the powerful example of the American CIO unions' approach to politics, and perhaps the direct pressure of international headquarters, may have played a part in inhibiting affiliation. A Canadian union will ordinarily conform to the norms and procedures of the international union of which it is a part. The CIO atmosphere encouraged political activism, but not in the form of direct formal affiliation to a political party. This may be a significant, perhaps a crucial, factor accounting for the shift of emphasis in the CCL's political policy from affiliation to PAC as the technique of support for the CCF.[73]

Thirdly, the leadership of the rival TLC had begun in 1944–45 to build a close relationship with the Liberal government.[74] This acted as a disincentive to intensified support for the CCF in the CCL.[75] Leaders like Pat Conroy tended to "drag their feet," particularly in working for *affiliation* to the CCF, because they were reluctant to do anything to add to the advantages accruing to the TLC from its "non-partisan" friendliness with the government.

Finally, the plans for trade union affiliation were made at the beginning of a period of tremendous growth in CCF strength and popularity. During the Second World War it appeared that the CCF was becoming a major party. The CCF expected to become the official opposition in the election of 1945. The full implementation of the affiliation plan may have hinged on the realization of this dream.

The defeat of the CCF in 1945 seems to have had two consequences so far as union affiliation was concerned: (1) Union enthusiasm for the CCF subsided. The bandwagon atmosphere was dissipated. Affiliation to a "becalmed" minor party is less exciting than affiliation to a major

[72]Report from TUC to Ontario Provincial Executive, March 20, 1945, *ibid.*
[73]For further discussion of the international influence see below, pp. 234–8.
[74]See below, p. 102–6.
[75]In a letter to GH, Aug. 16, 1966, David Lewis recalled "feeling stymied and frustrated by the situation, but it seemed wrong to press the CCL leaders unduly."

party advancing from success to success. (2) CCF enthusiasm about union affiliation subsided. When the CCF expected that it would continue to grow in strength until it became the government, it could welcome a steadily growing trade-union wing with few reservations, for its individual membership would be growing at the same time, and perhaps farm organizations as well as trade unions would affiliate. The balance between its trade union and other sections would thus be maintained. The sudden halt and slow decline of the CCF in the late forties probably brought about a change in attitude, if not in official policy. To try to build up a large trade union section under the new circumstances would threaten the basic CCF policy of resisting transformation into a purely labour party.

Even if the CCF had not been so badly disappointed in 1945, the materialization of a trade union section would not have been guaranteed. For even at the height of the CCF's popularity, there was a decided ambivalence in the attitude of most CCF members to the affiliation of unions and a corresponding lack of responsiveness in the attitude of unions which were "ripe" for affiliation. While the CCF was anxious to obtain trade union support, there always existed within its ranks a strong suspicion of "those others," the union men, and a determination to preserve both the *status quo* in the organizational structure of the CCF and its status as a "movement" of committed socialists rather than a mundane political party with a broad base among the masses. This attitude expressed itself in two ways: as opposition to the "watering down" of socialist doctrine by CCF leadership; and as opposition to the increasing power of labour within the party. The Provincial Council of the Ontario CCF approved the terms of affiliation of September 1942 by a one-vote margin.[76]

During the early forties the CCF leadership could disarm opposition to trade union affiliation with the argument that the CCF would continue to grow, and that affiliation would therefore not upset the balance of power within the party. After the defeat of 1945, this argument could no longer be used, and CCF leadership, even if it wanted to (which is doubtful), could no longer resist CCF opposition to affiliation.

The ambivalence in the CCF evoked a similar ambivalence among unions ripe for affiliation. Even when the Ontario CCF was actively seeking affiliations, there was a suspicion among unionists that they were not really wanted. This suspicion was exploited and intensified by Communist propaganda, and the terms of affiliation themselves provided

[76]Zakuta, "A Protest Movement Becalmed," PhD thesis, University of Toronto, 1961, Part VII, p. 14.

evidence that the suspicion was well grounded. There was always a feeling in CCF-labour circles that the terms of affiliation—specifically, the basis of representation at conventions—did not give affiliated unions an adequate role in the CCF organization. That the basis of representation at national conventions was considered a disincentive to affiliation is shown by the efforts of the CCL-PAC to revise the basis of representation as late as 1952, long after the original intention to build up a large affiliated-union wing had been abandoned.[77]

When the CCF did abandon this intention, the "ripe" locals lost whatever incentive to affiliate they may have had. The CCF was not asking them to affiliate; the initiative had to come from the locals themselves. Affiliation would have little practical meaning other than the per capita fee, and the invitation to participate in CCF conventions dominated by individual members. The local union, even if it were overwhelmingly and enthusiastically pro-CCF, would find ways of helping the CCF other than affiliation. If it had affiliated in the early period, it might well let its affiliation lapse.[78] According to David Lewis, most of the affiliations secured by the Ontario CCF in late 1942 were allowed to lapse within the next few years.

Although the CCF never formally abandoned the idea of trade union affiliation, affiliation was promoted to the status of an ultimate goal. It was not rescued from this lofty limbo until the CCF and labour decided to launch the New Democratic party.

[77]See below, pp. 156–7.
[78]Lewis interview, Jan. 15, 1963, and interview with William Mahoney, Jan. 9, 1963.

3. *The Struggle with the Communists, 1943-48*

1. INTRODUCTION: MILLARD AND CONROY

The only organized opposition to labour political action in support of the CCF during the forties was the formidable Communist "opposition" group in the CCL. The political energies of the CCFers in the CCL throughout this period were devoted primarily to battle with the Communists—a battle ranging in intensity from undercover intrigue to open civil war.

The Communists had been anything but inactive in the early days of the CIO organizing drive. While Millard and his colleagues were taking control of one group of CIO unions, the Communists were taking control of another; furthermore, while Ontario was becoming a centre of CCF strength in the labour movement, British Columbia was becoming a centre of Communist strength. The regional director of the CIO in Vancouver was Nigel Morgan of the IWA, a Communist; he was as useful to the Communists in British Columbia as Millard was to the CCF in Ontario. At the first convention of the CCL in 1940, Morgan ran against Mosher for the presidency. The results were Mosher 283, Morgan 175.[1]

Four CCL unions were Communist-dominated: the United Electrical Workers, Fur and Leather Workers, Shipyard General Workers' Federation of British Columbia, and the International Woodworkers of America. The total membership of these unions in 1946 was about 55,000. The total CCL membership was about 270,000. Two other unions, the United Automobile Workers and the Mine, Mill and Smelter Workers, with a total membership of about 63,500, could not be described as Communist-dominated, but both contained very influential Communist factions, and the heads of both were dependent on Communist support. Thus ten of the CCL's twenty-three unions, and more than a third of the CCL's membership, were under Communist domination or influence.[2]

[1]*Federationist*, Sept. 9, 1940.
[2]*Financial Post*, Sept. 16, 1946.

Arrayed against the Communists was a group of unions which varied in the degree of their support for the CCF. The new industrial unions which had been organized by Millard and his friends made promotion of the CCF as labour's political arm one of their major goals. Of these Millard's Steelworkers' union—the largest and most powerful in the Congress—was the acknowledged leader. The other important union in this group was Dowling's United Packinghouse Workers. The older unions in the CCL—unions like the CBRE, ACWA, the UMW—supported the CCF but with less vigour and less single-mindedness than the Millard group.

At a Congress convention there were likely to be three groups of delegates: Communists and their supporters, CCFers and their supporters, and an aggregation of delegates who were not committed to either party. Many of this last group would be French Canadians scattered through most of the Congress unions. These delegates are described as an "aggregation" because they lacked coherence and organization, did not act in concert, and were not vocal on political issues. Their role consisted in observing the battle from the sidelines. When an issue came to a vote, they could usually be counted on to support the CCFers. The only organized political blocs in the Congress were the Communists and the CCF.

The three most important men in the Congress were the president, A. R. Mosher; the secretary-treasurer and chief executive officer, Pat Conroy; and executive committee member Charles Millard. The attitudes of Millard and Conroy to the issue of political action differed considerably. These attitudes were both reflections and determinants of the two basic political approaches which were taken within the non-Communist leadership of the CCL unions.

Charles Millard was simultaneously a labour leader, a CCF politician, and a determined enemy of Communism in the labour movement. There was no conflict among these three roles; each complemented and gave meaning to the other. Millard's goals—and these became the goals of his union—were to strengthen the Steelworkers' union in particular and the labour movement in general; to build the CCF as the political arm of labour; and to drive the Communists from the labour movement. Each of these goals was intertwined with the others; each was pursued not only for its own sake but for the sake of the others. What was good for Steel and labour was good for the CCF, and *vice versa*; waging war against the Communists was good for both. In 1963 J. B. Salsberg still wondered[3] at the almost "religious" fervour with which Millard and

[3]Interview, Jan. 16, 1963.

his union carried on their campaign against Communism and for the CCF, and still puzzled over the "enigmatic figure" of Pat Conroy.

Conroy was described in CCF circles as a "unionist first"—first chronologically and first in terms of loyalty. When he came from District 18 of the United Mine Workers (Alberta and British Columbia) to become secretary treasurer of the CCL, he was not a supporter of the CCF. He did *become* a supporter of the CCF—partly because he was persuaded, partly because of the CCF's strength within the Congress[4]— but not in the same sense as Millard. Millard *identified* the CCF and labour; Conroy did not. Conroy's commitment to the CCF was conditional, partial, revocable. The CCF was to be supported only because and only in so far as it was good for labour. The party and the labour movement were two separate and distinct entities; their interests might come into conflict; when this happened, the interests of the labour movement must take precedence. Millard was a CCF leader and a labour leader. Conroy was a labour leader who supported the CCF. To the enthusiastic political actionists in Steel and other unions Conroy's support often appeared "lukewarm."

Conroy, subsequently the labour attaché at the Canadian embassy in Washington, confirmed this appraisal of his attitude when he was interviewed late in 1963. He said that he had regarded the young CCFers who had helped to organize the new CIO unions as "trade-union illiterates" (many of them "nuts"), whose primary motivation was not to build a labour movement but to capture it for the CCF. On the one hand, he had been sympathetic to the CCF, he had supported the principle of labour political action through the CCF, and he had valued the CCF's strength in the CCL as a bulwark against the Communist "menace." On the other hand, as a "unionist first," he considered the political enthusiasm of the "red hot" CCFers to be excessive, a "nuisance," a hindrance to the progress of the CCL as a *union* movement.

A complicating factor in Conroy's attitude to the CCL's political action program was his bitter personal rivalry with Millard. This rivalry appears to have stemmed, in the first instance, from a straightforward power struggle within the Congress between the new unions, grouped around Millard's Steel, and the older unions, primarily the CBRE and the UMW. The rapid growth of the new unions between 1940 and 1943 and the corresponding increase in their weight at CCL conventions, specifically in the election of executive members, aroused the resentment of the previously dominant older unions.[5]

[4]Interview with Lewis, Jan. 15, 1963.
[5]Stuart Jamieson, *Industrial Relations in Canada* (Ithaca, N.Y., 1957), pp. 46–7.

Against this background there developed a rivalry between Conroy and Millard for the position of "number one man in Canadian labour," and a rivalry between their respective "machines"—the Congress and the Steel union—for the position of organizational core of the industrial union movement.[6] Conroy conceived of the Congress, not as the passive servant of its affiliates, but as the central motive power of the movement, the co-ordinator and guide of the affiliated unions. From Conroy's point of view, the influence which was wielded by Steel over other new CIO unions amounted to usurpation of the functions of the Congress. He describes Millard as an "empire-builder," driven by a "power complex" to "interfere in the affairs of every union in the Congress" with a view to setting up a kind of "*ex officio* Congress of his own."[7]

The Millard-Conroy enmity did not, so far as I know, affect Conroy's relationship with the CCF as a political party outside the Congress, or with CCFers inside Congress unions which were not aligned with Millard. But it did affect Conroy's attitude to the Congress' own political action efforts, because Millard was the dominant figure, and Steel the dominant union, in these efforts. Conroy saw the Political Action Committee not simply as an instrument for labour support of the CCF, but also as an instrument for the aggrandizement of Steel as against the Congress. His "lukewarmness" (as a "unionist first") to PAC was reinforced, if not activated, by his view of PAC as a tool in Millard's empire-building kit.

In the late forties, when both the CIO and the CCL turned on their Communists and drove them out, Pat Conroy became famous throughout Canada as "labour's number one anti-Communist." But during the war, Conroy semed "lukewarm" in his anti-Communism as well as in his support for the CCF. At the first convention of the CCL in 1940, a resolution denouncing Communists as subversive of free institutions was introduced by the CBRE and supported by leaders of CBRE, ACWA, and Conroy's own UMW-18; Conroy denounced it as a "witch-hunting resolution."[8] Eamon Park describes Conroy's position during the war years in this way: as the leader of a Congress which contained a powerful group of Communist-dominated unions, Conroy felt that he could not

[6]Millard interview, Jan. 9, 1963.

[7]Conroy interview, Dec. 31, 1963. When Conroy dramatically resigned as secretary-treasurer on the floor of the 1951 convention after having been defeated by the Millard forces on an issue having to do with the composition of the Congress executive, the organ of Mosher's CBRE declared: "He quit because an unashamed drive for power . . . was aimed at changing the Congress from a vehicle for the many to a juggernaut for one." *CBRE Monthly*, Feb. 1952.

[8]CCL Convention Proceedings (1940), pp. 30–3. See also H. A. Logan, *Trade Unions in Canada* (Toronto, 1948), p. 398.

identify himself outright with the anti-Communists. In a showdown on any issue, he always lined up against the Communists, but he tried, so far as was possible, to maintain a manoeuvrable position above and between the warring factions, to preserve his acceptability to the Communists, to *avoid* showdowns.[9] For the more partisan CCFers, he was "lukewarm"; for the Communists, he was "enigmatic."

2. COMMUNIST POLITICAL STRATEGY

In 1943 a new party appeared on the Canadian political scene. It was a "new party of Communists," but it called itself the Labor-Progressive party, and it busied itself chiefly with attacks on the CCF—from the right. The German invasion of the Soviet Union had led to the adoption of a new party line, which can be summed up in a phrase: "Win the war." "Labor's number one grievance, which must take precedence over all others, is the defeat of Hitler fascism. Anything that endangers that victory is against the interest of labor."[10] Simple enough, but from it flowed a mighty river of "right-wing deviationism" and "class collaborationism." The river reached its crest with denunciations of the "divisive," "utopian" socialist program of the CCF, and appeals to the Canadian people to re-elect the government of national unity. That government, of course, was the government of Mackenzie King.

"Win the war" meant that trade unions must abandon their militancy for the duration of the war, and concentrate on production; it therefore meant a "no strike pledge," rigidly and absolutely enforced. It meant that the class struggle must be replaced by class collaboration, by "national unity." The war government must not be attacked; it must be supported in its war effort, and pressed to pursue that effort still more vigorously. To make "political capital" out of wartime discontent was to act, "objectively," in the interests of Hitler.

The CCF, and the CCF leadership of the CCL, were bitterly denounced by the Communists for their failure to call off the class struggle on the industrial and political fronts. On the industrial front, the CCL refused to swallow the "no strike pledge" whole; it insisted that, so long as collective bargaining was not compulsory, labour must retain the strike weapon. The CCL policy was "a pledge to settle if possible every

[9]Interview with Park, Jan. 14, 1963. My description of Conroy's position is also based on interviews with Mahoney, Jan. 9, 1963, and James Robertson, Jan. 14, 1963.
[10]*Pacific Advocate*, Jan. 27, 1945.

dispute without resort to strike action . . . but a readiness to strike if necessary. . . ."[11] On the political front, the CCF refused to abandon its intention of becoming official opposition in the election of 1945. It made a great deal of "political capital" out of wartime discontent. It was therefore accused by the Communists of trying "to weaken Canadian unity and cripple Canada's war effort in order to gain some narrow partisan advantage."[12]

The Communists soon dropped the saving clause "for the duration of the war" from their pronouncements on "national unity." The Teheran Conference opened up "new perspectives" of *post*-war co-operation between the West and the Soviet Union: "The dominant character of the peace . . . will be stamped upon it by the fact that it will be based upon cooperation between the socialist and capitalist sectors of the world."[13] Co-operation between the West and the Soviet Union must be assured by continued collaboration between Communists and capitalists in the West. The task of Communists in the United States and Canada thus became to ensure the re-election of "progressive" capitalist governments which would extend into the post-war years the policy of domestic and international class collaboration, and to ensure the defeat of "reactionary" capitalists who were not captivated by the "perspectives of Teheran." In the United States the Communists supported Roosevelt. The Canadian Communists, being good pan-North Americans, looked around for a Canadian version of Roosevelt, and found Mackenzie King.[14]

On May 28, 1944, the National Executive Committee of the Labor-Progressive party issued a statement calling for the election of a large bloc of LPP and independent labour members pledged to co-operate with a re-elected Liberal government. The King government must be returned to power—though made dependent, if possible, on an LPP-labour bloc—because the Liberals "represent those of the capitalists who understand that they can and must cooperate with labor."[15] They are "the most democratic and pro-Teheran among the capitalists."[16]

If the CCF leaders were sufficiently enlightened to adopt a "pro-Teheran" policy, they would co-operate with the LPP by "making possible United Labor election campaigns around single candidates, CCF,

---

[11]*CCF News* (Ont.), Dec. 27, 1945.

[12]*Pacific Advocate*, Jan. 20, 1945.

[13]*Canadian Tribune*, June 3, 1944.

[14]Salsberg admitted that he was at best an "ersatz Roosevelt" in an interview, Jan. 16, 1963.

[15]Text of LPP statement, May 28, 1944, NDP files.

[16]*Canadian Tribune*, June 7, 1944.

LPP, or independent labor," in every constituency.[17] But the CCF leaders were not enlightened. They could not be expected to co-operate. For their program was not a realistic program of "democratic national unity . . . maintained within the profit system"[18] but an unrealistic " 'socialism or nothing' utopianism."[19] The CCF program was not a basis for peaceful relations with the bourgeoisie but a basis for "struggle and conflict."[20] The Communist leaders of UAW local 195 in Windsor explained their differences with the CCF in these words: "The CCF intends to take over the industry with which the UAW proposes that Labour co-operate."[21] Obviously, "national unity including important sections of big capital could not be established around a CCF government."[22]

There was, of course, little danger that the CCF would form the government; but there was a great danger that its drive for major party status would divide "the democratic vote" and ensure a victory for reactionary, anti-Teheran toryism. At the very least, it would force the Liberals into a reactionary coalition with the Tories:

Labor looks forward and intends to work for a progressive, forward looking government, not necessarily socialist. . . . The CCF, on the other hand, is looking forward to a reactionary government with the CCF as official opposition. . . . They refuse to consider a government composed of . . . Liberals, CCF, LPP, and Labor as an alternative to reaction. They want to go it alone and to hell with the consequences.[23]

Labour must therefore reject the socialist program of the CCF in order to facilitate post-war co-operation with the pro-Teheran capitalists; and the labour vote must be directed away from the CCF towards LPP and "labour" candidates in certain constituencies (the LPP intended to nominate in sixty-five constituencies) and towards the Liberals in others. A small vote for the CCF would ensure a Liberal victory; a large vote for the LPP and "labour" would ensure a Liberal minority government dependent on LPP-"labour" support, perhaps even a "liberal-labour coalition government."[24] Within the CCL, the Communists waged a

[17]*Ibid.*, June 3, 1944.
[18]Text of LPP statement, May 28, 1944.
[19]*Glace Bay Gazette*, June 8, 1944.
[20]*Canadian Tribune*, June 3, 1944.
[21]*Local 195 News*, May 1945.
[22]*Glace Bay Gazette*, June 8, 1944.
[23]*British Columbia Lumber Worker*, March 12, 1945.
[24]This was not an unrealistic strategy in the political circumstances of 1945. Most observers believed that no party would have an absolute majority in the House of Commons after the election. If the Communists succeeded in electing even a few MP's, they might be in a strong "balance of power" position.

ferocious battle aimed at diverting its political action from support of the CCF to support of a "liberal-labour coalition."[25]

3. THE POLITICAL ACTION COMMITTEE

On February 10, 1944, the Executive Council of the CCL authorized the establishment of a Political Action Committee to "implement" the Congress' endorsement of the CCF. A struggle over the composition and policy of the PAC immediately began, the CCFers under Millard striving to tie it to the CCF, and the Communists trying to commit it to a "non-partisan" "liberal-labour" line. The CCFers apparently believed that they could keep representatives of Communist unions out of PAC, for it consisted at first of five CCFers appointed by the Congress executive. By the time of the second meeting, May 27, 1944, PAC consisted of seven members, representing the UPWA, CBRE, Mine-Mill, Steel, ACWA, Rubber Workers, and the UAW. George Burt, representing the UAW, was at this time a member of the CCF.[26] The chairman of the committee was Charles Millard. The vice-chairman was Robert Carlin of Mine-Mill, a CCF MPP; and the secretary was Andy Andras of the CBRE, an active CCFer.[27] The Communists immediately protested that the PAC was "loaded with the most partisan CCF elements."[28]

Meanwhile Secretary-Treasurer Conroy also expressed dissent, and it appeared for a time that PAC might founder because of the enmity between Conroy and Millard. I have not been able to discover the precise details of the Millard-Conroy controversy as it affected PAC. However, it seemed to centre on two crucial points: (1) Conroy seemed to be withholding his co-operation from PAC because of the prominent role which had been assumed in it by Millard. (2) Conroy's "unionist first" attitude to the CCF and his policy of preserving his acceptability to the Communists apparently led him to insist that the character of PAC *as a Congress instrument* for support of the CCF rather than *a body of CCF trade unionists* be clearly established, and that concessions be made to Communist demands for a "representative" PAC:

He stated that in his opinion the . . . method of forming the national PAC was . . . premature and provocative, that this was tantamount to a CCF committee, and not a Congress PAC. . . . In his opinion the committee should

---

[25]After the election of 1945, the Communists returned to their traditional anti-capitalist line, urging a CCF-Communist united front against both old parties.

[26]See below, pp. 108–12.

[27]CCL-PAC Minutes, April 15, 1944, and May 27, 1944, CLC-PEC files.

[28]*Canadian Tribune*, Dec. 2, 1944.

embrace representatives of every large union, and that those who are not in accord with the policy of the convention would be tied down to the policy put through the National PAC, since the majority on that committee would be in favour of convention policy.[29]

At its second meeting the PAC made a concession to the Communists by inviting UE to name a representative. But this concession did not appear to satisfy either Conroy or the Communists. The PAC had begun to set up provincial PAC's with chairmen appointed by the national PAC. In British Columbia, where the CCL's provincial organization was virtually dominated by Communists, the appointed chairman was James ("Shakey") Robertson, a violently anti-Communist Steel official who was also a key figure in Steel's anti-Communist drive on the West Coast. Conroy told him "that it was a foolish mistake for [him] to take the position, as all the party boys would be sniping at [him]."[30] Conroy felt that the provincial as well as the national PAC's should be bodies representative of all CCL unions rather than appointive bodies consisting of Millard nominees. In June 1944 the PAC was instructed to halt its preliminary organizational work pending a meeting between the PAC and the Congress executive which would settle the controversy. Salsberg described the situation as follows: "When the CCL formed its PAC, the CCF trade union spokesmen . . . hastily proceeded to transform it into a narrow CCF appendage. They excluded from it all leaders . . . who do not subscribe to the CCF line. . . . This . . . aroused such powerful opposition within the CCL unions that the . . . leaders of the Congress had to step in and try to bring the PAC leaders down to earth."[31]

At this crucial stage of the proceedings, David Lewis appeared to be trying to bring about a *rapprochement* between Conroy and Millard. On July 8, 1944, Lewis wrote Conroy that he was "very worried about the PAC, and for only one reason, the obvious difficulties between yourself and Charlie Millard, and the undoubted fact of your serious distrust of Charlie's motives. . . . It would be a tremendous disservice to the entire thing if personal differences were allowed to create obstacles in the way of . . . PAC." Lewis appealed to Conroy to have a "heart-to-heart talk" with Millard, and to "take the leadership at the meeting of the PAC to push the work . . . of the committee forward . . . to ignore completely any personal differences which may stand in the way."[32]

The result of Conroy's intervention and the ensuing discussions among the PAC leaders, Lewis, and the Congress executive appears to have

[29]Robertson to Millard, June 29, 1944, NDP files.
[30]*Ibid.*
[31]*Canadian Tribune*, Aug. 19, 1944.   [32]NDP files.

been an agreement that Conroy's line would be followed. The PAC, while it would not renounce Congress policy of support for the CCF, would be a *Congress* PAC, representing all large unions in the Congress, rather than a "CCF committee." The political action resolution submitted to the 1944 convention of the CCL authorized the establishment of provincial and local PAC's "representative of organizations affiliated with the Congress."[33] The PAC would try to "tie" the Communist minority to Congress policy; but in order to do this it must make concessions to the Communist demand for "independence" of the PAC from the CCF. George Harris, secretary treasurer of UE, became second vice-chairman of PAC. It was decided that despite the Congress' endorsement of the CCF, the PAC would draw up a legislative program of its own and submit it to the leaders of all political parties in Canada. The program was adopted on August 12. Vice-chairman Harris voted against the preamble and most of the twenty-nine clauses.[34] He objected to the preamble, which mentioned the Congress' endorsement of the CCF, because it "seeks to narrow the scope of . . . political action to one party and thus fails to create conditions which are indispensable in preventing the victory of reaction."[35]

On September 4 Harris asked Millard to call a special meeting of PAC to adopt a program which "will make possible the broadest national unity to defeat . . . the Tories." Millard refused. The task of the PAC, he said, was to support the twenty-nine-point program and to implement "the political action resolution passed at our last . . . convention." Harris remained vice-chairman "so that the fight can be carried on inside PAC for the correct policies," but George Burt, who had by this time adopted the Communist "liberal-labour coalition" line, resigned from the PAC in protest against Millard's attempts to make it "an appendage to the CCF and its policies."[36]

At the CCL Convention of October 16-20, 1944, thirty-four resolutions submitted by UE, IWA, Mine Mill, a majority of UAW locals, and even some Steel and UMW locals "opposed restricting support to one political party and advocated a non-partisan policy similar to that of the CIO . . . for the election of . . . progressive candidates regardless of party, and looking toward a coalition of all progressive . . . forces."[37] The resolutions committee brought in a substitute resolution endorsing the twenty-nine point political action program drawn up by the PAC

[33]CCL Convention Proceedings (1944), p. 53.
[34]CCL-PAC Minutes, Aug. 12, 1944, CLC-PEC files.
[35]*Canadian Tribune*, Sept. 23, 1944.
[36]*Ibid.*
[37]*Ibid.*, Feb. 3, 1945.

and authorizing the establishment of local PACs representative of Congress unions. The resolution did not mention the CCF, but the front cover of the political action program reproduced the 1943 endorsement of the CCF. President Mosher stated that adoption of the substitute resolution would confirm "the policy adopted at the 1943 convention." Defeat of the resolution would "constitute a reversal of policy." A heated, explosive debate followed, in which George Harris and other Communists accused the Congress leadership of trying to bind unwilling unions to support of the CCF, and demanded that "the Congress . . . not be tied to the tail of any political party but that its members should be mobilized in such a way as to express themselves freely."[38] The Communist offensive apparently had an effect on the centre aggregation of delegates who were neither Communists nor CCFers. The success of the substitute resolution appeared to be in doubt.[39] The Congress officers assured the convention that the Congress was not subservient to any political party, that the political action program would be submitted to all parties, that neither the 1943 resolution nor the resolution under discussion bound "any unit of the Congress to become a part of, to affiliate with, or support any political party."[40] These were not concessions, but statements of fact, aimed at dispelling Communist-inspired notions that the Congress had been "taken over" by the CCF and that Congress affiliates were to be forced to support the CCF. However, in the heat of the debate, Pat Conroy made a statement which was interpreted by the Communists as "agreement on the part of the leadership to free the PAC from the CCF anchor and permit it to play an independent role."[41] Conroy's statement was "that the resolution passed at the 1943 Convention endorsing the CCF had no place in the Political Action Program."[42]

The substitute resolution was carried by a roll call vote of 272 to 185. In the election of Congress officers, all the incumbents except Conroy faced Communist opponents. Conroy was re-elected by acclamation. The presidential vote was Mosher 308, Jackson (of UE) 121.[43]

One can only speculate about what the result would have been if the delegates had been asked to vote on a resolution specifically reaffirming the 1943 resolution, or if Conroy had not promised to remove the 1943 resolution from the political action program. Although Mosher had

[38]CCL Convention Proceedings (1944), p. 53.
[39]Interview with Donald MacDonald, Oct. 23, 1962.
[40]CCL Convention Proceedings (1944), p. 54.
[41]Canadian Tribune, Dec. 2, 1944.
[42]CCL Convention Proceedings (1944), p. 54.
[43]Ibid., p. 55.

made it clear at the outset that support of the substitute resolution would
not change Congress policy, subsequent debate and Conroy's concession
confused the issue, and the final result was susceptible to a variety of
interpretations. The official Congress interpretation, set down in an
editorial in the *Canadian Unionist*,[44] was: "There should . . . be no
doubt in anyone's mind as to the position of the Congress. . . . The
Congress endorsed the CCF last year, and nothing was done at the
recent Convention to change that decision. The official policy of the
Congress calls for support of the CCF and the Congress proposes to
co-operate with that party to the fullest possible extent."

A new edition of the political action program appeared; its front cover
now carried the resolution passed in 1944 instead of the resolution of
1943, but a brief opening paragraph reminded the reader that the 1943
convention had endorsed the CCF as "the political arm of labour."

The next meeting of the PAC took place on November 16, 1944.
Burt had returned, and he and Harris were joined by Nigel Morgan of
the IWA, Gary Culhane of the British Columbia Shipyard Workers, and
Starr of the Fur and Leather Workers. The remaining eleven participants
(including three Congress officers, Mosher, Dowd, and Conroy), were
supporters of the 1943 resolution. Burt opened the discussion by
announcing that the UAW had decided to contribute $5000 to PAC, but
the money "would not be forthcoming until the position of PAC was
clarified to his satisfaction." Mosher declared that the Congress had
endorsed the CCF, and PAC "should educate the rank and file to the
aims of that party." Harris and Starr then moved the following resolution:

Whereas . . . the PAC . . . has until now been a partisan instrument created
to advance the interests of one political party . . . and whereas there existed
a pronounced resistance to PAC within the CCL unions and a strong demand
for a non-partisan PAC . . . and whereas . . . Secretary Treasurer Conroy
assured the delegates . . . that page one of the printed program of PAC
which carried the pro-CCF resolution . . . would be removed . . . and this
assurance was accepted by most of the delegates to mean that PAC would
henceforth be nonpartisan, Be it therefore Resolved . . . that
1) The PAC of the CCL is a nonpartisan political instrument of all unions.
2) That PAC is not an agent to [*sic*] nor is its objective to advance the
interests of the CCF or any other single political party.
3) That PAC . . . will seek the cooperation of the nonpartisan PAC which
the TLC decided to establish,[45] and of other labour and democratic
bodies.
4) That the PAC . . . will join . . . with all other democratic peoples and
organizations to defeat the plot of reaction . . . to capture the government.

44Nov. 1944.   45See below, pp. 104–8.

In the discussion that followed, Conroy stated that "as he understood it, the Congress and the CCF were tied together." Morgan and Starr retorted that, if this were so, their unions would withdraw from PAC. The reaction of Millard to this threat indicates that he had agreed with Conroy on a strategy of encouraging the participation of Communist unions in PAC. By making formal concessions on the issue of the PAC's "independence" of the CCF, Millard would encourage the Communists to believe that they could prevent PAC from being used in support of the CCF alone. But PAC would not formally renounce the Congress policy of support of the CCF. At the appropriate time, after it had been organized across the country without Communist opposition, the PAC would decide to support the CCF. The Communists would then either be "tied down" to the majority view—their organizations would remain in PAC, and it would appeal to their rank and file over their heads—or they would have to withdraw their organizations without being able to complain that PAC had excluded them. Millard moved the following substitute resolution:

Be it resolved that . . .
1) The PAC of the CCL is the political instrument of all unions of the Congress.
2) That PAC is an agent of the Congress unions and is wholly independent of any political party.
3) That PAC . . . will seek the co-operation of the PAC [of] the TLC . . . and other labour and democratic bodies.
4) That the PAC . . . will join . . . with all other democratic organizations to defeat reaction and to ensure the election of a . . . government of the people.

This motion was carried without a dissenting vote.[46]

J. B. Salsberg hailed the Millard resolution as an "important advance" towards the transformation of PAC into a "non-partisan political instrument." But he pointed out that Millard and his friends had not altered their "untenable sectarian" views, and that they were likely to attempt to "nullify" the resolution "through their control and direction of the national PAC." The fact that the same meeting which passed the resolution also appointed Eamon Park director of PAC was "an indication of such a desperate attempt," for "a person like Park" could not be expected to adhere to a "non-partisan program."[47] The UAW, UE, and IWA district councils also hailed the "revised" policy, and called upon their locals to set up PACs without delay.

On December 28, 1944, Director Park sent a circular to all CCL

[46]CCL-PAC Minutes, Nov. 16, 1944, CLC-PEC files.
[47]Canadian Tribune, Dec. 2, 1944.

locals outlining the PAC's organization plans. All local unions of the Congress were advised to set up PACs; the chairmen of local PACs would form district PACs, and chairmen of the latter would form provincial PACs. The work of all PACs would be "co-ordinated" by the national PAC under the supervision of the CCL executive. The circular pointed out "that PAC activity is independent of any . . . party and PAC committees . . . will be agents of the unions of the Congress." The task of PAC would be to work for the election of "a parliament which will carry out the 29 point legislative program of the CCL." A "memo" enclosed with the circular cautioned local, district, and provincial PACs not to endorse any "candidates for office," since "the question of endorsation of candidates has not been thoroughly discussed by the national PAC."[48] Also enclosed with the circular was a copy of the *Unionist* editorial reaffirming the Congress policy of support for the CCF.

George Harris agreed that the matter of candidate endorsements should be discussed by the national PAC, but he called for a policy "which will be sufficiently broad to enable local PACs . . . to follow it without restricting . . . their right to make the final decision."[49] The Communists apparently hoped at this time that the national PAC could be restricted to publicizing the CCL legislative program and prevented from taking any position other than calling for the election of candidates supporting the program. The endorsement of particular candidates would be left to local PACs. Local PACs controlled by Communists could then support LPP or "independent labour" candidates running on the "liberal-labour coalition" platform, and claim that in doing so they were carrying out the political policy of the CCL. The authority and prestige of a CCL which had endorsed the CCF could thus be used to support Communist opponents of CCF candidates in the sixty-five constituencies in which the LPP intended to nominate.

The CCFers realized that their strategy of involving the Communist unions in the work of a PAC which would eventually come out in unequivocal support of the CCF might not succeed very much longer. Park wrote Andras that "We must face into the probability that there must be a split in PAC if it is going to work at all. . . . I think the Commies are afraid of us doing a straight job because they know we can bring the rank and file of their unions as well as our own along with us."[50]

48Park to all CCL locals, Dec. 28, 1944, CLC-PEC files.
49Harris to Andy Andras, Dec. 6, 1944, *ibid.*
50Dec. 11, 1944, *ibid.*

Events hastened the split. The conscription crisis was at its height. Mackenzie King called a by-election for February 5, 1945, in Grey North (Ontario), in order to obtain a seat in the House of Commons for his new Minister of Defence, General Andrew McNaughton. The CCF and the Conservatives decided to run candidates against him. For the Communists, of course, the CCF decision was a betrayal of the war effort and a dastardly attack on national unity.

The national PAC met again on January 16, 1945, and adopted the following resolution:

Whereas the PAC program of the CCL has been submitted to all . . . parties . . . for their endorsation and support and whereas the PAC-CCL as an agent of the Congress is bound by the decision of the CCL Convention in 1943 . . . which was maintained by the 1944 convention, now therefore be it resolved:

1) that we re-affirm the position of the PAC-CCL as an organization independent of all political parties and subject only to the direction of the CCL.
2) that in view of the replies of various political parties, of which only the CCF has given support of labour's legislative program,[51] the national PAC-CCL affirms its endorsement of the CCF and . . . will do all possible to elect a CCF government at the next General Election.
3) that in given constituencies the PAC will endorse individual CCF candidates and offer full organizational support to those candidates.
4) that local PAC committees shall make recommendations to the national PAC but . . . final . . . policy regarding candidates will be in the hands of national PAC.[52]

This resolution, and another endorsing the CCF candidate in Grey North (Air Vice Marshal Godfrey), were adopted by a vote of 15 to 3 (George Harris, Nigel Morgan, and George Burt). Harris and Morgan immediately resigned, and Burt stated his intention of resigning.

The UE and IWA district councils immediately confirmed the resignations of Harris and Morgan and officially withdrew from PAC, in spite of a request from Millard to both unions to repudiate their representatives' position and appoint new representatives who would be "prepared to work with us irrespective of [their] . . . personal partisan point of view."[53] A short time later the UAW District Council withdrew George

[51]The Conservative and Liberal parties merely acknowledged receipt of the program. The Labor-Progressive and Social Credit parties made no reply whatsoever. The *Tribune* claimed that LPP leader, Tim Buck, had not received the program and so could not make a reply. Park countered by announcing that a copy of a letter to Buck, dated November 6, was in the PAC files. J. B. Salsberg confirmed in an interview on January 16, 1963, that Buck had received the program.
[52]CCL-PAC Minutes, Jan. 16, 1945, CLC-PEC files.
[53]Millard to C. S. Jackson and Harold Pritchett, Jan. 20, 1945, *ibid.*

Burt from PAC, and Gary Culhane of the British Columbia Shipyard Workers resigned.

Apparent attempts to exert pressure on the UE and IWA leaders through their American superiors indicate that the CCFers really wanted to keep these unions in PAC, and that Millard's request that new representatives be appointed was not made solely for its propaganda effect. On March 3, 1945, Eamon Park reported that the international president of the IWA had "instructed Brother Pritchett that the affiliation of the IWA to the CCL is through the international union and that they do not concur in the actions of the District Council." Since the UE international was as Communist as its Canadian section, "nothing very much could be done," but Park intended to discuss the situation with James Carey, secretary of the CIO.[54] This strategy did not succeed. UE, IWA, and UAW stayed out of PAC; there was nothing to be gained by returning. As George Harris explained to his District Council, "I had no choice but to resign. . . . The railroading of this resolution through the PAC . . . actually placed local unions in a position where they cannot, unless they go contrary to CCL policy, support any but a CCF candidate."[55]

The *Canadian Tribune* greeted the re-revised policy of the PAC with these headlines:

> CCF LEADERS ARE DETERMINED TO DESTROY INDE-
> PENDENT TRADE UNION POLITICAL ACTION. CANA-
> DIAN LABOR MUST UNMASK CONTRABAND STUFF
> PEDDLED BY MILLARD AND CO. UNDER FINE PAC
> LABEL.

J. B. Salsberg denounced Millard and his "handful of CCF . . . politicians" for their "cynical and reckless raid" on the PAC. They had violated Conroy's pledge to the convention; they had "unashamedly discarded" the resolution of November 16; they had "kidnapped" the PAC and made it a "partisan instrument for CCF electioneering."[56] Leslie Morris declared that "a party dictatorship" had been set up in the CCL. The "only way now" was to "fight . . . the CCF vote catchers. These are sharp words, but the situation is sharp, brothers," for if the PAC were not opposed, labour would be "split to the benefit of the tories."[57] The CCF and PAC were also accused of trying to antagonize the King government so that it would make no further legislative concessions to labour.[58]

54CCL-PAC Minutes, March 3, 1945, *ibid.*
55PAC Report of Harris to UE District Council, Jan. 28, 1945, *ibid.*
56*Canadian Tribune*, Feb. 3, 1945.
57*Ibid.*, June 17, 1945.
58Order-in-council PC 1003 making collective bargaining compulsory had been

The Communist presidents of four Steel locals in Vancouver appealed to CIO president Murray to stop the use of Steel funds in Canada for support of the CCF, and demanded an examination of the books of the Canadian section. Millard replied that support of the CCF was the official policy of Steel in Canada, and the international knew it.[59] Under the banner headline "MILLARD IS DESTROYING THE UNION!" the *Tribune* appealed to Steelworkers to support Millard's opponents in the forthcoming union elections.[60]

In the Grey North by-elections, the warring CCL labour leaders faced each other on the hustings—Millard and his friends supporting CCF candidate Godfrey, Harris and his friends supporting Liberal candidate McNaughton. The local Liberals accepted Communist support without qualms: those labour leaders were after all spokesmen of *bona fide* unions who believed that King was Canada's Roosevelt. An aura of respectability and moderation surrounded the rightist LPP in that strange wartime period. A full-page advertisement in the *Owen Sound Daily Times*, "published by the authority of the North Grey Liberal association" on February 3, 1945, declared:

UNION LEADERS COAST TO COAST SUPPORT MCNAUGHTON

The Labor leaders pictured on this page represent tens of thousands of Canadian trade unionists. . . . As trade union leaders, men who have worked in the best interests of the membership of their unions . . . they appeal to you . . . to put Patriotism above Partyism and to vote for General McNaughton on February 5th.

---

passed a short time before. George Harris said: "Prior to the PAC meeting I spent three days on a special committee of the CCL . . . formulating proposed amendments to PC 1003. . . . When we were confronted with this resolution in the PAC meeting it was obvious that the work of the special committee . . . was . . . shattered because it placed 300,000 members of this Congress in the position of going to the . . . government and stating we want this and this amendment on the one hand and on the other those 300,000 workers regardless of what you give us are going to smash your administration. . . . It is highly improbable that in the face of this resolution . . . King . . . will accede to the requests of the working people. . . . Millard . . . and the braintrust of the CCF have one object in view . . . to secure personal power for themselves regardless of what effect that has on the . . . interests of the working people." (PAC Report by Harris, Jan. 28, 1945, CLC-PEC files) Salsberg wrote: "Millard believes that the worse things are the better it is for the CCF." *Canadian Tribune*, Feb. 17, 1945.

[59]*Vancouver Sun*, April 17, 1945.

[60]"The proud United Steelworkers . . . is in danger of destruction in Canada because of the policies of Canadian Director C. H. Millard. . . . More interested in his CCF parliamentary ambitions than in trade unionism . . . Millard has packed his staff with all kinds of CCF propagandists . . . leaving union business go hang. In 1943 . . . Millard had to get $39,005 from the International because he couldn't 'make ends meet.' Yet he handed over $10,000 to the PAC." *Canadian Tribune*, Feb. 10, 1945.

Among the "pictured" labour leaders were George Harris and C. S. Jackson of UE, Nigel Morgan and Harold Pritchett of the IWA, Michael Kennedy of UAW local 195, Malcolm McLeod of the British Columbia Shipyard Workers, and J. A. "Pat" Sullivan, Communist secretary treasurer of the TLC.[61] The results of the by-election were: Case (Conservative) 7338, McNaughton 6099, Godfrey 3136. The *Pacific Advocate*[62] pointed to the Conservative victory as a perfect example of the results of the "partisan policy" of the "Coldwell-Lewis Millard gang. . . . The splitting of democratic forces can only result in the election of a government of Tory reaction." But the *Tribune*[63] consoled itself with the thought that Grey North had proved that Communist labour leaders and Liberals "can work together."

From January 16, 1945, when the PAC resolution endorsing the CCF was passed, to the day of the Grey North by-election (June 11) the voices of Communists throughout the CCL were raised against the political policy of the Congress. No effort was spared in their drive to sabotage the work of the PAC at every level. "Sabotage" was the word used by Pat Conroy during the review of the PAC's work at the CCL convention of 1946:

My position in this Congress, as you all recognize, has been that of trying to conciliate and bring together all the diverse forces of this Congress in a common program. . . . Despite my efforts to make this program work, it has been sabotaged from beginning to end, because in the minds of those who opposed it . . . there was the demand for what they called a nonpartisan program, an independent program. Independent of whom?[64]

4. THE TLC'S LIBERAL-LABOUR COALITION

Both the CCF and the Communists were weak in the TLC,[65] so far as their numbers and organizational power were concerned. But while civil war raged between the CCL leadership and the Communists, peace, even brotherly love, characterized the relationship between the TLC leaders and the Communists. The "non-partisan" policy of the TLC was perfectly satisfactory to the Communists, and the non-political TLC

[61]See below, p. 103.
[62]Feb. 10, 1945.
[63]Feb. 24, 1945.
[64]CCL Convention Proceedings (1946), p. 80.
[65]Of the seventy-six TLC unions (284,000 members) only four, with a membership of 15,700, were Communist-dominated. These were the United Textile Workers, the United Garment Workers, the International Chemical Workers, and the Canadian Seamen's Union. *Financial Post*, Sept. 16, 1946.

leaders, believing that the "politics" of a union leader were of no more importance than his race or religion so long as "politics" were kept out of the union, saw no reason to spurn the Communists' outstretched hand of friendship. The TLC convention of 1944 adopted a Communist-inspired resolution authorizing the establishment of a "non-partisan" PAC. The *Pacific Advocate* rhapsodized: "TLC Meet Achieves Unity and Progress." This was a "refreshing contrast" with the CCL Convention, where CCF "domination [had] prevented adoption of a realistic program." The TLC convention had not only refused, in President Bengough's words, to "become the dog running behind the wagon of any political party"; it had gone so far as to condemn "red-baiting . . . by formal resolution."[66] The convention also reaffirmed the TLC's no-strike pledge.

The conservative-Communist entente in the TLC was symbolized by the election of J. A. "Pat" Sullivan, Communist head of the Canadian Seamen's Union, to the post of vice-president of the TLC in 1942. In 1943 Sullivan became secretary treasurer; he continued to hold this post until his resignation in 1947.[67]

During the first years of the war the TLC had been almost as bitterly opposed as the CCL to the King government. At the 1942 TLC Convention, Bengough compared the government's labour policy to "Hitler's labor policy. . . . We want to see this war against the Labor people in this country stopped."[68] When King made his concessions to labour in 1944, friendly relations between the TLC and the government were re-established. At the 1944 TLC convention Bengough announced that the Congress and the government had "arrived at a basis of friendly co-operation," and introduced the Minister of Labour, Humphrey Mitchell to the applauding delegates. (This was the same Mitchell whose resignation had been demanded by both labour congresses the year before.) The report of the Executive Council contained a veiled condemnation of the CCF:

We do not agree that any section or group of our society should endeavour to take advantage of the war situation. We cannot agree that now is the time for political parties to utilize this crisis and waste valuable time in advancing their own political prestige. . . . We would much prefer to aid and assist the government than devote time protesting undue infringements upon our liberties.

An enlightened Teheran policy indeed.

[66]Nov. 4, 1944.
[67]See his *Red Sails on the Great Lakes* (Toronto, 1955).
[68]TLC Convention Proceedings (1942), p. 10.

A guest speaker at the convention was C. D. Howe. He opened his speech with the remarks: "I must confess that after the public denunciation awarded me at [the CCL convention] a few days ago, it is a relief to know that I am at least on speaking terms with this, Canada's largest labor convention." He went on to quote William Green on the "priceless blessings" of "individual liberty and security" which are "inseparably associated with the vital principle of free enterprise and the private ownership of property." Secretary Treasurer Sullivan did not disagree. "I am willing," he said, "to go down the line with any government in advancing the welfare of . . . the people."[69] Thus the interests of the Liberal government, the non-partisan TLC leaders, and the Communists coincided. Everyone was happy, except the CCF.

"Friendly co-operation" with government is sought by all pressure groups, including those which are active in partisan politics. From the point of view of the British Trades Union Congress and the Canadian CCL, partisan political activity did not rule out co-operation with government. For the TLC, however, partisan politics and co-operation with government were incompatible. It therefore consistently advocated the election of "friends" and the defeat of "enemies," *in abstracto*, without ever pointing out *who* the "friends" and "enemies" were—consistently, until 1945. In that year the TLC actually advised its members to vote for a particular political party—the Liberal party.

Mackenzie King's diary reveals that on February 18, 1944, Bengough told King "he wanted to be helpful. Did not want to see the CCF make any headway."[70] When interviewed in 1962, Bengough denied having made this partisan remark. Whether he did or not, however, there can be little doubt that he at least discussed the political situation with King and gave King reason to believe that he "wanted to be helpful." King's government was in real danger of defeat; relations between the TLC and the government were good. Perhaps King asked Bengough to make some sort of gesture of support; perhaps Bengough felt that he could not refuse such a gesture to his new found "friend." This would explain how the non-partisan labour leader with friends in the government was drawn into political partisanship.

The first public hint of the non-partisan TLC's Liberal partisanship was a statement on the Grey North by-election by the TLC's Communist secretary treasurer:

Our Congress voted at its last convention to set up a PAC, but refused to attach itself to any political party. It is therefore impossible for our Congress

---

[69]*Ibid.* (1944), pp. 11, 43–4, 218–19, 225, 252.

[70]J. W. Pickersgill, *The Mackenzie King Record*, I (Toronto, 1960), p. 643.

. . . to join in any partisan move. Our attitude in this critical stage of the struggle against fascism is best seen in our reaffirmation of the "no strike pledge" at our last convention. We can only hope that the people of Grey North will put victory first and relegate party politics to a secondary position.[71]

In preparation for the election of 1945, the TLC implemented its convention resolution and set up a Political Action Committee. A committee of five was appointed by the Executive Council on April 22, 1944. Its duty was

to act in an advisory capacity with a view to having candidates elected who will support the aims and aspirations of organized labor. . . . There is nothing new in this procedure but there is this difference in that this Congress has not dealt with it in an organized way before. However, these are critical times. . . . A great deal depends upon the composition of the next Parliament. . . . [The] committee [does] not include members with definite party leanings.[72]

The PAC was given neither finances nor staff to carry on any kind of propaganda or organizational activity. It performed a single act—the publication, on May 19, 1945, of a statement calling for the re-election of the Liberal government.

The statement was long and involved and did not mention the names of any politicians or parties. But its import was clear. It referred to the "errors" of the government, but noted that the government had mended its ways. It emphasized the importance of "national unity," and condemned "any group who has no greater claim to fame than the destruction of National Unity." It concluded with these words:

Certain obligations were accepted by Government as to what will be the procedure when the time arrives to go forward to . . . peacetime economy. . . . [It] must be given the opportunity to redeem them. . . . [It] must be given the opportunity of keeping faith with the people. . . . There is a danger that a new group, put into power at this time, would institute policies that might have no relation whatever to the pledges that an overwhelming number of people . . . have put their faith in.[73]

The TLC statement was published as a Liberal advertisement in at least one newspaper, the *Winnipeg Free Press*, with the captions: "Trade Unionists: Attention. . . . Vote Liberal." On June 1, the *Toronto Star* greeted the statement with the headline: WITH ONE VOICE LABOR CALLS FOR KING REELECTION.

[71]*Canadian Tribune*, Feb. 3, 1945.
[72]*Trades and Labor Congress Journal*, May 1945.
[73]*Winnipeg Free Press*, June 11, 1945.

One reason for the momentary heresy of the TLC may have been the subtle Communist influence on the policy of the Congress. The Congress was favourably disposed to the government; the Communists, through Pat Sullivan or some other channel, may have encouraged it to take a step towards partisan political action. The step was a small and cautious, almost terrified, one, and it was never repeated. There can be little doubt that it would not have been taken at all if not for the presence of either or both of two unusual circumstances—the apparently close personal relationship of Bengough with King at a time when King was fighting for his political life, and the Communist influence, no matter how slight, within the TLC leadership.

5. THE CIVIL WAR IN THE CCL

The CCL-PAC, because of its novelty, its limited financial resources, and Communist "sabotage," was not able to make a significant contribution to the CCF election campaign of 1945. That campaign itself, though it resulted in a greatly increased popular vote and parliamentary representation for the CCF, was a failure, for it condemned the CCF to minor party status for the rest of its life. The CCF vote east of Manitoba was almost quadrupled (1940: 87,000; 1945: 300,000),[74] but no new CCF MPs were elected in the East.

Looking back, the CCF and Congress leaders decided that PAC had failed, that a new approach was necessary. Conroy wrote:

PAC has not "caught on." Perhaps more money . . . would have helped. . . . However I doubt this. PAC is a borrowed instrument, negatively successful in the U.S., yet it does not seem to "click" in Canada. It has an alien connotation of U.S. pressure in Canada, where such pressures rebound against the users more often than they are successful. Steady plugging, instead of the glamorous medium is as I see it the medium for Canada.[75]

The function of PAC in the United States was to "get out the vote" for Roosevelt. The votes were there; they need only be delivered. In Canada the CCF had not won the support of the majority of workers: PAC must therefore try to "educate" them, to win their support, before trying to deliver their votes. Political ignorance and apathy were not the only obstacles, for the workers in the CCL were subjected to a rival "educa-

[74]G. Caplan, "The CCF in Ontario, 1932–45," MA thesis, University of Toronto, 1961, p. 463.
[75]Conroy to Andras, Jan. 3, 1946, CLC-PEC files.

tional" force: the "non-partisan" Communists. As a Steel official, Larry Sefton, put it, "We are trying to tie in the labour movement to a socialist party which the Communists do not want, if they can stop it. Therefore a job of 'banging up' the vote . . . won't be enough."[76] Conroy suggested that "PAC . . . be reorganized, with a new name and a new function. I suggest for the name 'the Political Education Committee.' "[77] Millard agreed.[78] But PAC was neither reorganized nor given a new "educational" function. It was allowed to lie dormant until the Ontario provincial election of 1948. The CCL in the first post-war years devoted its entire attention to the industrial front—and to the internal struggle with the Communists.

The only organizational links between the unions and the CCF at this time were CCF trade union committees responsible to the CCF provincial councils. The first CCF-TUC was organized in Ontario in 1942. Within the next few years, similar committees were set up in other provinces. They consisted of CCF trade unionists from both the CCL and the TLC; their task was to act as liaison bodies, representing the trade union view in the CCF organizations and "educating" unionists to support of the CCF. In September 1945 the CCF National Council set up a National TUC, consisting of the chairmen of the provincial TUCs and a group of CCF MPs including Angus MacInnis and Stanley Knowles. Its purpose was to co-ordinate the activities of the provincial TUCs.

Among the activities of the TUCs was the establishment of CCF "industrial clubs" in plants and in local unions. The industrial clubs carried on propaganda work among their fellow workers and tried to prepare them for affiliation to the CCF if affiliation was to be sought. In Communist-dominated or -influenced units, they acted as organizers of opposition to Communist power.[79] Since the only organized opposition to the Communists in the unions was the CCF, many unionists whose sole motive was opposition to Communist domination found themselves co-operating with CCFers in an anti-Communist campaign led by CCFers, and eventually many of them became CCFers themselves.

The main arenas of struggle between CCFers and Communists were the UAW in Ontario and the entire CCL wing of the labour movement in British Columbia.

[76]Report on the Grey North By-election, Feb. 20, 1945, NDP files.
[77]Conroy to Andras, Jan. 3, 1946, CLC-PEC files.
[78]Millard to Andras, Jan. 9, 1946, *ibid.*
[79]National TUC Minutes, Sept. 7–9, 1945, NDP files.

a. The UAW

i. Non-partisan political action in the UAW
The UAW in Canada was dominated by its two big locals in Windsor, Ontario, locals 195 and 200. In both the Communists controlled the executive. In the UAW as a whole they were the best organized and most powerful political force. The Canadian director of the UAW, George Burt, had been the treasurer of Oshawa local 222 during the strike of 1937. In 1939 he had ousted Charles Millard as UAW director in Canada. From 1939 to 1947, though he never became a Communist and could therefore not be placed in the same category as C. S. Jackson and Harold Pritchett, he was dependent on Communist support, his staff was predominantly Communist, and he usually took a position identical to that of the Communists on the issue of political action.

The official UAW position on politics was laid down at a special convention on political action in September 1943. The convention "rejected" affiliation to the CCF on the ground that the terms of affiliation were "undemocratic." It decided to set up PACs in the locals to "educate their membership on the urgency of political action in the trade union movement," but "deferred" any "immediate" political action because of the "lack of unity" between Communists and CCFers. The task of the PACs would be to persuade the warring factions to "sink their differences."[80]

This position, while it could be interpreted as a statesman-like compromise between CCFers and LPPers, and was undoubtedly supported by many unionists for that reason, was in line with the traditional Communist strategy of bringing about "unity" of the CCF, LPP, and other "progressive" forces in support of a single candidate in every constituency where labour might be powerful enough to win an election. However, it also reflected the opinions of a large unorganized group which was inclined neither to the CCF nor to the LPP. By early 1944 this group had become, according to a CCF observer, "disgusted with CP and CCF alike." It wanted political action, but felt that such action should take the form of "straight labour candidates . . . nominated and elected by the unions themselves."[81] The Communists supported and encouraged the current of independent labourism in the UAW because it coincided with their own approach to political action and to the CCF.

By March 1944 the UAW had decided to run independent labour

80*Local 195 News*, Feb. 1, 1944.
81Report on Windsor, June 25–28, 1944, NDP files.

candidates in Windsor in the federal election and to obtain CCF and LPP agreement not to oppose them. The CCF leadership in Toronto decided to cater to the independent labour sentiment instead of opposing it as a Communist manœuvre. This decision was based on the knowledge that, although the Communists had participated in the formulation of the UAW line and were supporting it for their own reasons, it also had strong backing from non-Communists within the union; the CCF would endeavour to divert the current of UAW independent labourism to the CCF. The CCF leadership therefore agreed to consider endorsing a candidate proposed by the UAW, but insisted that he must run as a CCF candidate. If he did not do so, the CCF would oppose him, and the labour vote would be split.[82]

These were the circumstances in which George Burt became a member of the CCF—either on the advice of his Communist supporters or with their acquiescence. The CCF leadership did not know how to interpret Burt's action, but decided to accept it at face value for the time being.[83]

By March 17 the UAW had decided that "the right candidate for Windsor is J. L. Cohen."[84] The "right candidate" meant a candidate who could be supported by the CCF and by all factions in the UAW. Whether he was to run as a UAW candidate unopposed by the CCF, or as a CCF candidate, had not yet been definitely decided. J. L. Cohen was a prominent, popular labour lawyer who was friendly with both political groups in the CCL. He agreed to accept a nomination in Windsor on condition that he run as a CCF candidate with the full support of all factions within the UAW.

[82]*Ibid.*

[83]David Lewis wrote: "There is something going on in re George Burt. I had the brainwave of suggesting to the CCF people [in Windsor] to invite George to speak with me at the public meeting. They did so. George spoke. He made a very clear and unequivocal statement that the trade unions must support the CCF. He did more than this. . . . He signed an application to become a member of the CCF and signed a $100 pledge. . . . All this evidence did not allay the suspicions of our people in Windsor. I must admit that I do not blame them. I discussed George with Walter Reuther in Detroit quite frankly. Walter told me that George still is completely in the camp of Addes and Frankensteen. He always votes with the Communist gang on the international board. Even within the last two months he made quite an antagonistic speech about the CCF at a board meeting. . . . In short, I am a little puzzled about George's present actions. . . . I did my best to persuade the key [CCF] people in Windsor that . . . whatever suspicions they may have as to George's motives, his open and public actions are the important thing and it was their duty to take them at their face value. . . . I think it is impossible to know exactly what he is aiming at, and whether he is acting independently or in line with instructions from his CP advisors." Lewis to Jolliffe, March 9, 1944, *ibid.*

[84]Lewis to Jolliffe, March 17, 1944, *ibid.*

On June 25, 1944, a meeting of the executive boards and PACs of the UAW locals in Windsor resolved that J. L. Cohen be recommended to the membership as the UAW candidate, and that the CCF constituency organization be requested to nominate him as "CCF-Labor" candidate in Essex West.[85] This decision was ratified by a stewards' meeting on July 28 and a mass membership meeting shortly afterwards.[86]

The UAW leaders, including the Communists, and the top leadership of the Ontario CCF, each for their own reasons, had agreed that the CCF in Windsor should accept the UAW nominee as the CCF candidate. But the active CCFers in Windsor resisted—and without their support the whole elaborate arrangement might break down. A member of the CCF leadership in Toronto commented: "According to the standard pattern, those who fight the CP themselves acquire CP psychology. And at present the excuse 'this is a Communist plot' is used by many CCFers to damn any proposal whatever that emanates from union leadership."[87]

The CCF activists in the UAW not only resented having a candidate from the outside "rammed down their throats" by their Communist enemies but felt that in the new situation their own control over the CCF organization in Windsor was endangered. It was only after a great deal of pressure and persuasion by the CCF leaders in Toronto that the executives of the three CCF constituency organizations in Windsor met with J. L. Cohen (on August 22, 1944) and issued a statement which "welcomed" the recommendation of Cohen by the UAW. The statement announced that the recommendation would be presented to a nominating convention in Essex West.[88] That the convention would nominate Cohen was not a certainty. The Ontario CCF leaders therefore proposed to send a "skilled man to Windsor . . . for three or four weeks" to organize

[85]Report on Windsor, June 25–28, 1944.

[86]The organ of Communist-dominated local 195 hailed the decision as a victory for "non-partisan" political action: "UAW-CIO Locals Nominate J. L. Cohen as CCF-Labor Candidate. . . . The leaders of 195 . . . feel that J. L. Cohen is the one man that can get the most united support from all sections of the labor movement in this city. . . . We must realize that the time has passed when we can bind ourselves . . . to the election of any one particular party. Our strength must be used to elect men . . . who . . . best represent the interests of the Canadian people no matter to what party they belong. . . . The labor movement [should] unite for the one man in each constituency who has the best chance of being elected." *Local 195 News*, July 24, 1944.

[87]Report on Windsor, June 25–28, 1944. The Windsor CCFers also mounted a "sniping" campaign against George Burt. When Burt complained to the CCF leadership in Toronto, he was reminded that the Windsor CCFers' antagonism towards him "grew out of his past . . . and would take time to forget."

[88]Press release, Aug. 23, 1944, NDP files.

CCF clubs in the UAW locals and "greatly multiply [CCF] memberships among trade unionists." It was hoped that Burt would co-operate in this effort. If it were successful, the opposition to Cohen within the CCF organization would be swamped by new, pro-Cohen CCF members. The intention was to "sign up UAW members to a number which will be enough to beat the anti-Cohen gang."[89] This was not "packing"; on the contrary. CCF membership in Windsor was very small in relation to the number of CCF sympathizers in the union. An increase in membership might be resisted by "many of the old guard . . . as a threat to their monopoly of CCF power. But we [should] . . . be tough on this matter. . . . We are restoring democracy . . . not taking it away."[90]

These plans were never implemented, because the united front of Burt and Lewis collapsed, and Cohen's name never came before a CCF nominating convention. While the manœuvres and intrigues in Windsor were going on, the LPP's "liberal-labor coalition" line was hardening. On August 27, the PAC of the CCL adopted a political action program which was criticized by its vice-chairman, George Harris, for its failure to support the Communist line (unity of all progressive forces, opposition to Tory reaction, and the election of a Liberal government dependent on the support of a united independent parliamentary bloc of LPP and "Labor" MP's) and George Burt resigned from PAC in protest at its narrow CCF partisanship. On October 4, 1944, Burt publicly supported the Communist demand that the three opposition parties in the Ontario legislature—the Liberals, LPP, and CCF (official opposition)—unite to defeat the Tory government and establish a "progressive" coalition government. Mitchell Hepburn's Liberals were agreeable[91]; the CCF was not.

On October 6, 1944, J. L. Cohen announced that he would not accept a nomination as CCF-Labor candidate in Essex West. He wrote Burt[92] that in view of the increasing differences of policy between the UAW and the CCF—specifically, the adoption by both Windsor locals of resolutions in favour of an anti-Drew liberal-labour coalition—he could not accept the CCF-Labor nomination in Essex West; this would put him "in the anomalous position of opposing policies officially adopted by the union."

The Communists reverted, no doubt with relief, to their original plan to run "independent" UAW candidates. On December 10 a mass

---

[89]Morden Lazarus to Lewis, Aug. 24, 1944, *ibid.*
[90]Report on Windsor, June 25–28, 1944.
[91]Caplan, "The CCF in Ontario," p. 384.
[92]Oct. 6, 1944, NDP files.

membership meeting of the three Windsor locals decided to endorse a "non-partisan" UAW candidate for the federal election.[93] A committee of seven—the three local presidents, the three local PAC chairmen, and George Burt—were instructed to offer J. L. Cohen the UAW nomination.[94] Cohen declined, and the plan to run a UAW candidate in the federal election collapsed.

Eamon Park, director of the CCL-PAC, was in Windsor during the weekend of December 10. *Local 195 News* accused him of coming to Windsor for the purpose of organizing CCF opposition at the meeting of December 10th: "It seems highly irregular that the person who is supposed to organize the unions behind the policy of the CCL should try to sabotage the actions of a CCL affiliate in approving that policy."[95] Locals 195 and 200 protested to the CCL executive council. Park's actions, they said, showed that the "CCF clique" were preparing to "betray" the new non-partisan policy of the CCL-PAC.[96]

On December 16 the *Tribune* reported that A. N. Alles, a UAW member, CCF MPP for Essex North, had withdrawn from the CCF caucus because of its refusal to support the UAW-LPP demand for a progressive anti-Drew coalition.

The UAW District Council meeting of February 17–18, 1945, approved Burt's opposition to the CCL-PAC's decision of January 16 to support the CCF and "requested" him to resign from PAC. Burt rejected a suggestion that he remain on PAC to continue the struggle for a "non-partisan" policy. "Because of the extremely narrow partisan control by the Millard-CCF group," the PAC was beyond redemption.[97]

In March, the District Council decided to recommend to the locals that they nominate UAW candidates for the *provincial* elections of June 4. These candidates would be committed to the UAW policy of "uniting the anti-Tory vote" and electing an anti-Drew coalition government. The CCF, Liberal, and LPP parties would be asked to support the UAW candidates.[98] Of course, the CCF refused and the LPP agreed. But,

---

[93]*Local 195 News*, Jan. 1, 1945. This same meeting approved the UAW District Council's decision to send Burt back to the CCL-PAC and to authorize UAW participation on the basis of the Communist interpretation of the PAC's Nov. 17 resolution: "The UAW was successful in making the CCL-PAC a non partisan body. We can now go full into the PAC . . . and continue to fight so that this non partisan policy is carried out." *Ibid.*, Feb. 1, 1945.

[94]*Canadian Tribune*, Dec. 16, 1944.

[95]*Local 195 News*, Jan. 1, 1945.

[96]*Ibid.*, Feb. 1, 1945.   [97]*Ibid.*, April 1, 1945.

[98]*Ibid.* Oshawa local 222 did not follow the District Council's policy of securing unity of all anti-Drew forces. The Oshawa local endorsed the CCF candidate and contributed $200 (its share of the $5000 earmarked for CCL-PAC but withheld by Burt) to his campaign fund. *Oshaworker*, June 20, 1945.

strange as it may seem, the Liberals agreed too. In Canada as a whole, they made no efforts to repulse Communist offers of assistance in returning the King government. They had welcomed Communist assistance in Grey-North. In Windsor they went further, by actually entering into an electoral agreement with a Communist-dominated union.

The UAW nominated three candidates to contest the three Windsor provincial ridings: George Burt, Alex Parent (a member of the LPP and president of Local 195), and Windsor's mayor, Art Reaume, an ex-Conservative. All three were then nominated as official Liberal candidates by the Liberal constituency associations.[99] They ran as "UAW-Liberal-Labor" candidates endorsed by the LPP. Paul Martin, a member of King's government, "not only placed the whole Liberal organization at work for the UAW . . . candidates, but personally spoke on many mutual platforms."[100] Burt proclaimed that "the only people who are calling me Communist are Colonel George Drew, big business, and the CCF."[101]

In the 1943 election all three Windsor seats had been won by CCFers. In 1945 the results were:

Windsor-Walkerville	Burt	5691	CCF 4847	Tory 7428
Windsor-Sandwich	Reaume	6286	CCF 4949	Tory 7991
Essex-North	Parent	6049	CCF 5112	Tory 5544

The UAW-Communists, with the aid of the Liberals, had succeeded in defeating the CCF in all three ridings, and electing Tories in two. The successful UAW candidate was Alex Parent, the only one whose Communist affiliations were *not* hidden. He duly joined the Liberal caucus in the new Ontario legislature.[102]

ii. The civil war in the UAW

The beginning of the end for the Communists in the UAW was the Ford strike of September to December, 1945. The strike, called by the Communist-dominated Ford local, Local 200, was formally supported

[99]*Pacific Advocate*, May 19, 1945.
[100]*Canadian Tribune*, Sept. 1, 1945. Martin was supported by the UAW and LPP in the federal election. *Local 195 News*, May, 1945.
[101]*Pacific Advocate*, May 19, 1945.
[102]*Canadian Tribune*, Sept. 1, 1945. The Drew government was returned and the Liberals replaced the CCF as official opposition. In addition to the three "UAW" candidates in Windsor, the LPP named thirty-seven straight LPP candidates, twenty-seven of them in opposition to CCF incumbents. "In not less than eight ridings did an LPP candidate account for the election of an old party nominee. Had these candidates not split the labour vote the CCF would again have formed the official opposition." Caplan, "The CCF in Ontario," p. 462.

by the CCL, which set up a National Ford Strike Subcommittee, including Conroy and Millard among its members. A dispute over strike strategy immediately began between the Communists and the CCL leadership. The Communists advocated an unrelenting battle to the death with Ford; the CCL favoured an effort to reach a compromise. Against the advice of both the CCL and the UAW International, local 195 joined the strike, shutting down Chrysler and General Motors. The Communists also proposed a one-day general strike demonstration across the country in support of the Ford workers. The CCL leaders felt that the strike had been poorly timed—that it had been called for Communist political reasons and despite the weak bargaining position of the union. They opposed the general strike idea, proposing instead that strenuous efforts be made to reach a settlement with Ford.

In this dispute, George Burt aligned himself with the CCL and against the Communists in his union, mainly because he was supported by the secretary treasurer of the International, George Addes. Addes, like Burt, depended on Communist support for his position in the union; nevertheless, as the *CCF News* put it, "when the chips were down . . . both men showed themselves to be sound unionists, interested in maintaining their organization rather than letting the LPP strategists destroy it."[103]

While the CCL subcommittee was exploring the possibility of a settlement, Alex Parent, MPP, president of Local 195, and Roy England, president of Local 200, without consulting the CCL, sent nearly three hundred telegrams to union officials across Canada, calling for a national one-day general strike. This action was repudiated by the CCL subcommittee, no sympathy action was taken, and a strike settlement was accepted by a vote of 72 per cent of the union members. Steel official Murray Cotterill, in an article in *CCF News*, wrote: "The formula for settlement . . . stems . . . from the realization of men like Burt and Addes that the Communist control of the Windsor locals was dangerous for the future of the union . . . and from the . . . good sense of the Ford workers who . . . rejected the LPP leadership and reposed their confidence in sound union leadership."[104] The *Canadian Tribune* denounced Cotterill's article as "a vicious, anti-labor, red-baiting attack on the UAW and its leadership . . . by Murray Cotterill, a Millard spokesman and one of the most dangerous exponents of red-baiting and labor splitting." The *Tribune* warned that the CCL's opposition to national sympathy action, and Cotterill's article, were the "signals" for a "red-baiting" campaign by the CCF-CCL leadership: "Its gist: the 'responsible'

103*CCF News* (Ont.), Dec. 27, 1945.
104*Ibid.*

labor leadership must rid the trade union movement of its leftists."[105]
Alex Parent resigned from the Liberal caucus in the Ontario legislature
because the Liberals had "let down" the Ford workers.[106] He too warned
of "a conspiracy on the part of the monopolies, aided by a section of the
labor movement, to behead the UAW of its militant fighting leadership.
This conspiracy shall fail!"[107]

The Communists' fears were not groundless. The CCFers in Windsor,
guided by their friends in Steel and the Ontario CCF-TUC, were
organizing to overthrow the Communist leaders of locals 195 and 200.
Through the good offices of David Lewis the CCFers established contact
with Walter Reuther:

Our meeting was held with Walter Reuther last night as planned. . . . We all
came back with a firm determination to work harder than ever. . . . We are
determined to keep our group going and to caucus regularly throughout the
year and . . . to keep in contact with the Reuther group in Detroit. Thus we
will be able to take care of the two main points upon which the Communists
had an advantage over us: They were organized, we were not, and they had
a pipeline into the International office, we had not. . . . If we can keep it
up . . . we are in.[108]

The CCFers were joined by many "independent" anti-Communists, and
as part of a united anti-Communist caucus they were able to shake the
foundations of Communist power in the union. In the union elections
of March 2, 1946, Alex Parent and the entire Communist leadership of
local 195 were defeated. The new president was Earl Watson, who
"leans to the CCF"; the new vice-president was Bill MacDonald, secretary of the Essex East CCF. In local 200, Roy England retained the
presidency, but Jack Taylor, a CCFer, was elected vice-president. The
new executive was split between LPP and CCF sympathizers.[109]

The CCF opinion of Burt at this stage was that he

can be listed as a nice, pleasant guy who allows himself to be shoved around
unless he has strong support against the CP as he had in Addes during the
Ford Strike. . . . At the moment [the Communists] are holding the gun to
George Burt's head. . . . The threat is either Burt goes along with the party—
as he did recently . . . in lending his name . . . in speaking at LPP functions
—or the party will run against him at the coming [UAW international] convention. . . . Burt's past policy of trying to buy off CP opposition by staff
appointments to party stalwarts is now catching up with him. The party boys
. . . are ready to cut his throat.[110]

[105]*Canadian Tribune*, Jan. 12, 1946.
[106]*Ibid.*, Jan. 19, 1946.   [107]*Ibid.*, Jan. 26, 1946.
[108]Bill MacDonald (of local 195) to Lewis, Feb. 3, 1946, NDP files.
[109]Bill MacDonald to Park, March 10, 1946, *ibid.*
[110]*CCF News* (Ont.), Feb. 28, 1946.

CCF strategy was to defer attempts to replace Burt as Canadian UAW director[111] and in the meantime to help elect Reuther president of the international. The CCFers also tried to persuade Burt to divest himself of his Communist staff in exchange for CCF support in the elections for Canadian director in 1946. Burt was conciliatory, but said that "he does not like to just up and fire anyone"; besides, some of his staff were appointees of the international and could not be dismissed without its consent.[112] The CCFers therefore concentrated on their efforts to deliver the Canadian vote to Reuther:

While we have made a very good beginning in Windsor, the whole situation . . . hinges on the election of the president of the UAW at their convention in Atlantic City the end of the month. Burt is likely to remain as Canadian Director and can only be swung over if Reuther is elected. If [R. J.] Thomas remains as president . . . it is unlikely that [the Communist staff] can be got rid of. Burt won't remove them of his own free will.[113]

The UAW international convention elected Reuther president, but it also elected an anti-Reuther majority to the executive board. Among them was George Burt, re-elected Canadian director by the Canadian delegates to the convention. Burt was therefore not "swung over"; the civil war in the UAW continued on both sides of the border. At the CCL convention of 1946, Burt joined Jackson, Harris, and Pritchett in opposing a resolution reaffirming the CCL's endorsement of the CCF.

At the same convention, there were indications that Mosher and Conroy had decided, or were on the point of deciding, to wage all-out war on the Communists. Conroy, who had had a "bellyful" from the Communists during the Ford strike, seemed to have abandoned his strategy of "trying to conciliate and bring together all the diverse forces of this Congress." He closed the political action debate with what was, for him, an unusually strong denunciation of the LPP. He had tried for four days, he said, to persuade the Communists to refrain from opposing reaffirmation of Congress support for the CCF.

That they have refused to do. If we must have the facts, if we cannot have co-operation for a unified convention, then let us present the facts of the situation, and here they are as I see them, and I am taking the gloves off now! The issue in this convention is whether the LPP will dominate the CCL, or whether the CCL shall remain in the hands of its membership. Now I am getting sick and tired of this situation. . . . I say let us speak up for Canada

---

[111]"We could not expect to dislodge Burt this year. For some reason some of our fellows think he is alright." Bill MacDonald to Park, March 10, 1946, NDP files.

[112]*Ibid.*

[113]Lazarus to Lewis, March 14, 1946, *ibid.*

now. . . . Let us develop a political party that will . . . inspire the whole Canadian people. . . . We have but one choice to make.[114]

The pro-CCF resolution was passed. According to Eamon Park, the delegates consisted of "about 175 Communists, about 350 CCF, and another group of 200 who, at the end, were all on the side of the CCF."[115]

The 1947 CCL convention adopted two anti-Communist resolutions: one condemning "Communist imperialism" and another denouncing Communist party activity in the labour movement.[116] Burt was absent, but later said he would have opposed the resolutions.[117] Burt had been elected to the executive committee of the CCL at the 1944 convention. In 1947 the CCL leadership humiliated him by opposing his re-election and nominating a CCFer (Tom Brannigan of local 200) to take his place. Although a pre-election caucus of UAW delegates supported Burt four to one, the convention elected Brannigan.[118] Roy England issued a statement revealing that "Burt's defeat was hatched a month ago by the Millard-Conroy-Reuther group," and that the UAW might now "consider" terminating its affiliation to the CCL.[119]

At the UAW international convention of November 1947 a concerted effort to dislodge Burt from the post of Canadian director failed; he was re-elected by a narrow margin of eight votes. But his American friends, the Addes-Thomas group, were defeated, and Reuther emerged with firm control of the new UAW executive board. On December 10 David Lewis wrote to Reuther:

I cannot tell you how delighted we all were with your decisive victory. . . . We all look forward to the influence which the UAW should now be in a position to exert on the policies of the union movement both in the United States and Canada. I am only sorry that our people were unable to deliver a victory in the Canadian region. My impression is that it is only a matter of time now, and that continuing work will ensure a victory at the next convention.

Reuther replied: "Now that we have an opportunity to put our house in order in the UAW, I sincerely believe we will be in a position to make a major contribution both . . . in the U.S. and Canada. I hope to . . . chat with you in the near future."[120]

[114]CCL Convention Proceedings (1946), p. 81.
[115]Ontario CCF Provincial Council Minutes, Sept. 28–29, 1946, NDP files.
[116]CCL Convention Proceedings (1947), pp. 66 and 78.
[117]Ibid., p. 77; Globe and Mail, Oct. 13, 1948.
[118]Globe and Mail, Oct. 11, 1947.
[119]CCF News (BC), Oct. 17, 1947.
[120]NDP files, Dec. 23, 1947.

Confronted with rising CCF strength in the Windsor locals and the Reuther victory in the international, Burt "swung over."[121][122] At the CCL convention of 1948 he supported the administration's anti-Communist foreign policy resolution and was re-elected to the CCL executive. He "admitted he had 'taken left wing positions' in the past but now had changed his mind." Outside the convention he said "I never was a member of the CP nor a strong sympathizer, but I did go along on some matters."[123] In the Ontario provincial election of 1948, the UAW endorsed the CCF and participated in the OFL-PAC campaign which helped restore the CCF to the position of official opposition.

b. British Columbia

The three largest unions in British Columbia—IWA, Mine Mill, and Shipyard Workers—were under Communist domination until the late forties. Through their control of these unions,[124] and their influence in others, the Communists were able to exert virtual control over the provincial CCL organization itself.

In Ontario the CCF leadership had by the mid-forties become a hybrid of "bourgeois" socialists and labour leaders. A similar development in British Columbia was ruled out by Communist control of the CCL in the province. The British Columbia party, though it consistently received a much higher percentage of the labour *vote* than its Ontario counterpart, did not achieve close ties with the labour movement. On the contrary: in British Columbia the labour party and the major unions were enemies.

Only two local unions affiliated to the British Columbia CCF during the forties. This was in part the result of the normal fear which affected CCFers throughout the country, but it also reflected the unique situation in British Columbia—on the one hand, Communist control of the major industrial unions and, on the other, the influence within the CCF of a strong wing of doctrinaire leftists with an anti-union outlook. David Lewis described them as "pseudo-Marxists who considered unionism and unionists as unreliable from a socialist point of view . . . [and] really irrelevant to the socialist struggle."[125]

[121]*Financial Post*, April 1, 1949.
[122]Millard interview, Jan. 9, 1963.
[123]*Globe and Mail*, Oct. 13, 1948.
[124]In 1958 the IWA alone accounted for approximately 60 per cent of the CCL membership in British Columbia. Report of the BCFL-PEC, 1958, BCFL files.
[125]In a letter to GH, Aug. 16, 1966.

The British Columbia CCF convention of 1943 was presented with a constitutional amendment providing for affiliation, but it was tabled until the next convention. The rationale for this action was that the rank and file had "not had sufficient opportunity to consider this question which affects them so seriously." To put the amendment through without first permitting discussion of the matter at the constituency level "would be little short of railroading." In Britain and Ontario, the fact that many active party members were also leading trade unionists facilitated union affiliation, but in British Columbia the situation was "very much the reverse."[126]

The convention of 1944 adopted an amendment permitting union affiliation, and approved terms of affiliation virtually identical with those of the Ontario CCF.[127] But there was no drive for affiliations similar to the one which took place in Ontario, for most unions were either Communist-dominated or contained strong Communist factions. Very few were "ripe": "under such conditions," the CCF explained, "affiliation . . . would aggravate rather than remedy the situation. . . . Until this condition is removed we urge that . . . every step possible be taken to encourage our . . . supporters to activize themselves in their trade unions."[128] Affiliation had to be postponed until the Communist influence in the British Columbia labour movement could be removed; by the time it was removed, affiliation had ceased to be a practical goal of the CCF.

In the last months of 1943 the CCF leadership and the Steelworkers' union decided to launch a campaign to rid British Columbia labour of Communist domination. The campaign was to be managed by a revitalized CCF Trade Union Committee with the co-operation of Steel and Congress staff in British Columbia:

There is a definite need for following the lead set in Ontario and bringing

---

[126]British Columbia CCF Convention Proceedings (1943), p. 67. The Communist press opined that the real reason for the shelving of the affiliation proposal was "fear [that] Communist . . . infiltration into the ranks of the CCF would endanger the parliamentary ambitions and the machine control of the Websters, Winches, Gargraves et al." *People*, April 24, 1943. In any case, "under the terms of affiliation . . . trade unionists would provide a large portion of the finances . . . but would not be permitted a proportionate representation to determine policies in accordance with their numbers." *Fisherman*, Aug. 8, 1944.

[127]British Columbia CCF Convention Proceedings (1944), pp. 120 and 86.

[128]Joint Report of Economic Relations and Organization Committees on Affiliation of Trade Unions to the CCF, n.d. BC NDP files.

the trade union movement closer to the CCF. A vigorous campaign among trade unionists for membership in the CCF should be launched. . . . There are large numbers of trade unionists who are CCF supporters but due to lack of organization they are not always articulate and often allow a small minority to control the unions. . . . Communist party control . . . had only been brought about by organization. . . . We must organize along similar lines.[129]

David Lewis advised the TUC to

concentrate its efforts on wresting as many of the locals as possible from Communist control. . . . Shaky Robertson [Steel official, is being sent to BC] . . . with instructions from Charlie and the Congress people to start the ball rolling. . . . I will be discussing this whole matter with Mosher and Conroy. . . . I know they will welcome any assistance we can give them. . . . [and that] they will accept any reasonable advice we may give them.[130]
Their [Mosher's and Conroy's] fight is with Communist control of the coast unions and so . . . is our fight. Obviously, therefore, we should as far as possible co-ordinate our . . . activities.[131]

Shakey Robertson arrived in British Columbia and immediately assumed an active role in the TUC. A short time later he was joined by another Steel official from the East, Eileen Tallman, and together they acted as the "spearheads of the CCF" in the provincial CCL. The anti-Communist drive very early took on the character of a joint Steel-CCF enterprise. But the expected co-operation and co-ordination with the CCL was not forthcoming.

The chief executive officer of the CCL in British Columbia was the regional director, Daniel O'Brien, appointed by and responsible to the CCL's national executive. Although he was "under orders to co-operate with the CCF,"[132] he was also obliged, as a Congress official, to co-operate with the leaders of the major Congress affiliates. He soon fell under their influence, becoming in effect a member of the Communist labour elite and a public opponent of the CCF. But Mosher and Conroy not only refused to replace him; they supported him in specific disputes with the CCF. The result was that the Communists could act with the official sanction of the CCL in their struggle with the "political arm"

129BC CCF-TUC Minutes, Oct. 10, 1943, BC NDP files.
130Lewis to MacInnis, Sept. 21, 1943, NDP files.
131Lewis to Winch, Oct. 18, 1943, ibid.
132F. J. McKenzie to Lewis, March 29, 1945, ibid. "Danny O'Brien . . . is a weak man. . . . The major organizations affiliated with the CCL in this province are controlled by the LPP and it is natural enough that the CCL office here should be controlled by the LPP. It would take a very strong man to preserve a position of independence as Regional Director under the present circumstances."

of the CCL. When MacInnis and Lewis pointed out to Mosher that his chief representative in British Columbia had become "objectively, whatever his intentions, the main tool of the LPP," Mosher replied that "O'Brien is definitely anti-Communist and is very unhappy about having to rely so much on the LPP fellows." Mosher and Conroy still had "very great confidence" in O'Brien and would not consider "for one moment" the advisability of removing him from his position.[133]

It appeared that one of the main stumbling blocks to co-operation between the Congress officials and the CCF was the personal enmity of O'Brien, Conroy, and Mosher to the "foremost stumbling blocks of the LPP in the CCL,"[134] Robertson and Tallman. Lewis wrote:" Neither O'Brien nor the Congress officers here have any use whatever for Shakey Robertson and Eileen Tallman. . . . It seems clear . . . that it will be difficult, if not impossible, to win the confidence and support of O'Brien, the CBRE people in Vancouver, or the CCL officers if Shakey and Eileen remain the spearheads of the CCF." He suggested that efforts be made to bring about a *rapprochement* between the CCFers and O'Brien: "Some effort must be made, if it is not too late, to win O'Brien's confidence."[135] McKenzie replied that nothing was to be gained by such an effort: "When the CCF influence within the CCL here outweighs the LPP influence, Danny will succumb to the CCF influence." No *rapprochement* was achieved.

The personality factor was much less important than it appeared. The ultimate determinants of the CCL's failure to co-operate with the CCF in British Columbia are related to Conroy's feud with Millard, and to the different approaches to the Communist problem which these two men were taking in the early forties. Conroy was apparently willing to allow the Congress to promise co-operation in some sort of a drive against the Communists in British Columbia (Robertson was sent by "Charlie and the *Congress* people," and O'Brien was "under orders" to co-operate with the CCF). At the same time, however, Conroy was interested in balancing the Millard and Communist wings of the Congress, in "trying to conciliate and bring together all the diverse forces in this Congress." It was difficult to oppose the Communists without antagonizing them too much, yet this is what the "enigmatic" Conroy appeared to be doing. In the British Columbia situation, he found himself immobilized: how could he support the anti-Communist drive

[133]Lewis to McKenzie, March 22, 1945, *ibid.*
[134]McKenzie to Lewis, March 29, 1945, *ibid.*
[135]Lewis to McKenzie, March 22, 1945, *ibid.*

without antagonizing Pritchett, Morgan, Murphy, and the others beyond any possibility of reconciliation? Conroy's strategy therefore was to avoid involvement in direct aggression against the Communists,[136] and to argue that they should be quietly manœuvred into untenable positions which would cause them to lose the confidence of their rank and file. Robertson wrote: "They give us credit in Steel for cleaning up our mess, but don't appear to want it done in some of these others. Their attitude is that . . . the LPP . . . are digging their own grave. However, I believe we should have hold of the shovel to help fill the dirt in over them."[137]

Even if Conroy's attitude to the Communist unions had been different, however, there is reason to believe that he would not have acted differently. For this was a *Steel* drive; Millard was its mastermind, and his subordinates Robertson and Tallman were its "spearheads." The Congress officer's distaste for Robertson and Tallman was not based on the personal qualities of the two Steel officials, but precisely on their character as Steel officials, as creatures of Millard. Conroy may have approved of anti-Communist drives in principle, as anti-Communist drives, so long as he was not obliged to play an active or public role in them. But *this* anti-Communist drive was, as far as he was concerned, just another instance of Millard's "empire-building." If the price for a Communist-free British Columbia labour movement was to be the further aggrandizement of Steel, Conroy was not willing to pay the price. Conroy himself, when interviewed in 1963, explained that O'Brien was not a Communist, but was pushed into an alliance with them by his "hate of Millard." The enemy of my enemy is my friend. But why should O'Brien "hate" Millard? Because O'Brien was *Conroy's* man. David Lewis believes that if Steel and the CCF had made an effort to win Conroy's co-operation, to involve him in the formulation and execution of their plans, his attitude might have been different.[138] In the absence of such a Steel-CCF effort, it is not surprising that Conroy supported the officials of *his* organization in British Columbia and defended them from the attacks of officials of a *rival* organization (Steel).

On October 7, 1944, the CCL unions in British Columbia formed the British Columbia Federation of Labour (BCFL). The founding convention elected Daniel O'Brien president. The other three executive

[136]The ex-Communist Robertson, on the other hand, was so violent and single-minded in his anti-Communism that even Millard was horrified. Millard interview, Jan. 9, 1963.
[137]To Millard, June 29, 1944, NDP files.
[138]Lewis interview, Jan. 15, 1963.

posts were filled by Communists: Harvey Murphy (Mine Mill), first vice-president; Alex McKenzie (Oil, Chemical and Atomic Workers), second vice-president; and Harold Pritchett (IWA), secretary treasurer. The founding convention also adopted a resolution calling for "unity" of the LPP and CCF and the election of a liberal-labour coalition government in 1945.[139] In 1945, the BCFL asked the CCF to reach an electoral agreement with the LPP. The CCF refused, and the BCFL denounced its reply as "discourteous."[140] In the election, fourteen LPP and "independent labor" candidates ran on a "Liberal-Labor Coalition" platform. Among them were Harold Pritchett, Nigel Morgan, Gary Culhane, and Harvey Murphy.[141] According to the CCF, these candidates accounted for CCF defeats in six seats. Together with eight smiilar defeats in Ontario, "non-partisan" political action accounted for the loss of fourteen seats in the 1945 election.

The CCF's anti-Communist drive made slow but steady progress in 1944, 1945, and 1946. In November 1944, the executive of the British Columbia LPP issued a statement formally charging that the CCF party in British Columbia was trying "to either dominate or wreck the major trade unions" in the province. The CCF was accused specifically of "entering into an agreement with the notorious Trotskyite Socialist Labor Party in the U.S.A. which controls the international leadership of the IWA" to co-operate to gain control of the IWA in British Columbia. CCFers were "deliberately disrupting" local meetings throughout the province, making impossible the conduct of union business. Unionists were warned to "be on their guard and defend their unions against the 'rule or ruin' policy of the CCF."[142]

CCF strength on the Vancouver CCL Labour Council increased steadily. In March 1945, Eamon Park announced that "the IWA delegation to the Labour Council which was solidly Communist a year ago is now 80 per cent in support of Congress policies."[143] A year later (on

[139]*People*, Oct. 7, 1944.
[140]*British Columbia Lumber Worker*, Oct. 8, 1945.
[141]*Vancouver Herald*, June 6, 1945. Among them also was a veteran CCF MLA, H. W. Herridge, who sat for a strong Mine Mill constituency He was expelled from the party, but reinstated on his re-election to the Commons.
[142]*Pacific Advocate*, Nov. 4, 1944. In August 1945, an open letter from the executive committee of the Shipyard General Workers' Federation to the CCF provincial executive stated that CCFers within the union were "dishonestly exploiting grievances" against the leadership "in such a manner as to promote suspicions and hostilities, and by capitalizing on the political loyalties of the workers with results which threaten to disrupt and break the organization. . . . At the present moment the [Victoria] local is split wide open and its activities completely disrupted." SGWF to F. J. McKenzie, Aug. 28, 1945, BC NDP files.
[143]CCL-PAC Minutes, March 3, 1945, CLC-PEC files.

March 12) the *Vancouver Sun* reported that the Labour Council, "until recently" Communist-dominated, was evenly split between LPP and CCF supporters, though its executive was still Communist. The Council spent much of its time in vigorous political infighting—so much so that "independent" members feared that its usefulness as a labour council was threatened. The LPPers and CCFers on the Council fought for three hours, with cries of "rat, scab, fink, quisling," over a resolution condemning the CCL-PAC's endorsement of the CCF.[144] In June 1945, the Council requested the CCF and LPP to submit statements on their "relations to the trade union movement."[145] The CCF insisted that it was not fighting to gain "control" of the unions, but to free them from the domination of an unrepresentative Communist minority.

Despite the fact that in almost every instance the majority in every union apparently support the CCF, many unions are controlled by the . . . LPP. . . . This was only possible because we lacked cohesion in our efforts. . . . Every CCF member should be in there punching. . . . Only in this way will we ever effect our full weight and worth inside the trade union movement.[146]

The CCF does not want to release unions from LPP control to put them under CCF control. We *do* want their assistance in building a socialist party and forming a socialist government in Canada. . . . Our task . . . is to . . . fight for trade union democracy to release unions from LPP control, to organize ourselves inside unions for that purpose.[147]

144*Vancouver Province*, May 23, 1945.

145The CCF statement assured the Council that "the CCF deeply regrets the reports that political strife within the Council has reached the pitch where it threatens the usefulness of the Council. . . . It would be a mistake to imagine that any instruction can be issued by the CCF executive to members of the CCF who may be delegates to this Council with regard to the legitimate business of this Council. . . . All CCF members who may be eligible are asked to join and support trade unions, not as CCF members, but as trade unionists. . . . The CCF does not reach into the trade unions and urge them to do this or that as members of the CCF for purposes of the CCF. . . . The CCF quite openly and frankly appeals for the support of trade unionists. . . . The whole point is that this appeal . . . is based entirely on the record of faithful political service and a program shaped to meet the needs of labour. The success of this appeal never has and never will depend on intrigue within the trade unions, deception, or machine tactics. . . . [However], a member of the CCF who is active in a trade union is influenced by his . . . beliefs to uphold trade union policies as an important force towards working class emancipation. These convictions . . . lead him of his own account to oppose vigorously . . . policies detrimental to the interests of the workers. . . . The CCF has always upheld a policy of strict non-interference as a party with the internal business of trade unions. It is pointed out that any such policy to be successful must be respected by *all* political parties. Any intrigue always leads to counter-intrigue." Statement on behalf of CCF Provincial Executive Committee at June 26 meeting of Vancouver Labour Council, BC NDP files.

146*British Columbia TUC Bulletin*, July 1945.

147*Ibid.*, June 1946.

Though CCF strength in the IWA and other British Columbia unions was growing, Communist control of the IWA and the BCFL was not seriously threatened until 1947.

The Communist-dominated BCFL and the coalition government of the province shared a common interest in diverting the labour vote from the CCF. The increasing popularity of the CCF among the workers threatened both Communist control of the unions and Liberal-Conservative control of the government. The government was prepared to make concessions to labour, but it preferred to avoid the appearance of making concessions as a result of CCF pressure in the legislature. The BCFL obliged the government by giving it an opportunity to remove labour issues from the legislature to a "government-labour committee" composed of representatives of the government, the CCL, and the TLC. The government could then make its concessions to Harvey Murphy and Harold Pritchett of the BCFL (and, incidentally, of the LPP) rather than to the CCF opposition.

The government-labour committee was set up as a result of a joint CCL-TLC "lobby" which visited the legislature in March 1945. The leaders of the CCL section of the lobby, O'Brien, Pritchett, and Murphy, reached agreement with the government that no immediate action would be taken on labour's legislative proposals; instead, a government-labour committee would recommend labour measures to be proposed by the government at the next session of the legislature. The decision was endorsed by the mass membership of the joint lobby,[148] and the labour leaders informed the CCF caucus that no action was desired in the current session.

The *Pacific Advocate* hailed the decision on March 3

as a striking success for non-partisan . . . political action. . . . [Labor] has won a partnership in the administration of the affairs of the province. . . . The BCFL has been established as the leading political organ of labor in BC and the basis for greatly intensified independent labor political action. . . . [It] offers a sharp rebuke to those elements within organized labor . . . who would narrow the scope and effectiveness of political action by limiting its activities to support of one political party.

The CCF in the legislature and in the unions immediately denounced the plan for a government-labour committee as desertion from the battle for labour legislation. George Wilkinson of the Victoria Trades and Labor Council, leader of the TLC section of the labour lobby, disassociated himself from the lobby's decision, carrying his council with

---

[148]The Steelworkers under Robertson had left the lobby a day before. *Pacific Advocate*, March 17, 1945.

him. Both the Victoria Council and the Vancouver TLC (whose Secretary was R. K. Gervin, a Liberal) announced that they would continue
to press for labour legislation in the current session.[149] The Steelworkers'
union declared that the agreement with the government was unacceptable
and that it would press for the original objectives of the lobby. In a
radio broadcast, Angus MacInnis, MP, declared that:

> the rank and file of the delegation were duped by their leaders. . . . After
> all the effort to prepare a comprehensive brief of labor's *immediate* needs,
> after stressing the *urgency* of *immediate* action, after all the importuning of
> members of the Legislature of the *need* for action *at this session,* after taking
> to Victoria the largest lobby ever . . . a few leaders . . . went into a huddle
> with the Cabinet and agreed . . . that *no action* should be taken at this
> session—that the delegates would return home, be good fellows, and not
> embarrass the government. . . .
> The delegation went to Victoria with requests for urgently needed legis-
> lation now. They got the promise of a committee. An achievement to be
> jubilant over, what? . . . Labour asked for bread. Their leaders accepted a
> stone. Why? Intelligent trade unionists know the answer. But whether the
> LPP and the Government like it or not, the CCF has already given notice
> that it will raise in the Legislature some of the proposals made to the Govern-
> ment. What happened in Victoria is completely in line with the LPP's present
> policy of collaboration with capitalists and the capitalist parties.[150]

At the Vancouver CCL Council, a heated debate took place on a
motion by Steel's Eileen Tallman to repudiate the labour lobby's decision.
Daniel O'Brien accused James Robertson of leading a Steel conspiracy
to sabotage the government-labour committee and remove O'Brien from
his position as president of the BCFL.[151] Tallman's motion lost by a
vote of 48–45.[152] But F. J. McKenzie, the CCF provincial secretary,
called the Council debate

> the most important victory achieved in trade unions here against the
> LPP. . . . [The Council meeting] has given heart to many of the CCL ranks
> who had been weighed down by the sense of futility of the struggle with the
> LPP. . . . The whole LPP policy of heading off the demands of organized
> labour . . . and of restraining organized labour from using the facilities for
> expression which the CCF provides in the legislature has been exposed. . . .
> The position of Daniel O'Brien as a tool of the LPP has been exposed. . . .[153]

149McKenzie to Lewis, March 15, 1945, NDP files. Later the TLC group decided
to name representatives to the committee and to participate in its work. It appears
that the TLC leadership was split on this issue. A strong Liberal element led by
R. K. Gervin of the Vancouver TLC co-operated with the LPP leaders and the
coalition government. An opposition group led by George Wilkinson of the
Victoria TLC co-operated with the CCFers in the CCL and the Legislature.
150Script of radio broadcast, n.d., BC NDP files.
151*CCF News* (BC), March 15, 1945. O'Brien closed with an invitation to
Robertson to "step outside."
152*Pacific Advocate*, March 17, 1945.
153McKenzie to Lewis, March 15, 1945.

The executive of the BCFL responded to the Steel-CCF attacks by condemning them as "a movement started by certain individuals for purely partisan political reasons, aimed at disuniting labor and bringing about confusion. . . . We did not go to Victoria with a political axe to grind. . . . We are . . . anxious to cooperate with the government of the day and with all groups . . . that will further our cause. . . ."[154] The editors of *Pacific Advocate* declared the same day: "As soon as this committee can swing into action it will become evident that more concrete results for organized labor will accrue than from fifty . . . bills introduced by the CCF."

The government-labour committee was set up shortly thereafter with O'Brien, Pritchett, and Murphy as the CCL representatives, and R. K. Gervin and B. Showler as the TLC representatives. The national leaders of the CCL, Mosher and Conroy, aligned themselves with "their" BCFL rather than with Steel and the CCF. An editorial in the *Canadian Unionist* of June 1945 hailed the establishment of the government-labour committee and recommended it to the attention of CCL unions in other provinces. That it was an instance of LPP efforts to weaken political action through the CCL's official "political arm" and an attempt to substitute the BCFL for the CCF as "the political organ of labor in British Columbia," was not deemed worthy of mention.

The government-labour committee met three times. At its last meeting (January 3, 1945) the labour representatives accepted government proposals of a forty-four-hour week and one week's vacation with pay, though the BCFL's program called for a forty-hour week and two weeks vacation with pay. The agreement was not made public. On February 25 the joint labour lobby, led by labour's representatives on the government-labour committee, returned to Victoria; neither the mass membership of the lobby nor the CCF members of the legislature were informed of the decisions of the government-labour committee. The lobby pressed for a forty-hour week and two weeks vacation with pay— objectives which its leaders had secretly abandoned on January 3. After the lobby, the CCF opposition asked the government to table the minutes of the government-labour committee. The minutes were tabled on April 2. The CCF caucus was, in House Leader Harold Winch's words, "astounded" to find that the labour representatives on the government-labour committee had agreed, at the January 3 meeting, to legislation which was "out of line with the demands of the labour lobby led by them seven weeks later."[155]

The CCF immediately launched an attack on the "collaborationist"

[154]*Pacific Advocate*, March 17, 1945.
[155]*CCF News* (BC), April 14, 18, 1946.

leaders of the BCFL. Harold Winch wanted to know what labour's demands were—those of January 3 or those of February 25. According to the BCFL, Winch stated in the legislature that labour should fight for a thirty-hour week, thus "trying to sow confusion amongst the ranks of the workers . . . and suggesting that we were a bunch of phonies and reactionaries afraid to go forward and press for labor's demand."[156] The Victoria TLC condemned the government-labour committee as a "farce" and sent a circular to all British Columbia unions condemning the behaviour of Gervin, Showler, Murphy and O'Brien: "Why was a Labor Lobby called in view of this situation? Why was an elaborate pantomime enacted by . . . these men when they *knew* that an agreement had previously been reached? Why? We feel that the trade unions who spent thousands of dollars on the Lobby should have these questions fully answered." The Steelworkers' council adopted a resolution which expressed "dissatisfaction with the results of the government-labour committee, and decided to work more closely with CCF MLA's to assist them in securing better labour legislation."

The Vancouver CCL Council rejected by a narrow margin a motion by Eileen Tallman "regretting" the BCFL leaders' acceptance of the government's proposals and their failure to inform the labour lobby of their actions. Daniel O'Brien said that "the motion was a deliberate and planned attempt by the CCF-TUC to discredit the BCFL. . . . If we are to be dictated to by any political party, my resignation is on the table."[157] He produced a letter from Pat Conroy supporting the BCFL stand.[158] O'Brien explained that the decision of the government-labour committee had not been made public because the government "did not want it broadcast so the opposition could make political capital out of it. . . ." The government's offer had been accepted because "we are not a revolutionary organization and we were making gains. . . . These bills were presented to the House and not one of the CCF opposed the vote. . . . They voted for it as progress."[159]

At the BCFL's Executive Council meeting of April 22, 1946, O'Brien

[156]BCFL Executive Minutes, April 22, 1946, BCFL files.

[157]*CCF News* (BC), April 18, 25, 1946.

[158]"I have your letter of January 19 with attached copy of your legislative proposals submitted by the [government-labour] committee to the B.C. government. . . . You appear to be making a favorable impression. . . . The main issue I think is to maintain good relations with the Cabinet, and cooperation [with] . . . the Cabinet will ensure a sympathetic hearing and produce substantial results. If the B.C. government should introduce . . . the 44-hour week it would be a . . . notable development and would be the means of changing the attitudes of different provincial governments in this respect." BCFL Executive Minutes, April 22, 1946.

[159]*Ibid.*

launched a counter-attack on the CCF. Its policy, he said, was "to destroy this Federation as quickly and as expeditiously as possible. . . . There is no percentage in the Federation for the CCF. They are afraid that the Federation will get advanced legislation . . . and the CCF are unable to elect more members." Harold Pritchett supported his President. The CCF, he said, was guilty of "the most unprecedented and most vicious attack ever made on labor in this province. . . . The Congress have endorsed our position and accepted the forty-four hour week as a tremendous step forward." Harvey Murphy also rushed to the defence of labour: "The CCF has challenged the right . . . of the Federation . . . to fight for legislative gains for labor except through their party. They don't countenance labor having an independent existence outside of that." The Executive Council adopted a resolution condemning "the unmitigated attack by the CCF leader and other officials against . . . the entire trade union movement."

According to David Lewis, Pat Conroy was furious about the Steel-CCF attacks on "his" Congress people in British Columbia, and had to be pacified by his CCF friends in Ottawa. But it must have been difficult for the CCFers in British Columbia to understand Conroy's position. Colin Cameron, MP, described the political situation in British Columbia as follows:

The trade union movement has deserted the only friends it has in the legislature. What do [the government] see when they study the CCF as a potential threat to the Coalition government? They see this curious, and to them very comforting spectacle. Here is a group which comprises the only friends and champions the trade union movement has in the B.C. legislature. But . . . [Premier] Hart and his colleagues see something else. They see important trade unions in this province permitting their officials to launch vicious and scurrilous attacks on the unions' only legislative friends. . . . It must be a matter of great comfort . . . to . . . the Coalition . . . to know that on the ballots at the next election there will appear again . . . [LPP and "independent labour" candidates] who . . . can be fairly sure of attracting enough votes to defeat some CCF candidates and thus ensure the election of the Coalition government. . . . The Cabinet . . . can safely stick a knife into organized labour because these friends of theirs in the trade union movement can be relied on to save their electoral bacon for them by diverting union support away from the CCF.[160]

The government-labour committee never met again, partly because it lost much of its attractiveness to both the Communists and the government. From the Communists' point of view, it was out of line with the new post-war policy of militancy; CCF attacks on Communist "class

[160]*CCF News* (BC), Nov. 6, 1947.

collaborationism" did not embarrass the LPP in wartime, but in the
new situation such attacks were not only very effective as propaganda,
they must also have aroused guilt feelings among the Communists themselves. From the government's point of view, co-operation with a
Communist-led labour movement was acceptable while the Communists
were respectable, patriotic, and more "moderate" than the CCF. It
became unacceptable in the new "cold war" atmosphere. In any case,
the government itself adopted a new "hard line" in labour policy which
made it impossible for the BCFL to retain its publicly friendly attitude.
In 1947 the government enacted the first of a long series of restrictive
labour measures (Bill 39). The BCFL held an emergency convention
which called for the defeat of the coalition government. Of course, it
did not endorse the CCF, but repeated the tired clichés about unity of
the LPP and the CCF.[161]

Meanwhile the CCF's campaign to sever the labour movement from
its Communist vanguard began producing significant victories. One of
the largest locals of the IWA, local 1–357 in New Westminster, over-
threw its Communist executive and installed a CCF slate headed by
Stewart Alsbury. William Mahoney was sent by the CCL as Western
Director to work with Alsbury's group. Aid and comfort was also
obtained from the anti-Communist international executive of the IWA.
In October 1947 the CCL convention gave notice of the leadership's
new resolve to wage war on the Communists by adopting two anti-
Communist resolutions. By January 1948 the CCFers on the Vancouver
Labour Council had become the majority, and replaced the Council's
Communist executive with a CCF slate headed by George Home of the
Packinghouse Workers. Home defeated the Communist president, E.
E. Leary, by a vote of 79–65. The new executive immediately secured
the adoption of a resolution endorsing the CCF as labour's political
arm.[162]

The 1948 convention of the BCFL also produced victories for the
CCF. Communist voting strength was lower than usual because of the
exclusion of delegates of Mine Mill, which had been suspended from the
CCL. Daniel O'Brien was re-elected president (68–64), and William
Stewart, a Communist from the SGWF, was elected first vice-president
(66–65). But George Home replaced Harold Pritchett as secretary
treasurer (66–65) and Stewart Alsbury replaced Alex McKenzie as
second vice-president (66–65). Of the five remaining executive posts,

---

[161]*British Columbia TUC Bulletin*, May and June 1947, BC NDP files.
[162]*CCF News* (BC), Jan. 29, Feb. 12, 1947.

three were won by CCFers. The CCF thus had a 5–4 majority on the executive.[163]

A short time later, the Communist bastion in British Columbia, the IWA, crumbled. The CCF had managed to capture only the 5,000-member New Westminster local. The remaining 22,000 IWA members were still led by Communists. But the IWA leadership was so hard pressed by its enemies in the international union that the leadership decided to withdraw the British Columbia locals from the international and set up an independent Woodworkers' Industrial Union of Canada. In the ensuing competition between the IWA and WIUC for the loyalty of the locals, the great majority of locals rejected their Communist leadership and voted to stay with the international. The new executive of the IWA consisted almost entirely of CCFers and CCF supporters, including Stewart Alsbury and Joe Morris (later district director of the IWA and an officer of CLC). On November 11, 1948, Daniel O'Brien resigned as president of the BCFL, giving as his reason the executive's decision to support the IWA against the WIUC.[164] By 1949 the BCFL executive had rid itself of the last traces of Communist influence.

The capture of the IWA and the UAW by CCFers broke the back of Communist power in the Canadian labour movement. In both these unions, the Communists probably could not have been dislodged without the aid of the international. In UE and Mine Mill,[165] the Communists were supported by the international; these unions could therefore not be liberated from within, and they were expelled from the CCL early in 1949.

[163]*Ibid.*, Sept. 9, 1948.

[164]*Ibid.*, Oct. 7, Nov. 17, 1948.

[165]Mine Mill in British Columbia was solidly Communist. Mine Mill in Ontario, however, was headed by a CCF MPP, Robert Carlin; it contained a substantial number of CCFers; Carlin represented it on CCL-PAC and it followed the CCF rather than the LPP line on political action. Nevertheless, Carlin depended on Communist as well as CCF support within his union, and he was also tied to the Communist leadership of the international. Before the CCL began its anti-Communist drive this caused few difficulties. Carlin left the Communists alone, and they permitted him to support the CCF. The international even contributed to CCF funds. (C. C. Ames to Lewis, Dec. 13, 1946, NDP files). In 1948, when Carlin was forced to choose between joining the CCL's anti-Communist drive and retaining his loyalty to the Communist-dominated international, he threw in his lot with the Communists. (Special Executive Meeting of the Ontario CCF Caucus and Executive with Robert Carlin, April 13, 1948, *ibid.*) The CCF refused to endorse his candidacy in the provincial election of 1948; he ran as an "independent CCFer," lost, and was subsequently expelled from the party.

4. *Labour and the CCF, 1947-53*

1. THE REBIRTH OF PAC

A short time after the CCL convention of September 1946, the Congress leadership began discussing plans for the re-establishment of the PAC, which had gone out of existence following the federal election of 1945.[1] Steel, as always, led the way. It appointed a full time "political representative," Murray Cotterill, to promote political action by the Steel locals.[2] The next step was the Ontario provincial election of 1948.

Relations between the Conservative government of George Drew and both wings of the Ontario labour movement were very strained; so much so that even the TLC roused itself to an unusually high degree of political activity. The Ontario Provincial Federation of Labor (OPFL—the TLC's provincial federation) convention of January 1948 called on TLC unionists in Ontario to defeat all provincial legislators—both Tories and Liberals—who had failed to support the federation's legislative proposals, and the OPFL executive decided to provide its locals with the voting records of the three parties in the provincial legislature.[3]

The Ontario Federation of Labour (OFL—the CCL's provincial federation) went much farther. It set up a PAC with Murray Cotterill of Steel as director, and launched a vigorous independent public campaign in support of the CCF. All CCL unions in Ontario participated except Communist-dominated UE and Fur and Leather, which were not allowed to participate.[4] Every CCL local in Ontario was asked to contribute to the OFL's campaign fund. About $80,000 was collected, most of which was used for radio and newspaper advertising. Similar small-scale advertising campaigns were carried on by labour campaign committees in the constituencies. The OFL and a few large unions also assigned some of their staff to election work.

This campaign was the first and last unqualified success of CCL political action in Canada. Twenty-one CCF candidates were elected to

---

[1]Millard to Conroy, Jan. 6, 1947, CLC-PEC files.
[2]Lewis to MacInnis, Nov. 12, 1947, NDP files.
[3]Cotterill to Mahoney, May 19, 1948, CLC-PEC files.
[4]*Ibid.* UE ran a campaign of its own in support of the CCF. *UE News,* June 11, 1948.

the legislature, the great majority of them in industrial constituencies in which the OFL-PAC had concentrated its efforts. The CCF was once again the official opposition in Ontario. The CCF leadership recognized that the OFL-PAC had been "a decisive factor in our success."[5]

The CCL convention of 1948 resolved that there be "an effective program of political action . . . with a view to implementing Congress policy of supporting the CCF and electing the largest possible number of CCF members to the next Parliament of Canada and . . . that this same program be instituted on the provincial level for . . . each coming provincial election."[6] The CCL executive then decided to set up a PAC to support the CCF in the federal election of 1949. Murray Cotterill was appointed director. All locals, labour councils, and provincial federations were asked to "elect or revitalize" PACs, which "should not consist of persons who are members or known supporters of political parties not endorsed by the Congress." Each affiliated union supporting the CCL's political policy was asked to appoint one or more persons to serve on a "CCL Federal Election Campaign Committee" headed by Cotterill. The CCL launched a drive among the locals to secure as many election workers as possible and to collect an election fund of $350,000, or one dollar per member.[7]

These plans were over-ambitious. Only $59,463.85 was raised—less than had been raised in Ontario alone the year before. Steel was the most important single source of funds—$22,045.89 from ninety locals. Packinghouse locals provided $4,414.52.[8] The election results were disappointing too. St. Laurent's Liberals won an overwhelming victory and the CCF group in the House of Commons was reduced from thirty-two to thirteen. The CCF vote fell from 16 per cent to 13 per cent. Nevertheless, a Gallup survey showed that in areas where CCL members were heavily concentrated, the swing to the Liberals was not as great as in other areas.[9] Cotterill told the 1949 CCL Convention that the CCF had held its own in the main industrial areas thanks to the efforts of PAC.

By November 1949, the CCL executive had decided to make PAC a permanent part of the Congress organization.[10] Cotterill was to remain

[5]Ontario CCF Provincial Council Minutes, July 4, 1948. NDP files.
[6]CCL Convention Proceedings (1948), p. 75.
[7]CCL-PAC Federal Election Plan Approved by CCL Executive Council, Dec. 14, 1948, CLC-PEC files.
[8]Financial Statement, CCL-PAC Election Fund, 1949, CLC-PEC files. Other unions which donated more than $1,000 were CBRE, Retail-Wholesale, Textile, UMW, ACWA, UAW, and Rubber.
[9]Ontario CCF Provincial Council Minutes, Sept. 24–25, 1949, NDP files.
[10]Cotterill to D. C. MacDonald, Nov. 15, 1949, CLC-PEC files. D. C. Mac-Donald, now leader of the Ontario NDP, is not to be confused with Donald

as director. All affiliated unions supporting the CCL's political policy
were invited to send representatives to an inaugural meeting on March
22, 1950.[11] The meeting elected three officers to serve with Cotterill as
the PAC executive. They were: chairman, Lloyd Fell of UPWA; vice-
chairman, Arthur Williams, MP, of UMW-50; and secretary-treasurer,
Henry Weisbach of Steel. It was also decided to ask provincial federations to name representatives to the committee.[12] The PAC by-laws,
drawn up by Cotterill, Fell, and Weisbach, provided that the national
PAC consist of representatives of affiliated unions, directly chartered
unions, and provincial federations (or designated labour councils in
provinces which did not have federations). The national director was
to be appointed by the CCL executive. The other three officers were to
be elected by the PAC itself. The full committee would meet at least
twice yearly; the officers would conduct business between meetings and
co-ordinate the activities of provincial and local PACs. PAC funds were
to be obtained by asking locals to collect one dollar per member per
year, with a rebate of 45 per cent to local unions. Provincial federations,
labour councils, and local unions were to be encouraged to set up
PACs.[13]

A liaison committee of the CCL and CCF was set up to co-ordinate
the political activities of the two organizations. The CCF representatives,
named in August 1949, were David Lewis, Angus MacInnis, MP, and
Andrew Brewin, with Stanley Knowles, MP, as an alternate.[14] The CCL
representatives, named in January 1950, were Charles Millard, Pat
Conroy, Sam Baron, George Burt, and Murray Cotterill.[15] This liaison
committee did not develop into a functioning body. There are no refer-
ences to it in the correspondence after February 1950.

2. RELATIONS BETWEEN THE CCF AND PAC, 1948–1952

The official theory of the relationship between PAC and the CCF was
that PAC in Canada (as in the United States) was the political instru-

MacDonald, who succeeded Conroy as CCL (and subsequently CLC) secretary
treasurer.
[11]The following responded: Lithographers, Brewery Workers, Retail-Wholesale,
UMW, Building Construction Workers, UAW, Steel, Rubber, and UPWA. At the
second meeting they were joined by CBRE, ACWA, and Communications
Workers.
[12]CCL-PAC Minutes, March 22, 1950, CLC-PEC files.
[13]National PAC Bylaws, n.d., ibid.
[14]Lewis to Norman Dowd, Aug. 5, 1949, NDP files.
[15]Dowd to Lewis, Feb. 23, 1950, ibid.

ment of the labour movement, independent of all political parties, but used in *support* of the political party which labour considered most friendly at any particular time. The *official* purpose of PAC was not to capture the labour vote for the CCF, but to capture it for PAC; not to educate workers to support the CCF, but to educate them to support the party endorsed by labour, which happened to be the CCF. In theory, labour's endorsement could be withdrawn from the CCF and transferred to another party. The PAC report to the CCL Convention of 1949 stated that the primary objective of PAC was to emancipate unionists from control by business-dominated "political machines"; the secondary objective was to elect the candidates of a political party which supported labour's legislative program. PAC would not be used to build up the CCF party organization, but to build up an independent labour political organization side by side with the CCF. Since the CCF was the party most favourable to labour, labour's political organization would support the CCF.

This view of PAC-CCF relations was accepted by both the CCL and the CCF leadership, for the unofficial theory behind the official theory was that an independent PAC approach similar to that of the CIO was the only effective means of winning the votes of the rank and file. The purpose of PAC was to convince the majority of workers who voted Liberal and Conservative to switch their votes to the CCF. A "straight" CCF appeal might alienate them; it would certainly be less attractive than an appeal to join with fellow unionists in building labour's independent political power. Old party supporters would be involved in PAC; this involvement would lead them to support of the political party which supported labour; that party was the CCF. An independent labour political organization separate and distinct from the CCF and not too closely associated with it in the public mind was seen as a device for weaning the union rank and file from traditional old party loyalties and laying the groundwork for the achievement of the ultimate goal: a socialist party with a massive trade union section, a Canadian counterpart of the British Labour party.[16]

Although the CCF and the CCL agreed on the necessity for a PAC approach modelled on that of the CIO, there was in the early period (1949–1952) considerable disagreement between PAC director Cotterill and the CCF leadership about the precise form which CCF-PAC relations should take. Poor personal relations between Cotterill and the CCF leadership aggravated—indeed, they were one of the main causes

[16]Interviews with Cotterill, Jan. 10, 1963; Lewis, Jan. 15, 1963; and Park, Jan. 14, 1963.

of—the tension. The CCF, although it accepted the necessity of a formally independent PAC structure, insisted that the PAC should not *in fact* operate as an independent force. It should carry on its activities in close consultation with the CCF; independence should not be carried so far as to preclude co-ordination. The CCFers were irked by what they felt was Cotterill's over-emphasis on the "independence" of PAC, his tendency in public statements to dwell more than was necessary on the revocable character of the CCL's endorsement, and above all his tendency to take action without prior consultation with the CCF leaders. The absence of consultation meant that the PAC under Cotterill actually behaved in some respects as a separate political organization acting on the CCF from the outside, rather than a formally independent organization which in practice worked in close co-operation with the CCF. Some CCFers interpreted this situation as one in which "labour" was trying to "dominate" the party.

Disagreement centred on the degree of participation in CCF policy-making bodies, especially nominating conventions, which would be allowed to unions participating in PAC. Here there was a genuine conflict of interest between the labour political activists and the non-union CCF officials. The unionists argued that labour support for the CCF justified the participation of the unions as such in CCF nominations, and that labour's rank and file would not support the CCF if they were not given an opportunity to participate as unionists in the formulation of CCF policy. The CCF officials, although they anxiously desired labour support *and* labour participation, were equally anxious to preserve the individual membership's control of the CCF organization.

In the Ontario provincial election of 1948 the following scheme was agreed upon. The nomination of candidates was recognized as the sole prerogative of CCF constituency organizations. The nomination of unionists was recognized as highly desirable in heavily industrialized areas. Locals contributing to the OFL-PAC campaign fund were entitled to suggest the name of a CCF member to CCF nominating conventions in their locality. These locals were also entitled to representation on local CCF campaign committees, as long as the union representatives were not supporters of other political parties.[17] The CCF provincial executive urged all constituency associations in industrial areas to consult with the unions about nominations and election plans: "We are counting

[17]Lewis to Liesemer, June 23, 1948, NDP files. Cotterill to Mahoney, May 19, 1948, CLC-PEC files. Ontario CCF Provincial Executive Minutes, April 20, 1948, NDP files.

upon substantial support from . . . friendly trade unions. One way to ensure it is to . . . consult them."[18]

This arrangement was not accepted without qualms by those CCFers who were fearful of labour domination and jealous of the prerogatives of the individual membership. The CCF leadership was subjected to opposing pressures, from unionists on one side and constituency activists on the other. The scheme which was finally accepted was a compromise which the CCF leadership had to "sell" to both groups. CCFers in Oshawa who objected to the arrangement were told:

The final nomination of the candidate can only be made . . . by a . . . convention confined to CCF members only. Does this mean that we should not take steps to consult the unions . . . about possible candidates? Do you think it would be sensible or proper or democratic for us to accept the support of the unions in every way, but to refuse to consult them all down the line? Do you think it would be defensible to accept the union's support and merely present them with a *fait accompli* as regards the candidate?[19]

The arrangement of 1948 was not accepted as final by the CCL leadership. Cotterill wanted the CCF convention of 1948 to "clear the decks in a manner which will permit them to extend to the unions which [participate in PAC] the rights and privileges extended to unions affiliated to the CCF."[20] This proposal did not come before the convention. The scheme which was adopted for the 1948 Ontario election remained in effect for the federal election of 1949: locals contributing to PAC were entitled to make suggestions to CCF nominating conventions which had not yet chosen candidates, and to appoint representatives to CCF campaign committees.[21] At the Ontario Provincial Council meeting of September 24-25, 1949, Millard and Cotterill made a proposal even more radical than the Cotterill proposal of 1948. The 1948 proposal had been that locals participating in PAC be given the same rights as affiliated locals—that is, the right to *representation* on CCF bodies. Millard

[18]Circular, March 1, 1948. In at least two important instances, union suggestions about nominations were not accepted. However, according to Lewis, "this did not cause the slightest difficulty . . . and the unions gave their wholehearted support to the choice of the convention in spite of the choice being against them." (Lewis to Liesemer, June 23, 1948) In at least one other instance, CCF failure to consult with the unions aroused protest: Council 6 of the United Rubber Workers Union passed a resolution "protesting the nomination of a CCF candidate without prior consultation with the unions in the area." Ontario CCF Provincial Executive Minutes, Dec. 4, 1948, NDP files.
[19]Lewis to Frank McLellan, Jan. 13, 1948, *ibid.*
[20]Cotterill to Millard, Aug. 13, 1948, CLC-PEC files.
[21]CCL-PAC Federal Election Plan, Dec. 14, 1948.

and Cotterill now proposed that "union members who pay $1.00 a year to PAC should be allowed to vote at nominating conventions." Cotterill intended to submit this proposal to the 1949 CCL Convention.[22] Although he did not do so, he made his dissatisfaction with the *status quo* quite clear: greater participation in "whatever political party we endorse" was essential. In most constituencies, Cotterill complained, nominations had already been made "prior to the entry of PAC into the picture." As a result, the choice of candidates in some important areas "left something to be desired." Where locals were affiliated to the CCF, union representatives participated in nominations, but in other areas there was no provision for "direct union influence. This should be corrected."[23]

The implementation of either of the two labour proposals of 1948–49 would have meant that unions participating in PAC, though they were parts of a political organization parallel to and independent of the CCF, would have been given a "direct influence" in the CCF organization. The 1948 proposal meant, in effect, that unions were to be given the rights pertaining to affiliation without actually affiliating, without accepting the obligations of affiliation. They would be given power within the CCF organization without becoming parts of that organization and while retaining their status as parts of a parallel organization whose support of the CCF was revocable. The proposal of 1949 went even farther, in giving members of non-affiliated unions participating in PAC greater power than affiliated unions. This proposal, if implemented, would have obliterated the distinction between individual members of the CCF (whose membership fee was three dollars in Ontario) and unionists who had contributed one dollar to PAC, an organization independent of the CCF. It would have given non-members the same rights within the CCF as members, and would have made it possible for the former to swamp the latter at nominating conventions. The CCF at this time was not even prepared to accept large-scale affiliation of unions. The labour proposals were obviously unacceptable.

What especially irritated the CCF leadership was Cotterill's failure to attempt to reach agreement with them before broadcasting the proposal of 1949. This tended to confirm suspicions that the PAC was intent on "dominating" the CCF from the outside; that it would make decisions independently and press them on the CCF instead of making decisions in concert with the CCF. From Cotterill's point of view, the CCF attitude tended to confirm the long-standing suspicion that the CCF wanted

22Donovan Swailes to Lewis, Sept. 28, 1949, NDP files.
23CCL Convention Proceedings (1949), p. 50.

something for nothing—labour support without labour participation. Poor co-ordination, fears of labour "domination" on the one hand, and resentment at the CCF's "exclusion" of labour on the other: these were the main problems in PAC-CCL relations from 1948 to 1952.

The first efforts to correct the situation were made early in 1951. On April 9, 1951, the CCL Executive Council "considered the whole matter of political action in the light of the fairly widespread dissatisfaction with it since the 1949 federal election."[24] In order to increase both the efficiency of PAC and its co-ordination with CCF organization in the field, the Council decided to "decentralize" PAC, that is, to place primary responsibility on the provincial federations of labour[25] rather than "attempting to organize PAC out of a central office for all of Canada." On May 15, 1951, a joint meeting of the OFL and Ontario CCF executives agreed to set up a co-ordinating committee of OFL and CCF officers to meet at least once a month for "joint planning." They also agreed to set up similar PAC-CCF co-ordinating committees in nine areas of the province to facilitate co-operation on the local level. Through these committees the unions would suggest candidates to the CCF, and the two groups would co-ordinate their election activities.[26] The CCF national office informed the CCF organizations in other provinces of the scheme which had been adopted in Ontario and urged them to try to duplicate it in order to avoid "misunderstandings" and "lack of co-operation."

On January 10, 1952, Murray Cotterill announced his resignation as national director of PAC. He was replaced by Henry Weisbach, who was given the new title, executive secretary. Weisbach reported, after a tour across the country, that there was within the CCF a "definite current" of unfriendliness to the unions,[27] "more and more talk" of labour domination. This aroused a corresponding resentment in the unions: "What good can it do if we go out and induce our members to work . . . for the CCF when . . . the CCF refuses to give recognition to the . . . union movement?" In some areas, Weisbach discovered a labour demand for an independent labour party. He was fighting against it, but the struggle was "made harder day by day by the attitude of certain CCF people." He concluded that one of the main reasons for this situation was the absence of liaison between the CCF and the CCL-PAC at the

24D. C. MacDonald to Grant MacNeil, July 30, 1951, NDP files.
25CCL-PAC Minutes, Jan. 10, 1952, CLC-PEC files.
26*PAC Newsletter*, Oct. 1951.
27CCL-PAC Minutes, June 19, 1952.

national level.[28] "On all levels of CCF and PAC organization we have to come to a much closer understanding than so far."[29]

The absence of liaison and consultation was precisely the main grievance of the CCF leadership. The CCF national secretary, Lorne Ingle, agreed that there was an "unhealthy attitude in some sections of the CCF toward the CCL," and assured Weisbach that the situation could be remedied by "closer teamwork." Weisbach suggested that PAC-CCF consultation could be assured if officials of the PAC executive and the CCF executive would sit in on each others' meetings. This proposal was accepted by both organizations.[30] In January 1954, Weisbach reported that "mutual cross-representation on the national level is working well. . . . A fairly close relationship has been established with the CCF on provincial and national levels."[31] The achievement of the kind of consultation between PAC and the CCF which was desired by the CCF leadership ended the latter's apprehension that PAC would behave as a separate political organization acting on the CCF from the outside. As far as the question of union participation in CCF nominations was concerned, it was agreed that the *status quo* must be preserved: unions would be consulted, but the final decision would remain the sole prerogative of CCF members.

3. THE SPECTRE OF LABOUR DOMINATION

There has always been some suspicion of organized labour and some fear of trade union domination within the CCF-NDP, especially among its leftists. During the first few years of PAC the tension was at its height, because of the novelty of massive labour support and the early "misunderstanding" and "lack of co-operation" between PAC and the CCF. As a co-operative working relationship between the two developed, and as CCFers across the country became accustomed to working with labour organizations, the fears receded. But they never completely disappeared; they remain to the present a constant irritant, usually latent but sometimes rising to the surface in minor explosions. The top leadership in the unions and in the party have learned to accept this situation as inevitable, and to consider the minimization of tension and the constant lubrication of party-union relations as part of their job.

28Weisbach to Lorne Ingle, April 25, 1952, NDP files.
29Weisbach to D. C. MacDonald, May 1, 1952, *ibid*.
30CCL-PAC Minutes, June 19, 1952.
31*Ibid*, Jan. 18–19, 1954.

What are the causes of the tension which is always present, to a greater or lesser extent, in the relations between unionists and party activists in the CCF-NDP?[32]

First, there is the party activist's vested interest in his position within the party organization. This position can be threatened by large-scale union affiliation or even by the influx of large numbers of new individual members, whether they are unionists or not. In any organization there is a strong tendency to protect the existing structure of power and prestige against innovations which might alter it. The CCF-NDP organization is no exception.

Second, there is the situation which exists in all socialist parties: the unions tend to be moderate, reformist, practical, unconcerned with theory; the party activists tend to "doctrinaire socialism." This is, of course, a very sweeping generalization, and there are many exceptions. But there has always been fear in the CCF-NDP, slight in the powerful right wing but great in the declining left wing, that an influx of unionists would bring about a "betrayal" or at least a "watering down" of the party's socialist philosophy and program. The leadership of the party has been increasingly reformist. At the same time its relation with the labour movement has become increasingly intimate: left-wing dissidents point to this as confirmation of their fears.

Third, the social background and behaviour of the unionist, and the values which underlie his behaviour, are quite different from those of a middle-class member of the CCF-NDP. The non-unionist may perceive the unionist as gruff, tactless, uneducated, more interested in power than in virtue; a bit of a bully and a bit of a boor. The unionist may perceive the non-unionist as an impractical dreamer, more interested in endless pious discussion than in action; a bit of an old woman and a bit of an egghead. The CCF-NDP is a more democratic and a less monolithic organization than the average union. Discussion and democratic procedure are more highly valued in the party than in most trade unions; solidarity, discipline, and decisive action are more highly valued in the unions than in the party. The unionist feels that discussion should come to an end and decisions should be made. Once they are made, there is

[32]Many party activists who have a negative attitude to the unions are themselves members of trade unions. David Lewis has written: "In dealing with the suspicions between the party and the unions in the early years, I was personally often struck by the . . . fact that . . . there was frequently *more* resentment in active CCF members who were also members of unions than in other CCFers. The former seem to have had a sense of virtuous superiority which made them angry at other union members who were either not in the CCF at all or who were not active enough." In a letter to GH, Aug. 16, 1966.

no value in further discussion; it is the duty of all members to abide by them. The unionist may feel that discussion in the party is too long, that decisions are never final, that action is always being postponed pending further discussion, and that too much dissent is permitted after decisions have been made. The non-unionist may feel that the techniques used by labour leaders to achieve solidarity in their unions are undemocratic, and he fears the use of these same techniques by labour leaders in the CCF-NDP.

Fourth, the close relationship between the party leaders and the labour leaders results in a situation in which anyone with any kind of grievance against the party leadership is likely to extend his resentment to the "power-mad labour bosses" of popular parlance, and ascribe the errors of his party's leaders to "labour domination." A case in point is that of Hazen Argue, who resigned from the New Democratic party after losing a bitter contest with Tommy Douglas for the post of national leader. His opponents in that contest were the CCF leadership (Coldwell, Knowles, Lewis, etc.), and they were supported by most of the labour leaders who were active in the formation of the NDP. Argue claimed that he resigned not because he had lost the national leadership but because the party was "dominated" by a "labour clique."

Fifth, the non-unionists in the CCF-NDP may share to a certain extent the view of labour unions which is current in the general population. If the public "image" of the labour movement is unfavourable—as it has been since the war—the relations between unionists and non-unionists inside the party are likely to suffer. Even those party members who have a positive attitude towards unions may fear that a closer association between the CCF-NDP and the "labour bosses" would decrease the popularity of the party.

Sixth, there is a tendency among some party members to resent labour's failure to support the CCF-NDP more strongly than it has; paradoxically, this resentment is likely to be felt by the same persons who fear "labour domination."

Seventh, the fact that in many localities the leadership and membership groups of CCF-NDP and union organizations overlap or interlock, results at times in friction within each of the two organizations and between them. Rivalry between two factions within one organization is carried over into the other. Active party members within a union organization may form a separate caucus in opposition to the established union leadership: unionists within a party organization may act in concert against the party leadership. In principle, the "political arm" and the "economic arm" are strictly separate; the one must not interfere in the affairs of the other or attempt to use the other for its own purposes. The same person must be, in the union, a "unionist first," and in the party a "CCFer first." In practice, because the same people are active in both "arms" and because they are human, they tend to use their positions in one organization as levers with which to improve their positions in the other or to use one organization as the subsidiary of the other. Union matters which should in principle be irrelevant in the party, and party matters which should in principle be irrelevant in the union, become in practice very relevant indeed. Flagrant abuses are uncommon, but the ideal of strict union-party separation is never achieved.[33]

Finally, there is the special case of Saskatchewan. The bulk of CCF members and voters in that province have been farmers and wary of labour's increasing influence in the national and to a lesser extent in the provincial party. Moreover, the general attitude of farmers as such to labour unions has been negative, and this attitude has spread to the farmer-dominated Saskatchewan CCF. The situation is further complicated by the fact that the CCF has been the *government* in Saskatchewan and has as a government been involved in serious economic disputes with CCL unions. In 1949, during a dispute between the government-owned power corporation and the oil workers, a high government official (George Cadbury) asked David Lewis to comment on "the very strong suspicion here" that the CCL was planning "to take over the urban CCF

[33]Two examples.
July 7, 1961: a meeting of the CCF Constituency Organization in Oshawa, Ontario. "Problems of area clearly indicated by coolness between [two UAW officials] Pilkey in chair and Brady. . . . We must attempt to find federal candidate outside of labor who will not be handicapped by bitterness aroused by UAW-222 internal politics." OFL-PAC report from Tom Edwards, Part Time Organizer, Ontario Riding July 9, 1961, OFL-PEC files.
"All hinged around an internal squabble of personalities within the Steelworkers Union. Our candidate was *X* a Steelworker, President of the McIntyre local, who up until a year ago . . . stood very high in the esteem of the local union leadership. This may seem very silly, but the actual reason why he fell from favour was because he had the temerity . . . when he decided to contest the CCF nomination [not to] clear with the local union hierarchy." [The "hierarchy" opposed and defeated him at the nominating convention, but the nominated candidate became ill and a new nominating convention had to be held. At this convention *X* ran again and won. The "hierarchy" made a show of closing ranks behind him, but] "we received no assistance whatever . . . from the Steelworkers throughout the campaign. On election day they never came near the committee rooms, and in fact worked actively and vocally against *X* throughout the whole campaign." Report on Ontario 1959 Election Campaign by Murdo Martin, MP, June 20, 1959, NDP files.

movement and leave the farm movement to tail along with little option
but to play second fiddle." Lewis responded with assurances that the
Congress fully appreciated the need for preserving the CCF's character
as a party in which "farmers will feel just as much at home as industrial
workers." He pleaded with Cadbury and his friends "to discard these
doubts . . . the Congress attitude to the CCF is genuine and is thoroughly
co-operative."[34]

A few weeks earlier Lewis had been informed that members of the
Saskatchewan CCF executive were worried about labour domination
of the national party, and that the executive had decided to ask Saskat-
chewan's representatives on the National Council for a report on CCF-
CCL relations. Lewis had to assure Carlyle King, president of the
Saskatchewan CCF that

at no time has any responsible spokesman of the CCL . . . taken an attitude
which even remotely suggested a desire for control. . . . They have on their
own initiative emphasized the importance of farmer-labour co-operation inside
the CCF and the importance of avoiding even the semblance of labour control
of the party. They have entirely approved those provisions . . . in our CCF
constitutions which make it impossible for the trade union wing to control
the party. . . . There is not a shred of reason for any fears.[35]

One of the major tasks of the national leaders of the CCF (especially
David Lewis and Lorne Ingle) and of the CCL (especially Pat Conroy
and A. R. Mosher) has been to act as informal mediators between the
Saskatchewan government and the Saskatchewan CCL unions in a series
of disputes beginning with CCL charges that the Minister of Labour (C.
C. Williams) was partial to TLC unions in the competition to organize
Saskatchewan civil servants in 1944, and ending with a bitter dispute
between the Oil, Chemical and Atomic Workers (OCAW) and the
government-owned power corporation in 1955. During the latter dispute
the government at one point threatened to enforce compulsory arbitration. The CCF national secretary, Lorne Ingle, warned Premier Douglas
that this "would mean the end of CCF support in the labour movement
for years to come. Right now in many places in Canada, for example the
whole Ontario movement, that is the same as saying that it would mean
the end of the CCF. . . . If this pessimistic outlook seems exaggerated
to you, I can assure you that it is the feeling of almost all the members
of our national executive."[36] The dispute was eventually settled without

[34]Cadbury to Lewis, March 30, 1949, and Lewis to Cadbury, April 7, 1949,
NDP files.
[35]Lewis to King, March 14, 1949, *ibid.*
[36]Feb. 14, 1955, *ibid.*

compulsory arbitration, as a result of the efforts of the Canadian and international leaders of OCAW and the national leaders of the CCF and the CCL.

From 1944 to 1955 the national leaders had to appeal to the "higher loyalties" of both sides in Saskatchewan, to remind them constantly that poor relations between the unions and the government in Canada's only socialist province would cause incalculable damage to the CCF—by weakening its labour support outside of Saskatchewan, in areas where labour support was of crucial importance—and to the CCL—by driving a wedge between it and the CCF, its "political arm."

The Saskatchewan unionists, dissatisfied as they were, realized that they had no alternative but to try to increase their influence within the provincial party. Saskatchewan labour legislation was far more favourable to the unions than that of any other province,[37] and the alternatives to the CCF were parties in which labour had no influence whatsoever. The PAC in Saskatchewan was therefore unique: its most difficult task was not to win the unionists' vote for the CCF but to strengthen union influence within the CCF in order to counteract anti-labour trends in its farmer majority and in the CCF government.[38]

A position of power for labour within the Saskatchewan CCF was not easily achieved. In 1952 there were a number of TLC unionists in the Saskatchewan legislature but not a single CCL unionist. Efforts to capture a nomination for a CCL unionist in Regina were thwarted by powerful elements in the government,[39] and insult was added to injury by charges that the CCL's efforts were "part of the power play of the CCL to take over the CCF."[40] A CCL unionist, Bill Davies (Executive

[37]From 1945 to 1954 trade union membership increased by 68 per cent in Canada, 118 per cent in Saskatchewan. CCL Convention Proceedings (1954), p. 39.

[38]A conference of Saskatchewan PAC representatives in 1955 listed among their objectives: "2) That within the CCF we intensify the raising of union issues and endeavour to make local CCF branches acquainted with certain anti-labour trends within the CCF and ask co-operation in their correction. 3) That we suggest . . . unions apart from direct CCF activity request audiences with the government protesting trends inimical to Labour's interest. 4) That in each constituency where our unionists are active in the CCF we should consider each nominating convention in respect of whether candidates reflect Labour's interest. 5) That where we have the best opportunity to elect suitable men and women as CCF candidates we should promote their nomination and election and that these should be concentration points. . . . 10) That we continue to co-operate with the Saskatchewan Farmers Union to illustrate the real viewpoint of the farm movement not the bogus attitudes said to be farm opinion by certain elements in the CCF and commercial farm organizations." PAC Proposals, Aug. 22, 1955, CLC-PEC files.

[39]C. C. Williams and Clarence Fines.

[40]Weisbach to Ingle, April 25, 1952, NDP files.

Secretary of the Saskatchewan Federation of Labor [SFL]), was nominated in Moose Jaw but lost the election.

When Weisbach found "difficulties and misunderstandings" between PAC and the CCF in 1952, he found them at their worst in Saskatchewan. The long-standing ill-feeling between the CCL and Douglas' Minister of Labour, C. C. Williams, was at its height. The CCL unions were demanding, without success, that Williams be given another portfolio and that an acceptable minister of labour be appointed. There was much resentment at the opposition of certain CCF elements to CCL efforts to secure nominations. Weisbach wrote: "I am almost certain that the patience of our unions in Saskatchewan has come to the breaking point. They have kept it under their hats long enough now. . . . How much longer they can hold out I don't know. . . . there is talk about running independent labor candidates in the next election."[41]

By 1956 CCL efforts to penetrate the Saskatchewan CCF were crowned with a measure of success. In the election of that year Bill Davies was elected to the legislature and appointed to the cabinet. But relations between labour and other groups in the Saskatchewan CCF continued to be troubled; and the fear that labour would overshadow the farmers in the national party was the main source of the Saskatchewan opposition to the formation of the New Democratic party between 1958 and 1961.

4. TENSIONS IN ONTARIO

The Ontario CCF began as a poorly organized, poverty-stricken protest movement with a small and dwindling membership. In 1942 and 1943 it rapidly developed into a major political force. There was a great influx of new members, many of them trade unionists, and a great increase in popular support—most of it from the working class. The rank and file party veterans welcomed these developments, of course, but not without qualms. There was considerable opposition to the leadership's proposal that the party seek trade union affiliation. And though unionists were welcomed as individual members of the party, there was fear that they would bring with them trade union domination and an opportunistic willingness to abandon socialist principles. As labour leaders and union officials, most of them from Steel, gained positions of influence within the party, the fears of the old guard increased.

Myrtle M. Armstrong, a member of the CCF who was appointed

[41]To Lloyd Fell, Nov. 5, 1952, CLC-PEC files.

secretary of SWOC in 1940, was elected some years later to the Provincial Council of the CCF. In the late forties she was involved in efforts to organize a leftist opposition to the administration, and she later resigned from the CCF. In 1959 she wrote a master's dissertation for the University of Toronto[42] which reflects the left-wing antipathy to labour in the Ontario party.

Armstrong describes the dilemma of the "old guard" in 1943 and 1944: they realized that without trade union support the party had little hope of coming to power; but they knew that labour support would bring about unpalatable changes in the organization, policy, and character of the CCF. The chief spokesman for this group was the provincial secretary, Bert Leavens (himself a trade unionist), who

feared the undemocratic domination of trade union leaders because he was a political idealist. Money and organization he claimed could win a political election but could not win a socialist victory. . . . Mr. Leavens' position and influence in the CCF were gradually undermined and replaced. His tours around the province to discuss provincial affairs with the members of local clubs were called disruptive tactics and a misuse of his office and party funds. . . . A private whisper campaign by CCF trade unionists and their supporters completed his destruction. Mr. Leavens retired from the CCF shortly before his death, a defeated and broken man. . . . The only outspoken critic of the changes which had occurred in the CCF . . . was unable to rally about himself those members who desired socialism rather than political power.[43]

The "change which had occurred" was the development of a protest movement, an élite of the committed, into a major political party with a mass membership. The primary motivation of the party, in Zakuta's terms, was no longer ideological—belief in future victory—but political —hope in present success. The chief activity was no longer "protest" or "socialist education," but vote-seeking. The organization was no longer a decentralized, loosely disciplined association of clubs but an increasingly centralized and disciplined electoral machine. According to Armstrong the new membership of the CCF considered "programs, policies, principles and intellectual honesty . . . merely trappings in the struggle for power."[44] Armstrong also criticizes the unionists for using in the CCF "techniques of minority domination" similar to those which are common in the labour movement: "To the members in the CCF who prized individual freedom, the trade union techniques were undemocratic and unsuitable in the party." Examples of those techniques are the "slate" in party elections and the "bloc vote" on the provincial council.

[42]"The Development of Trade Union Political Activity in the CCF."
[43]Ibid., pp. 59–60.
[44]Ibid., p. 62.

The slate was first used at the provincial convention of 1946. A "self-appointed" group of unionists drew up a list of candidates for the provincial council and executive and distributed it to the unionist delegates (about one third of the total) and their supporters. The slate was "exposed" and charges of "trade union dictatorship" were made. At the 1948 convention the slate was accepted without protest as a normal part of election routine. It was the only slate distributed and most candidates wanted to appear on it. The slate committee contacted "various groups" within the CCF and requested that they suggest members for positions on the slate. In this manner, says Armstrong, the trade unionists, as the only organized group within the convention, indirectly controlled the elections of party officers. A candidate whose name did not appear on the slate was unlikely to be elected: "My own election to the Provincial Council for three consecutive years was a result of my name appearing on the trade union slate." Those who "prized individual freedom" also objected to the solidarity of the trade unionists on the provincial council: Their unanimity on every issue "aroused the suspicion of other Council members who were accustomed to voting against everyone at least once during their year in office."[45]

According to Armstrong, opposition to "labour domination" was weak in the early forties and had become almost non-existent in the late forties, chiefly because the leftists realized that the party was and must be dependent upon trade union support. In the late forties and early fifties leftists in the CCF objected to the leadership's attempts to discourage such activities as the "celebration of May Day, meetings to discuss World Peace, and support of the Housewives' Consumer Organization." The leftists believed that the CCF leadership's support of NATO and the cold war generally was due at least in part to the CCL's new anti-Communist policy. "Labour domination" was driving the party to the right in foreign policy: "The policy of the CCL once enunciated could not easily be contradicted by CCF . . . conventions. Activities which resembled or paralleled those of the Communists were for-

[45]*Ibid.*, pp. 62, 70, 71, 73, 75. David Lewis writes: "The suggestion . . . that union members were unanimous on every issue is simply incorrect, although it is true that they were probably unanimous [in opposing] the minority group to which Miss Armstrong belonged. Otherwise they frequently disagreed." In a letter to GH, Aug. 16, 1966.

In 1948 five of the twenty-two provincial council members were trade union officials (most of them from Steel) and Charles Millard was vice-president of the Ontario CCF. On the national council there were no trade unionists in 1947–48, but in other years one of the ten members was usually a trade unionist: e.g., in 1946–47, Millard, and in 1948–49, Dowling.

bidden."[46] In 1950 and 1951 a small leftist "ginger group" was organized to oppose the policies of the leadership. Murray Cotterill, reporting to Pat Conroy on the 1951 provincial convention, wrote: "This . . . group did not turn out to be any great menace. . . . They are composed of some impatient younger people, a few older people who resent the growing influence of the unions and some pacifist-minded individuals who are uneasy about American foreign policy. They cannot be compared in any way to the B.C. 'leftists' headed up by Colin Cameron and Rod Young."[47]

In April 1952 a distinguished founding father of the CCF, Professor Frank Underhill, denounced union domination of the party in the pages of the *Canadian Forum*. Underhill had been a member of the board of directors of the Woodsworth Foundation (a CCF educational organization), which had just been involved in a bitter dispute with the Ontario CCF leadership. The dispute ended with the defeat of most of the directors in the 1952 election of board members. Underhill charged in his article, "Power Politics in the Ontario CCF," that the CCF in Ontario had "fallen into the hands of a small clique who perpetuate themselves in party office" by manipulating conventions. This "clique" was "too much under the influence" of the Steel union and its close allies in the CCL. It was "perfectly proper," of course, that a socialist party should attempt to obtain union support, but the "big new industrial unions have come up a little too easily for their own . . . good. . . . They show some signs of being intoxicated by power." Underhill closed by quoting the *CBRE Monthly*'s attack on Millard's "unashamed drive for power" within the CCL.[48]

The CCF leadership replied in the May issue of the *Forum*. F. A. Brewin wrote that the deposed directors of the Woodsworth Foundation had evinced "an attitude of hostility" to the CCF leadership which coincided with "an openly expressed hostility to the trade unions." Brewin acknowledged that in a socialist party "there is a danger" of control by

[46]"The Development of Trade Union Political Activity in the CCF," pp. 72, 76, 77. Again, according to Lewis, "the suggestion that the CCF's foreign policy was in any way governed by CCL policy decisions is sheer nonsense. Indeed, these policies differed on many occasions and even today the NDP foreign policy is in important respects different from [that of] the CLC, despite [the] much closer connection [between the two organizations]. The fact is that the foreign policy of the CCF became less and less tinged by the pacifism which had earlier influenced it and which Miss Armstrong still supported." In a letter to GH, Aug. 16, 1966.

[47]March 28, 1951, CLC-PEC files.

[48]On the *CBRE Monthly* editorial, see above p. 88n.

trade unions. But the leaders of the Steel union had never "made their support conditional upon any control or the adoption of any policy by the Ontario CCF." Brewin chided Underhill for "sneering" at Steel, the union which had "led the movement for effective trade union support for democratic socialism," and for "exploiting" the Conroy-Millard dissension within the CCL in order to make his point.

While CCFers like Armstrong and Underhill perceived their party as one which was dominated by labour, some CCF unionists complained that it was dominated by intellectuals and professional people:

If the Ontario CCF does not become more of a labour party . . . it will not be a party at all. I think that we are cursed with an excess of professors, lawyers, and other assorted professional people. Too many of the CCF leaders take the attitude that as the CCF is a labour party labour will vote for it even without proper strength on the councils of the party. With so many educated gentlemen who have a habit of tangling themselves up in numerous committees there is no practical approach. . . . About all [they] can do is sit around and talk. . . . They are a bunch of old women. . . . The CCF in my opinion should be taken out of the hands of the intellectuals and made more of a union party.[49]

Anti-union sentiment was never powerful or even organized in the Ontario CCF, and by the fifties it appeared to have become almost completely inarticulate. But it persisted in a condition of latency, and the leadership was careful not to arouse it unnecessarily. For example, when Steel assigned one of its staff members to the CCF as a party organizer to be paid by the union, the CCF leadership made sure that it be fully understood that he was to be responsible to the CCF alone: "Otherwise, there is a potential kickback from people in the movement who tend to be on guard against growing union influence."[50]

5. PAC, 1952–1955

In the Ontario provincial election of 1951, the CCF sustained a crushing defeat. Its popular vote was reduced from 27 per cent to 19 per cent, and its representation in the legislature from twenty-one to two. Coming so soon after the federal defeat of 1949, the Ontario defeat strengthened the fear—which had been growing since 1945—that the

[49]James Kidd (president of the Sudbury Mine Mill local and of the Sudbury CCF Club) to Lewis, Nov. 14, 1945, NDP files.
[50]D. C. MacDonald to C. C. Ames, June 19, 1952, *ibid.*

party would be forever incapable of raising itself from minor party status.

Two years after the election of 1945, the Ontario CCF had lost half its membership. During the year following the election of 1949, it lost one third of its members. Across the country, constituency associations in areas of CCF weakness faltered or disappeared. With the loss of members came a serious decline in party finances. The party found that a great deal of effort had to be expended simply in maintaining membership and organization, especially in areas of weakness. It had to run in order to stay in the same place. In its weakness, the party turned increasingly to its only powerful ally in the community—the trade union movement. By 1951 there could no longer be any doubt, even among those suspicious of "labour domination," that salvation could come only from the unions. Reinforcements were not long in coming—first in the form of increasing PAC activities, second in the form of steadily larger direct and indirect contributions to party funds. PAC's share of election expenses in 1945 was 10 per cent; in the mid fifties it was 50 per cent. With union assistance, the decline in membership was halted and the financial situation greatly improved by the early fifties.[51]

One of the most important channels of union support for the CCF was the National Organization Fund, established in 1952. Since the 1949 election the party had had no full-time organizers in the field: without them it was impossible to prevent the attrition of CCF membership and organization. At least five organizers were needed—one in British Columbia, one in Manitoba, two in Ontario, and one in the Maritimes. The cost to the party would be $30,000 a year—an amount which the CCF could not provide from its own regular budget.[52] "There was only one legitimate source to which the CCF could turn with any hope of a response. That was the trade unions."[53] Steel and the UAW agreed to assume the burden of the National Organization Fund with annual contributions of $12,000 apiece.

The CCF's failure in the Ontario provincial election of 1951 led to a "new approach" to political action methods. The five main elements of the new approach were:

1. The integration of PAC and CCF activities. The original concept of PAC had resulted in the establishment of an electioneering organization "paralleling that of the CCF but usually not too well integrated with it."

[51]Zakuta, *A Protest Movement Becalmed*, chaps. VI and VII.
[52]Confidential Memorandum of CCF Organization Fund, Jan. 1952, NDP files.
[53]CCF Convention Proceedings (1952), p. 18.

Both organizations had limited resources at their disposal, and neither was "as effective individually as they might have been with closer integration."[54] Furthermore, the great need of the party was to increase its membership and to strengthen its organization. PAC activity, since it was parallel to CCF activity, contributed nothing to the satisfaction of this need. As D. C. MacDonald pointed out, there was "little possibility of building a CCF organization" while "its greatest body of supporters," the industrial workers, devoted their efforts to building a separate PAC organization.[55] It was therefore decided that "PAC must be closely integrated with organization work of the CCF all the time rather than being conducted as a separate effort paralleling that of the CCF. . . . PAC's new objective is a solid organizational job, increasing CCF memberships among unionists and integrating them in [the] basic poll committee structure [of the CCF]."[56] The new emphasis on union support for the CCF's organizational work also expressed itself through contributions to the National Organization Fund.

Integration of CCF and PAC activities meant also that PAC participation in election campaigns would take the form of support for the CCF campaign rather than the conduct of a separate PAC campaign. Henceforth the main contribution of provincial PAC's to election campaigns would be to pay the bills for the CCF's newspaper and radio advertising. Thus, in the provincial election of 1955, the OFL-PAC provided $16,000 to cover almost the entire cost of the CCF's advertising program.[57] The total cost of that election was $26,000.[58] In the 1957 federal election the cost of the CCF campaign in Ontario was $26,661.06. Of this amount, $2,400 was contributed by the UPWA, and $13,600 was spent by the OFL-PAC to pay for the CCF's advertising campaign.[59]

Efforts were also made to bring about integration of CCF and PAC efforts on the local level during campaigns. The OFL-PAC's *Election Guide for Labour Council and Local Union PAC's* emphasized the importance of integrating PAC workers into the CCF's electoral machinery:

CCL unionists must play a part in building CCF riding associations during the campaign. . . . Try to sign up as many CCF members in the plant as

---

[54]D. C. MacDonald, "Democratic Organization of the CCF," *Comment*, Aug. 1953.

[55]In a letter to Lazarus, Aug. 3, 1951, NDP files.

[56]CCF Convention Proceedings (1952), p. 18.

[57]Ontario CCF Provincial Executive Minutes, April 19, 1955, NDP files.

[58]Report on 1955 Provincial Election, June 25, 1955, CFL-PEC files.

[59]Report on Conduct of 1957 Federal Election Campaign in Ontario, Aug. 6, 1957, *ibid.*

possible. Active trade union participation in CCF ridings provides us with the opportunity of influencing the choice of candidates. . . . PAC's should concentrate on enlisting volunteer help for the CCF. Where local circumstances permit, local unions in an area may wish to assign a group of election workers to work as a team responsible for a section of a constituency: e.g., where a high percentage of workers from a plant live in a concentrated area near the plant, the CCF riding association may, with the agreement of the local union . . . decide to make the election work in that district the job of the local. This arrangement has the advantage of permitting unionists from a certain plant to work together.

Besides assisting the CCF campaign, PAC's should run campaigns of their own directed at their fellow unionists. They should distribute literature provided by OFL-PAC, insert election propaganda in union publications, and invite CCF candidates to address local union meetings, plant-gate meetings, and special election meetings. Throughout the campaign, close contact with CCF constituency officials should be maintained.

2. Continuous PAC activity rather than the restriction of that activity to election periods. Unionists had been asked to vote for the CCF without having been conditioned to respond favourably. The basic task of educating unionists to support of the CCF was not being performed. It was therefore decided that the PAC would operate continuously, not only by involving itself in the CCF's long-term organizational efforts, but by instituting a program of political education for rank and file unionists. The unconverted would be converted, and the converted would be encouraged to involve themselves in the CCF as well as the PAC organization.

3. The reduction of the public visibility of labour support for the CCF. It was felt that in 1948 and 1949 the PAC's "high pressure publicity campaigns" had driven away as many middle-class and farm votes as they had gained among workers.[60] The decision to aid CCF campaigns rather than conduct separate PAC campaigns would solve this problem as well as bring about greater integration and efficiency of the two organizations.

4. The moderation of PAC's approach to the rank and file unionist. Previous PAC efforts had met with some rank and file resentment at being "told how to vote"; the "high pressure" of PAC campaigning tended to alienate the unconverted. It was therefore decided that PAC's efforts to convert the unionists should be more moderate, more "objective," more "low-keyed." The unionist would not be "told how to vote"; the

[60]CCF Convention Proceedings (1952), p. 18.

facts of the Canadian parliamentary system of government and of the
CCF's record on labour issues as compared to that of other parties would
be presented; the pressure to vote CCF would be indirect rather than
direct. Not "don't *scab* at the ballot box" but "look at these facts and
vote intelligently."[61] A local union president described the shift from
"hard sell" to "soft sell" in his local:

Last year this local . . . followed a "blunt PAC policy" with some degree
of success. However . . . in some cases it did more harm than good. . . . It
tended to create animosity in the membership. This year we decided to use
more subtle tactics. We "educated" by leaflet saturation; we "confounded"
rather than "ridiculed" individual resistance. . . . We set up Political Forums
to which we invited all political parties, thereby forestalling any suggestion
of a "down the line" policy in respect to the CCF. . . . The method of PAC
employed this year was one that was completely acceptable to the rank
and file member.[62]

5. The stabilization of the PAC's financial base. From 1949 to 1952
locals were asked to contribute one dollar per member per year to PAC.
In practice, "bucks for PAC" were collected only during election campaigns, and from a fraction of the CCL membership. Henceforth, locals
would be requested to make a *monthly* contribution of ten cents per
member to their provincial PAC. In this way a permanent political
action fund would be built up, and PAC would not be dependent solely
on the response to election appeals. Of the ten cents monthly per capita,
four cents would go to Labour Council PAC's, and six cents to the provincial PAC. The latter would forward two cents directly to the CCF—an
amount exactly the same as that required for direct affiliation. Affiliation,
however, would be established only on request of the local; meanwhile,
"the financial equivalent of affiliation dues" would be reaching the CCF
via the provincial PAC.[63] This new system was implemented only in
Ontario and there only partially. Most of the locals which adopted the
scheme were Steel locals. By January 1954 one third of the membership
of Steel and one quarter of the membership of the OFL were paying a
monthly per capita to the OFL-PAC.[64] By 1957 about half the income
of OFL-PAC came from per capita contributions, and the remaining
half from election donations by local and labour councils:[65]

61Weisbach interview, Jan. 10, 1963.
62William Lowry (president of IWA local 1–367, Haney, B.C.) to George
Home, June 23, 1953, BCFL files.
63D. C. MacDonald, "Democratic Organization. . . ."
64CCL-PAC Minutes, Jan. 18–19, 1954, CLC-PEC files.
65OFL-PAC Financial Statements, April 1 and June 21, 1957. OFL-PEC files.

Per capita tax	$11,154.11
Election donations	12,901.46
Literature sales	24.00
	$24,079.57

D. C. MacDonald described this system as "indirect affiliation" to the CCF: "In the strange and devious ways in which developments sometimes emerge in Canada we are arriving at much the same position as in Great Britain."[66]

It appears that before deciding on the scheme of per capita contributions to PAC, CCF and union leaders had considered reviving the idea of direct affiliation. When the UAW made its first contribution to the National Organization Fund George Burt "raised the question of what representation the UAW would get in the CCF if it made a financial contribution." The CCF replied that representation could be secured only through direct affiliation. Burt "seemed quite intrigued with the idea of affiliating the whole of the Canadian District of the UAW, making provision . . . for locals who so desired to withdraw."[67] At the same time the District Council of the UPWA decided to pay the affiliation fees for any local approving affiliation by a 75 per cent referendum vote. At the 1952 Convention of the CCF, D. C. MacDonald announced that there was a "much more active consideration of affiliation now than at any time since the end of the war." By 1953, however, affiliation had been deferred, and the system of "indirect affiliation" through monthly contributions to PAC adopted instead. The reasons for this appear to have been:

1. The CCL and TLC had begun to move towards the merger of 1956. A strengthening of the alliance between CCL unions and the CCF would have placed obstacles in the way of merger and would also have made it more difficult to convert the TLC to some form of political action in support of the CCF.

2. It would be easier to convince many locals to pay a per capita amount to PAC than to convince them to affiliate to the CCF. "Indirect affiliation" would lay the groundwork for direct affiliation at some future date.

3. As far as the CCF was concerned, the financial benefits of "indirect affiliation" were identical with those of direct affiliation: a stable income of two cents per member per month. Moreover, indirect affiliation made it possible to avoid the problem of convincing the CCF's membership

[66]In a letter to Freeman Jenkins, April 7, 1953, NDP files.
[67]Ingle to Lazarus, July 10, 1952, NDP files.

to accept large-scale affiliation of unions and overcoming the CCF's reluctance to increase the representation of affiliated locals at CCF conventions.

The basis of representation set down in 1946 was unsatisfactory to the unions. Since affiliation to the CCF was being seriously considered in 1952, the question of representation at national conventions was raised in the CCF convention of that year. One proposed resolution called the basis of representation "irrational and discriminatory" and requested the executive to study the matter and recommend changes. The convention adopted a substitute resolution instructing the National Council to investigate the basis of representation and report to the next convention.[68] The main union grievance was that affiliated locals with less than five hundred members could not be represented unless they pooled their memberships. Many locals had less than five hundred members and the pooling provision was difficult to implement: it was hard, for example, to ask an upholsterers' local to pool its membership with a railway workers' local. Locals with less than five hundred members were virtually deprived of representation.

In May 1952 the national executive ruled that the constitution should be interpreted to mean that locals with five hundred members *or major fraction thereof* were entitled to one delegate; this reduced the minimum from 500 to 251.[69] But the problem remained for locals with fewer than 251 members. The 1954 CCF convention adopted a constitutional amendment proposed by the National Council. The amendment lowered the minimum of members required for representation of constituency associations from fifty to one, and the minimum for local unions from 500 (or 251 according to the executive ruling of May 1952) to 200 or major fraction thereof.[70]

The PAC was not completely satisfied with the change. Locals with

[68]CCF Convention Proceedings (1952), p. 39.
[69]D. C. MacDonald to Harold Thayer, Sept. 22, 1953, NDP files.
[70]CCF Convention Proceedings (1954), p. 41. The 1954 provisions: Constituency associations: one delegate for each association with 1–50 members. One additional delegate for every additional 200 members or major portion thereof up to a total membership of 450. One additional delegate for every additional 300 or major portion thereof up to a total number of 1050. One additional delegate for every additional 500 or major portion thereof.

For local unions: One delegate for the first 200 members or major portion thereof. One additional delegate for each additional 800 or major portion thereof up to 1,800. One additional delegate for each additional 1,200 or major portion thereof up to 4,200. One additional delegate for each additional 2,000 or major portion. Pooling for locals with less than the minimum: Where a local is the only local of its union which is affiliated to the CCF within a province, the minimum of 101 is waived. *Ibid.* For the 1946 provisions, see above, p. 75.

less than 101 members were still required to pool their memberships in order to secure representation: "This . . . leads to a reluctance of local unions to affiliate with the CCF. [We are] endeavouring by influence to further improve the situation."[71] As the PAC itself noted, the problem of representation at conventions was "not . . . very pressing," since it had been decided not to embark on a campaign for large-scale affiliation. Only with the formation of the New Democratic party did the question of representation become once again an important one.

6. THE UAW AND THE IWA, 1948–1954

The end of Communist domination in the UAW and the IWA did not mean that these unions automatically became strong supporters of the CCF. Both unions went through a transitional period during which close relations with the CCF were developed. At the end of the period, the UAW and the IWA joined Steel and the smaller unions associated with it as the most energetic supporters of the CCF in the labour movement.

1. *The UAW*
The anti-Communist victories in UAW locals 195 and 200 in 1946 had not been brought about by CCFers alone. There was a substantial body of "independents" who co-operated with the CCFers in the anti-Communist caucus, and many of these independents probably had Liberal and Conservative sympathies of varying degrees of strength. The *Canadian Tribune*[72] described the defeat of Alex Parent's executive in local 195 as the result of a cabal of "the Liberal, Tory, and CCF parties, with the active aid of the Windsor Daily Star and sections of the reactionary clergy." Although CCFers had been elected to both local executives, the new president of local 195, Earl Watson, was "apparently a Liberal and not in favour of CCL policy of support for the CCF"; the presidency of local 200 was retained by Roy England, who had been an LPP supporter before the Reuther revolution. In both locals the situation was aggravated by . . . "the popularity and strength of Paul Martin," the incumbent Liberal MP.[73]

Although Burt had swung to Reuther and to the CCF in 1947–48, and Roy England had made his peace with the Reuther forces at about

[71]PAC Brief to the CCL Executive, March 7, 1955, CLC–PEC files.
[72]On March 23, 1946.
[73]Lewis to Millar Stewart, March 24, 1949, NDP files.

the same time, and although the UAW had supported the OFL–PAC in the provincial election of 1948, the CCF was not confident of UAW support in the federal election of 1949. Careful cultivation of the CCF's relations with England[74] and Watson, the example of Reuther's and Burt's support for the CCF, and consultation with the locals about the nomination of candidates resulted in the endorsement by both locals of the CCL's political action plans for the 1949 election. The UAW District Council also supported the CCF in 1949. But these election endorsements did not represent the achievement of a close and stable relationship between the union and the CCF, nor did they represent a firm policy of permanent political action through the CCF such as that of Steel. This stage was not reached until 1951. The spur seems to have been the decision of the international union, at its 1951 convention, to intensify its political action program and to set up a "Citizenship Fund" to which each member would contribute ten cents a month.

The Canadian UAW decided that its share of the Citizenship Fund would be used in intensified political action in support of the CCF. On April 10 and 11, 1951, Lorne Ingle, M. J. Coldwell, Angus MacInnis, and Stanley Knowles met with George Burt and the presidents of about fifteen UAW locals. Ingle wrote: "The upshot of the two meetings will be . . . a much closer relationship between the UAW and the CCF, both on the local level and on the national level. . . ."[75] In June 1951 the UAW District Council endorsed the CCF as the union's political arm and pledged full and active support to CCF candidates in future elections.[76]

The union decided to appoint a full-time staff representative to take charge of political action. The appointee was Art Schultz, a prominent CCFer. By January 1952 half the UAW locals had set up political action committees. In the 1951 provincial elections, seven UAW members ran as CCF candidates, including Earl Watson. In 1952 the UAW became one of the two chief contributors to the CCF's National Organization Fund. The other was Steel. And in 1961 the UAW was one of the three unions singled out by Hazen Argue as the "dominators" of the New Democratic party.

2. The IWA

At the first convention of the IWA after the secession of the Communists, there was a "heated debate" on a resolution endorsing the

[74]In 1951 England was appointed to the UAW staff and was replaced by CCFer Jack Taylor. Archie Cherniak to D. C. MacDonald, May 11, 1951, *ibid.*
[75]To Cherniak, April 17, 1951, *ibid.*
[76]*PAC Newsletter*, Oct. 1951.

CCL's political policy. The opponents of the resolution argued that the rank and file "had become so disgusted with the . . . tactics of the LPP" that any suggestion of "tie-up" with *any* party would arouse their antagonism. The leadership gave assurances that the CCF had "no intention of interfering with the IWA in any way whatsoever," and the resolution was finally passed without a dissenting vote. But the *CCF News* warned: "It would be idle to pretend that the bulk of the membership is convinced. . . . There remains a great deal of work to be done . . . within the IWA."[77]

The participation of the IWA in the federal election of 1949 was minimal. The BCFL-PAC reported that the IWA leaders were busy re-organizing the union after the WIUC split; they were reluctant to set up a PAC or become involved with the CCF, since the membership might consider this an attempt to re-establish a party dictatorship in the union. "It will require time and education to point out to their members the difference between a union taking political action and a union being used by a political party."[78] As a result of these difficulties in the IWA, the BCFL-PAC collected only $4,376.58 of its projected $50,000 campaign fund. The great majority of the contributions came from CBRE, Steel, and Packinghouse locals ($3,134.32).

The Communist past of the IWA and its resulting suspicion of "tie-ups" with any political party were not the only obstacles to close relations between the IWA and the CCF in British Columbia; factionalism in the IWA was also a factor. The new leadership had not consolidated its position. It was unwilling to translate its CCF sympathies into political action for fear that this would be used against it by opposition groups within the union.

Wherever the ties between labour leadership and the CCF are weak, or relations between the two are strained, there may appear within the unions a tendency towards political action independent of the CCF— the nomination of "straight labour candidates" by the unions themselves. This current of independent labourism is encouraged by anti-CCF elements such as the Communists. The CCF can deal with it only by trying to absorb it, by convincing the labour leaders that they can express themselves politically through the CCF.

Independent labourism soon appeared in the IWA. It was especially strong in that union not only because its former Communist leadership had prevented the development of any connections with the CCF, but because the Communist experience had resulted in fear of domination

---

[77]*CCF News* (BC), Jan. 19, 1949.
[78]BCFL-PAC Report on the 1949 Federal Election, n.d., BCFL files.

by *any* political party; independent political action seemed to be the
only alternative. Moreover, independent labourism was fostered by
anti-administration factions within the union.[79]

At the BCFL convention of February 1952, the demand for independent labour candidates was raised as expected. The resolutions committee reacted by proposing a compromise resolution instructing the
executive to "call delegate conferences in the industrial areas to discuss
political candidates . . . in line with CCL policy."[80] CCL policy, of
course, was support of CCF candidates; the purpose of the resolution
was to satisfy the demand for independent labour candidates without
rejecting CCL policy. CCF candidates would be supported by labour,
but labour wanted an undefined degree of influence in the nomination
of those candidates. PAC and CCF spokesmen, including George Home
of the BCFL and James Bury of the Vancouver Labour Council, opposed
this concession to independent labourism, emphasizing that only CCF
members had the right to nominate candidates, and that unionists could
legitimately influence nominations only by joining the CFF. The IWA's
George Mitchell, president of the BCFL and chairman of the resolutions
committee, assured the opponents of the resolution that no interference
with the rights of CCF members was intended: "We are not going to
try to run the CCF, but labor wants to . . . have a say in picking candidates."[81] The resolution was adopted. Home and Bury later realized that
it "might eventually be used to advantage."[82] It offered the CCF an
opportunity to render independent labourism harmless by absorbing it,
in much the same way that the CCF had tried to absorb independent
labourism in the UAW in 1944. "Consultation" with the unions about
candidates would do much to eliminate the unions' desire to run candidates of their own. The *CCF News* asked CCF members to meet the

---

[79]In January 1952 Grant McNeil of the British Columbia CCF wrote: "The
Whalen element is aligning itself with the Commies and Liberals to break with
CCL-PAC policy. . . . They are fanning the idea of independent labour candidates,
as they say named by the 'masses of the workers.' At present the IWA membership has not been influenced to assist PAC, and certainly would not endorse the
CCF at this juncture. A great deal of ground work must be done, along educational lines, before the IWA is solidly on our side. Remember, there is still the
strong suspicion of political action because of the long record of Communist
domination. . . . [These developments] may easily ruin the CCF chances. . . .
We're doing what we can through our trade union . . . committee despite the
[leftist] screwballs in our own camp who persist in insulting the trade unions. We
keep in close touch with the PAC leaders." From a letter to Ingle, Jan. 12, 1952,
BC NDP files.

[80]*CCF News* (BC), Feb. 6, 1952.

[81]*Vancouver News-Herald*, Feb. 4, 1952.

[82]J. Williams to Weisbach, Feb. 5, 1952, CLC-PEC files.

BCFL proposal "with patient wisdom and understanding. It is the business of the CCF to win and not alienate working class support."[83]

In compliance with the resolution, the BCFL executive called a delegate conference of fourteen locals in the Vancouver area. Grant McNeil read a list of CCF candidates who had already been nominated, pointing out that many of them were CCL and TLC unionists. The conference decided to discuss candidates in constituencies where nominations had not yet taken place, and agreed on a number of names to be forwarded to the CCF for consideration by nominating conventions. George Home emphasized that direct participation in nominations could only be achieved by joining the CCF: "The best we could do [here] was to suggest nominees. . . . Next time . . . we will be in the CCF."[84]

In the provincial elections of 1952, three of the successful CCF candidates were members of the IWA. The provincial secretary of the CCF, Jessie Mendels, wrote: "There is an excellent feeling now between the IWA and the CCF. . . . The fact that there are IWA people among our members [of the legislature] is already bearing fruit."[85] Within the next few years CCF-IWA relations grew closer; at the same time the leadership of the IWA became stable and factionalism within the union decreased. In 1954 the union decided to set up a district PAC. Henry Weisbach wrote: "Our efforts of [sic] getting the IWA to accept PAC on a full scale are now beginning to be successful. [This is] a major achievement because you know . . . how hard it was to sell the IWA on the idea of PAC."[86] By 1956 the IWA was "firmly and wholeheartedly in support of the CCF,"[87] and by 1960 the British Columbia industrial union movement, which ten years before had been Communist-dominated, was as closely tied to the CCF as the Ontario movement. At the founding convention of the New Democratic party, the fourth largest union delegation was that of the IWA, with thirty delegates (Steel had 165, UAW 60, and Packinghouse 69).

[83]*CCF News* (BC), Feb. 6, 1952.
[84]Minutes of Delegate Conference of Affiliated Locals within the Vancouver Area, March 31, 1952, BCFL files.
[85]To D. C. MacDonald, July 14, 1952, BC NDP files.
[86]To D. C. MacDonald, Nov. 8, 1954, CLC-PEC files.
[87]Thayer to Art Schultz, Sept. 27, 1956, BC NDP files.

5.   The Merger

1. EVENTS OF 1953

In December 1953 the TLC and CCL appointed representatives to a Unity Committee to discuss ways and means of bringing about eventual organic unity between the two congresses.[1]

The leadership of the TLC had remained firmly committed to its long established non-political policy, and this policy had been reaffirmed in convention year after year. At the same time, however, the desire to take some sort of political action was growing stronger within the Congress, and sympathy for the CCF was increasing. The 1949 TLC Convention was "split down the middle" on the issue of support for the CCF; the non-partisan policy was reaffirmed, but by a narrow margin.[2] Sympathy for the CCF was especially strong in the Ontario TLC, which had by the late forties come to "unofficially look towards the CCF . . . as the political party for labour."[3] In 1948 the OPFL convention denounced both the Liberal and Conservative parties in Ontario and called for the defeat of all MPPs unfriendly to labour. In 1949, after "violent controversy," it adopted a resolution calling upon the executive to lead a campaign to "defeat reaction in administrative bodies and governments" and to elect "genuine and sincere" friends of labour.[4] These resolutions stopped short of endorsement of the CCF, and little or nothing was done to implement them, but there could be no doubt that they reflected growing sympathy for the socialists.

A former TLC leader estimated that by 1952 about one third of the delegates at TLC conventions were in favour of political action in support of the CCF.[5] The CCF's national organizer suggested early in 1953 that there was almost as much support for the CCF among the

[1]See Eugene Forsey, "The Movement towards Labour Unity in Canada," A. Kovacs. ed., *Readings in Canadian Labour Economics* (Toronto: 1961).

[2]Douglas Hamilton, "Why Labour Must Be Political," *Canadian Labour*, July–Aug., 1959.

[3]Myrtle M. Armstrong, "The Development of Trade Union Political Activity in the CCF," MA thesis, University of Toronto, 1959, p. 102.

[4]*Globe and Mail*, Jan. 19 and 24, 1948.

[5]Interview with R. K. Gervin, Oct. 2, 1962.

TLC rank and file as there was in the CCL ranks. "The attitude of the leadership and the official policy of the Congress is the big problem."[6]

In January 1953 the CCF leadership decided that the time had come to try to commit the TLC to some form of political action. Tom Alsbury and Harold Thayer of the British Columbia CCF–TUC drafted a resolution for submission to the TLC convention. The draft was revised by the National TUC, which asked a dozen or so TLC locals across the country to submit their own versions of the resolution to the TLC convention. Rewording of the National TUC draft by each local was urged "so that we are not open to the accusation of an organized conspiracy along the lines which the Communists have followed in the past. . . ." "Let the resolution come 'spontaneously.' "[7]

The National TUC's draft made no mention of the CCF. It referred to the failure of the Canadian government to implement such TLC proposals as a national health plan; it then pointed out that American unions were taking political action to elect their "friends," and instructed the executive to set up a "Labor Political Education committee" to work for the election of candidates supporting the TLC's "program and ideals."[8] It was felt that such a resolution, avoiding endorsement of the CCF and urging political action modelled on that of the AFL, would not arouse the ire of Bengough and the TLC executive; if the executive were not "provoked . . . into bulldozing the ranks" against the resolution, the convention would "split right down the middle."[9]

The TUC resolution was so cautious that it did not even call for support of the *party* endorsing labour's program—the word "candidates"

[6]D. C. MacDonald to Ames, Feb. 24, 1953, NDP files. The increasing sentiment for political action in the TLC was perhaps partly due to the example of the AFL, which was becoming more active in politics to the extent of endorsing a presidential candidate (Adlai Stevenson, 1952) for the first time since 1924.

[7]From letters written by D. C. MacDonald, Feb. and March, 1953, *ibid.*

[8]Proposed Resolution on TLC Political Action: "Whereas the Trades and Labor Congress of Canada has made representation to the governments on federal and provincial levels; and Whereas no action has been taken on such matters as a national health plan, provision for adequate housing and adequate pensions for the aged; and Whereas in the industrial centres of the United States labor, through its political action program, has made real progress to elect its friends; Therefore be it resolved that the incoming executive be instructed to forward immediately on adjournment of this convention the legislative program of the Trades and Labor Congress of Canada to the leaders of political parties, asking their endorsation and support for our program; and Further be it resolved that the replies be given the widest possible publicity to the rank and file members, and that the Labor Political Education committee be instructed to support the election of the candidates who support the program and ideals of the Trades and Labor Congress of Canada." *Ibid.*

[9]D. C. MacDonald to Ames, Feb. 24, 1953, NDP files.

was substituted for "party" in the original draft in order to avoid antagonizing the TLC leadership. TLC locals submitting revisions of the
resolution were asked to make no specific reference to the CCF unless
they were affiliated to it. Thus only a few of the proposed resolutions
would mention the CCF, and the resolutions committee, it was hoped,
would opt for a "compromise" similar to the National TUC draft.
CCFers in the TLC were also asked to work for the election of sympathetic convention delegates in order to create a convention atmosphere
favourable to the resolution, and also, if possible, to work for the
election of sympathetic people to the TLC executive.[10]

No CCF sympathizers were elected to the executive, but the resolutions committee did propose a "compromise" resolution authorizing
(not instructing) the executive to set up a "League for Political
Education" which would, like that of the AFL, publicize the voting
records of legislators. This resolution was adopted. The *Globe and Mail*
described this development on August 15 as a concession to the
"growing grass roots sentiment for some form of political action," and
a "triumph" for CCF supporters within the TLC. The TLC executive
did not set up a League for Political Education. As one of the drafters
of the National TUC's resolution said before the convention, nothing
would be gained by more resolutions "until Percy Bengough either has
a change of heart or is surrounded by an executive that will force him
to take some action."[11]

2. ENTER CLAUDE JODOIN

After the TLC's 1953 convention, Percy Bengough announced his
intention of retiring as president. The three contenders for the succession
were Claude Jodoin, vice-president for Quebec, A. F. MacArthur,
president of the OPFL, and R. K. Gervin, vice-president for British
Columbia. The CCF was anxious to "ensure the election of someone who
will at least not do the CCF any harm."[12]

R. K. Gervin was an active, partisan Liberal, a friend of the Minister
of Defence, Ralph Campney. As president he "would be as actively anti-
CCF as Bengough—indeed likely more so. He would probably use every
opportunity to cut our throats."[13] A. F. MacArthur was a Conservative,

[10]D. C. MacDonald to Jim McDuffe, Feb. 3, 1953, *ibid.*
[11]Thayer to D. C. MacDonald, Jan. 15, 1953, *ibid.*
[12]Ingle to Tom Alsbury, May 25, 1954, *ibid.*
[13]Ingle to George Bothwell, Aug. 15, 1954, *ibid.*

considered as cabinet material at one time by Premier Frost of Ontario.

Claude Jodoin had been a former Liberal member of the Quebec legislature. However, he had "got . . . into trouble" with the Liberal leadership, became an independent Liberal and then a straight independent MPP. He was defeated in the provincial election of 1944. Years later, Jodoin explained his rebellion in these words: "I felt the Liberal Party was not doing all it could for labor and since I could not have two loyalties on the question of labor legislation I cut free from the party."[14] In 1948 the Liberals stretched out the hand of forgiveness and offered him another nomination. He spurned the offer, ran as a labour candidate, and lost. Shortly afterward he considered joining the CCF, but was dissuaded by a CCF friend (Kalman Kaplansky) "because . . . in Quebec such a move would prejudice his future in the labour movement without helping the CCF very much."[15]

Jodoin's 1948 flirtation with the CCF was not a matter of general knowledge in either the labour movement or the CCF. Only a handful of people know about it to this day. In 1949 Jodoin became a vice-president of the TLC; from that time onward he did not associate or identify himself with the CCF in any way. His public image in 1954 was "that of a middle of the road labor man . . . more politically conscious than Percy Bengough."[16] He himself described his ideological point of view as "somewhere between that of a right wing CCFer and a left wing Liberal."[17]

Though he was not a CCFer, Jodoin's position on political action was quite progressive for a TLC leader. In August 1954 he told a *Globe and Mail* reporter that the TLC should at least circulate the voting records of MPs among the rank and file, leaving it to them to decide who were the "friends of labour." The reporter asked whether this would not in effect force the Congress to endorse one political party "since the caucus system . . . leaves little room for variation in the voting record of M.P.'s." Jodoin agreed that "this might indeed be the outcome."[18] Jodoin had been an official of the ILGWU, one of the few TLC unions sympathetic to the CCF. He had been active in a labour group fighting racial discrimination. He had also served for a time as chairman of the Presse Cooperatif Ouvrière, the French version of the Cooperative Press Association (CPA), in which CCF trade unionists were active.

[14](Toronto) *Star Weekly*, April 9, 1955.
[15]Ingle to Swailes, July 5, 1954, NDP files.
[16](Toronto) *Star Weekly*, April 9, 1955.
[17]Ingle to Bothwell, Aug. 15, 1954, NDP files.
[18]*Globe and Mail*, Aug. 30, 1954.

Therefore, the feeling of CCFers in the TLC was that Jodoin would be "the lesser of the three evils."[19]

In July the national secretary of the CCF, Lorne Ingle, spent several hours in conference with Jodoin:

My net impression was that he was a better man from our point of view than I dared hope to find. He put his cards on the table and I felt he was dealing with me honestly. This augurs well for the future of relationships with the Congress if he should be elected. . . . Indeed, it was he who raised this point, that if he should be elected he would count it a privilege to consult with us at any time when either he or we felt there would be advantages in such consultations. . . . He stated quite plainly, and I respected him for it, that he did not agree with the CCF on many things and the fact that we did talk things over did not mean that he was necessarily going to take our point of view, but that when and where we differ he would be frank in telling us so. At the same time he does have a great deal of admiration for the work done by the CCF in parliament on behalf of labour and would like to see closer relations established between ourselves and the TLC.

He indicated that he . . . hoped that if he were elected he could work fairly closely with us. . . . He would appreciate an arrangement where we could consult one another informally at any time, where he could get on a first name basis with our MP's and officers etc. He . . . thought . . . that CCF ideas should be reflected more in top TLC positions than it has been— simply because the CCF strength is fairly substantial in the TLC and the top brass has not been democratic in recognizing this fact.

To make a long story short, I think we could do a lot worse than swinging whatever weight we have behind Jodoin. . . . As Jodoin himself put it to me . . . "I am no partisan but from your point of view you might consider me a lesser of two evils."[20]

What weight did the CCF have in the TLC? According to the *Globe and Mail*'s labour reporter, Wilfred List, that was "one of the great uncertainties." But he predicted that, although the next president of the TLC would not be a CCFer, he would "probably be elected by followers of that party."[21]

The Congress's political policy had never been made an issue in elections to the TLC executive. The CCF had always played down rather than accentuated the political division in order to avoid the isolation of CCF supporters from their non-CCF fellows. The CCFers would therefore help to elect Jodoin, but not as CCFers. Ingle told Jodoin that "as indeed he already knew . . . there was no 'bloc' of CCF votes that could be delivered to him and that if any open or vigorous

[19]Ingle to Alsbury, May 25, 1954, NDP files.
[20]Ingle to Swailes, July 5, and to Bothwell, Aug. 15, 1954, *ibid.*
[21]*Globe and Mail*, Aug. 9, 1954.

attempt were made to make him a 'CCF' candidate in any sense, it might easily defeat him. I did let him know however what I had previously ascertained from key CCFers in the TLC—that insofar as we had influence it would . . . be on his side."[22]

At the TLC convention in August, Jodoin, with the support of the Quebec delegates, the CCFers, and other groups within the Congress (including most of its officers), was elected president. The vote was Jodoin 355, Gervin 172, MacArthur 151. Jodoin's margin was thus 32 votes out of a total of 678.[23] The only other change in the TLC executive was the replacement of Jodoin as Quebec vice-president by George Schollie, non-partisan Canadian vice-president of the IAM. Secretary treasurer Gordon Cushing and vice-presidents Carl Berg, James Whitebone, William Jenoves, and R. K. Gervin were re-elected. None of these men were in any way inclined to support the CCF. All of them were, or were thought to be, Liberal or Tory sympathizers. Only the new president was favourable to a closer relationship with the CCF, but this was not generally known, even within the TLC. The *Canadian Forum* of October that year opined: "The CCF can expect little more aid from Jodoin than from his predecessors. . . . He does not regard with favour the idea of independent political action. . . . He has little in common with the socialist-minded officials of . . . large CCL unions. . . ." The *Forum* was wrong. According to Donald MacDonald, one of the crucial developments which made possible the TLC-CCL agreement on political policy for the new merged Congress was the replacement of Bengough by Jodoin in the midst of the merger negotiations.[24]

3. CCF STRATEGY IN THE MERGER

The difference between the CCL and the TLC on political policy was thought to be a serious potential obstacle to the merger of the two organizations. The strategy of the CCL and CCF leaders in this situation was to "avoid any frontal attack" in the form of a demand for adoption of the CCL's policy by the new Congress. "The political policy of the CCL should not be permitted to stand in the way of the merger."[25] The

[22]Ingle to Bothwell, Aug. 15, 1954, NDP files.
[23]*CCF News* (BC), Sept. 1, 1954.
[24]Interview with Donald MacDonald, Oct. 25, 1962.
[25]Lewis to Ingle, Feb. 24, 1955, NDP files.

CCL leaders would not demand endorsement of the CCF as a condition of merger, for they were

confident that a program of political action in support of the CCF will within a year or two carry a . . . convention of the new united Congress. Our support within the CCL is so dominant that combined with the strong minority we have in the TLC, it would . . . quite easily carry any convention of the new body which was not deliberately rigged against us. The strategy would be not to press the matter initially until most of the headaches of union had been ironed out, but ultimately it would mean much more united and stronger support for the CCF in the labour movement . . . than we have ever had.[26]

What was immediately important was to preserve the existing CCL political action program as an organization consisting of unions willing to participate in its work, even if it should not become an organization of the new Congress.

On March 9, 1955, the CCL-TLC Unity Committee agreed on a statement of principles which would govern the merger of the two congresses. On May 9, the complete merger agreement was announced. There was no reference to political policy in either document; the Unity Committee had agreed that no political policy would be determined in advance for the merged congress. The matter would, in Jodoin's words, be "left to the free and democratic decision of the regular conventions of the Canadian Labour Congress."[27] It was informally agreed that the *first* convention of the CLC would endorse no political party. On the other hand, there was tacit agreement that the CCL unions would be allowed to carry on their political action program.[28] On May 9 the Unity Committee decided that a political education department would be established within the new congress, and on July 4 there was a further decision that Henry Weisbach of CCL-PAC would be the director of the new department.[29]

By July 1955, then, the Unity Committee had agreed that the political policy of the CLC would be left to CLC conventions, that affiliated unions would be free to carry on any type of political activity, and that the CLC itself would have a PEC headed by a CCFer.

Towards the end of July, David Lewis and Claude Jodoin arrived at an informal agreement that "although the merger convention itself should avoid any direct partisan commitment for the new Congress, a further step would have to be taken in 1958, either through the CCF or

26Ingle to T. C. Douglas, Feb. 14, 1955, *ibid.*
27CCL Convention Proceedings (1955), p. 120.
28Memo to National PAC officers from Fell, March 14, 1955, CLC-PEC files.
29Unity Committee Minutes, May 9 and July 4, 1955, CLC files.

through some broader political alignment." They also agreed on the main lines of the political strategy to be followed by the CLC and CCF leaderships for the next few years. The president-designate of the new Congress had thus committed himself to a policy of positive political action by the CLC following the merger convention.[30]

Though the top leaders of the CCF and CCL had agreed that the CCL's political policy would not be pressed on the TLC, many lower-ranking CCFers in both congresses feared that political action would be lost in the merger. They were therefore inclined to intensify rather than moderate their vocal support of the CCF, to fight for endorsement rather than avoid the issue. Their enthusiasm had to be suppressed. In June 1955 the TLC convention approved the terms of merger and reaffirmed the non-partisan policy of the congress. Before the convention the CCF leaders had agreed that a debate on TLC endorsement of the CCF should be avoided. An endorsement resolution had been submitted, but the CCF leaders hoped the resolutions committee would prevent it from coming up for a vote. If it did reach the floor, CCFers should not support it, but argue that the matter should be left to the new congress. Any other course might endanger the merger.[31] The CCF leaders succeeded in preventing the endorsement resolution from reaching the floor. The resolutions committee proposed a substitute resolution "that the TLC continue to encourage and organize non-partisan political action and education."[32] This was adopted, but not without some dissent from delegates sympathetic to the CCF who were either unaware of or opposed to the CCF strategy. It was clear that the CCFers were aroused and anxious for a guarantee that the new congress would support the CCF. The political action debate had been the longest since 1939.

Although the CCF leaders avoided rather than pressed the issue of political action at the TLC convention, they did organize a quiet "non-partisan" campaign to depose one of the TLC's vice-presidents, Carl Berg. Berg defeated his opponent, CCF MLA Donovan Swailes, by a vote of 272–270.[33]

At the 1954 convention of the OPFL, a resolution urging support for

[30]Lewis to G. H., Aug. 16, 1966.
[31]Lewis to Ingle, May 16, 1955, NDP files.
[32]TLC Convention Proceedings (1955), p. 205. After the 1954 convention the executive had set up a "Department of Political Research" which had made a study of labour legislation in the various provinces. Its report to the convention stated that "some provincial governments and some political parties are much more friendly to labour than others," but the friendly governments and parties were not identified. Ibid., pp. 47 and 168.
[33]Ingle to Lewis, May 23, 1955, NDP files.

the CCF had been defeated by a tie vote of 133–133.[34] The Federation's 1955 convention also divided equally on the question, but before it could be settled "relief was given to a harassed and bewildered chairman and an embarrassed executive by a narrowly successful motion to adjourn."[35]

At the CCL convention in October, the PAC executive requested the Congress officers to present a resolution urging members of CCL unions to press for a vigorous political action program in the merged congress. But the CCL leaders insisted that any effort to predetermine the CLC's political policy might upset the harmony of the two congresses and make merger difficult.[36] At a conference on October 9, MacDonald, Burt, and Millard tried to assuage the fears of PAC workers that political action would be "lost in the merger." The terms of the agreement on political action with the TLC were outlined, and an appeal was made for support of the leadership's strategy: it had been agreed with the TLC that neither Congress would come to the merger convention with a pre-determined political policy. If the CCL convention passed a resolution dealing with the political policy of the new congress, this agreement would be broken and the merger would be endangered. Burt expressed confidence "that we could unify the new . . . congress on political views since we are going to participate in [its] leadership." Millard gave assurances that "the merger provides the opportunity for increased political . . . effectiveness. . . . The few remaining trade unionists who preach political neutrality find fewer and fewer followers." The conference was not satisfied. A resolution "that this meeting go on record as supporting the recommendations" of the CCL executive was defeated.[37]

It was evident that there was great dissatisfaction with the leaders' strategy and that delegates might raise the issue of the merged congress' political policy on the floor of the convention. The executive decided that the only way to prevent this was to prevent any discussion at all on the perennial resolution reaffirming the CCL's support for the CCF.

[34]*CCF News* (B.C.), Dec. 7, 1955.

[35]*Canadian Aeronaut*, Dec., 1955. The *Aeronaut*, organ of IAM local 717 which had submitted the resolution, declared: "The days of political inaction are numbered. . . . The leadership of the OPFL is trailing miserably behind the demand of delegates for a more positive stand on politics. . . . No one who is familiar with the machinations and private meetings which took place during the TLC Convention (at which even leading figures in the CCF . . . lobbied against support of a resolution calling for endorsation and succeeded in preventing this question from coming before the convention, believing . . . that it might somehow endanger the merger) could consider the recent vote at the OPFL as either a surprise or insignificant."

[36]CCL-PAC Executive Minutes, Oct. 7, 1955, CLC-PEC files.

[37]PAC Conference Minutes, Oct. 9, 1955, *ibid*.

President Mosher called for a vote on the resolution without debate. A noisy demonstration of protest followed, "thirty minutes of foot-stamping, desk pounding and shouting during which President Mosher's ruling of no debate was twice challenged."[38] Mosher's ruling was finally put to a vote and upheld, and the resolution was adopted without debate.[39]

On the day after the official closing of the convention, David Lewis appeared before a special PAC meeting to outline the strategy for the merger convention of the new Canadian Labour Congress, scheduled for April 1956. He stated that an attempt to force endorsement of the CCF at the CLC's founding convention "may lead to bitter fights and differences. . . . It was more important to establish a proper PAC policy in the new Congress than to create differences." A "proper PAC policy" would involve the establishment of a CLC political action or education department, freedom for unions with PAC machinery to continue their political action in support of the CCF, and freedom for the CLC's department to assist such political action. Thus the congress, while it would not itself support the CCF, would assist former affiliates of the CCL in their continued support of the CCF. Unions which decided to remain "non-partisan" would be encouraged to participate in a "non-partisan" political education program. The PAC made no decisions after hearing Lewis; it decided to hold two further meetings to decide on the line to be followed by CCFers at the merger convention.[40]

In December the CCL and TLC leaders decided to modify their agreement that no political policy would be determined in advance for the CLC. In order to "prevent confusion and division at the convention," that is, in order to avoid a fight between CCFers revolting against their leaders' strategy on the one hand and non-partisans on the other, the combined leadership group would promulgate a definite compromise policy which would be acceptable to both sides. Such a policy would be "a positive policy of such a nature as not to designate a particular party."[41]

4. TOWARDS A NEW PARTY

Disappointment at the failure of both the CCF and CCL-PAC to increase the CCF vote had been growing among the top leaders of both

[38]Armstrong, "The Development of Trade Union Political Activity in the CCF," p. 102.
[39]CCL Convention Proceedings (1955), pp. 39–40.
[40]Special PAC Meeting Minutes, Oct. 13, 1955, CLC-PEC files.
[41]Unity Committee Minutes, Oct. 9, 1955, CLC files.

organizations. The merger offered an opportunity to search for new methods and, if necessary, for new institutions. At the 1955 CCL convention, Henry Weisbach referred to the failure of CCF and PAC efforts to gain more than two additional seats for the CCF in the Ontario provincial election of that year. "Perhaps," he said, "a new approach to political action is necessary." At the PAC conference held in conjunction with the convention, the secretary treasurer, Donald MacDonald, explained that "even without the merger," the time had come for a reappraisal of political action methods; the merger provided an opportunity for change "without embarrassment to us or our political arm."

The idea that the CCF should be replaced by a new movement which would bring together the CCF, trade unions, and farm organizations, and that the merger of the CCL and TLC presented an opportunity for the launching of such a movement, was first broached by a few CCF and CCL leaders at a meeting of the Ontario CCF-TUC on December 8, 1955.[42] In the same month it was decided that the CCF National Council meeting of January 13–15, 1956, would be devoted to "as frank and profound a reappraisal as possible of our philosophy, program, strategy, and propaganda." What could be done about the CCF's "failure to make progress in the last few years"? Had the time come for a modernization of the CCF's democratic socialist philosophy? In view of the new developments in the labour movement, had the time come for "a new approach to weld labour, farmer, and CCF into a large mass political movement"?[43]

The major address at the National Council's reappraisal meeting was given by Tommy Douglas:

We have to look very realistically over the period of the last ten or fifteen years and recognize that we have lost ground. . . . We have also to recognize that the capitalist groups have learned a great deal. . . . They have applied some of the Keynesian techniques and they have been admirably successful up to a point. . . . We . . . like socialist parties all over the Western world, are on the defensive. . . . [The] indictment of capitalism [in the Regina Manifesto] is still basically true, but it is not as apparent as it was in 1933 and it is harder to sell.

Our movement must be deepened and broadened. . . . No one knows better than I that you just can't elect a CCF government with only the people who are avowed socialists. You have to have the support of the hundreds of thousands of people who will accept the objectives that we have without necessarily understanding the political philosophy or ideology. And that of course is where we must then use this hard dynamic core [of convinced socialists] as the yeast that will . . . work as the leaven in other organizations

---

42Ingle to Alsbury, Dec. 27, 1955, NDP files.
43Lewis and Ingle to National Council members, Jan. 6, 1956, ibid.

to get us the mass support which we need. We have to get those people to
. . . exercise their influence in . . . the labour congresses, the farmers unions.
. . . When the tide starts to come back in, as I think it will, we must be
ready for it. In 1932–33 we had as our objective a federation of farmer,
labour and socialist organizations. It was a good objective. I'm not completely without hope that if the tide begins to turn the farm, co-operative,
and labour organizations might . . . come in with the CCF, or merge in
some alignment of which the CCF would be the dynamic core—a new type
of federation or the same type of federation enlarged for a genuine farmer-
labour-socialist movement in Canada. I think that ought to be our aim.

If we could accomplish that by 1958 or 1960 we would have the basis of
a great movement in Canada. . . . Unless we can restate our position and . . .
unless we . . . adopt better techniques and adopt them fast . . . unless we can
stimulate and direct some of the mass movements to which I have referred
. . . we will continue to be a diminishing group, a small well-respected,
highly-thought-of minority, with increasingly less influence. But the possibilities are here, they're here if we're prepared to do something about it. . . .[44]

The consensus of the National Council meeting was (1) that the CCF
should look towards the "establishment of a far more broadly based
people's movement among the workers and farmers of this country," a
movement which would bring into one political party—either a reformed
CCF or a new party—the major labour and farm organizations. Thus
construction of a massive affiliated union wing, deferred since the end of
the war, became once again an immediate objective of the CCF. (2)
That the Regina Manifesto of 1933 should be replaced by a new statement of the party's philosophy:

While retaining its basic goals, the CCF should endeavour to make its
appeal more pragmatic, more empirical, more geared to the issues of the
day. . . . The CCF should define more clearly the extent and place of social
ownership in its program. . . . Some new basic literature . . . should be
published which would restate the application of democratic socialism in
today's world and today's terms.[45]

At the CCF's 1956 convention the Regina Manifesto, with its traditional socialist phraseology, was replaced by the Winnipeg Declaration
of Principles, in which the phraseology was modernized and moderated
and the emphasis shifted from public ownership to public control of
the economy, economic planning, and public investment: "The aim of
the CCF is the establishment . . . of a cooperative commonwealth in
which the supplying of human needs and the enrichment of human life
shall be the primary purpose of our society. Private profit and corporate

[44]CCF National Council Minutes, Jan. 13–15, 1956, *ibid*.
[45]Ontario CCF Provincial Council Minutes, March 17–18, 1956 (Report of
the delegates to the National Council meeting), *ibid*.

power must be subordinated to social planning. . . . Investment . . . must be channelled into socially desirable projects. . . ." Public ownership should be increased to the extent necessary to facilitate economic planning and prevent monopoly control of the economy.

The willingness of the CCF to accept a mixed economy, its readiness to regard nationalization as a "tool" rather than an end in itself, were not new. The policy statements of the party (e.g., *Security with Victory* [1944] and *Security For All* [1948]) and the publications of its leading theoreticians[46] had been becoming steadily more reformist, emphasizing nationalization less and less. What was new was the willingness to allow a new statement to *supersede* the Regina Manifesto, which was widely regarded within the party as sacred writ. "The metamorphosis of the CCF did not occur . . . in Winnipeg; it merely shed its cocoon there, revealing the transformation that had long since taken place."[47]

The leaders of the CCF denied that the Winnipeg Declaration represented a shift to the right. It was, they claimed, not a betrayal but a restatement of socialist philosophy. The left-wing opposition disagreed. According to Ernest Winch, the "grand old man" of British Columbia socialism, the CCF had "surrendered the stand which distinguished it from all other political parties and sounded its death knell as a vital and revolutionary force."[48] For the leftists, the Declaration was "a bit of expediency to woo labour."[49] The Regina Manifesto, they charged, "was an embarrassing document to [those] . . . who hoped to gain the support of organized labour."[50]

The increasing reformism of the CCF was in line with the liberalization of socialism throughout the Western world; but, of course, it was also intended to enhance the party's attractiveness to the middle class, and to the labour movement as well. There is no doubt that the convention which adopted the Winnipeg Declaration did so with one eye on the new Canadian Labour Congress. The *United Auto Worker*[51] applauded the new look of the CCF: "Many in organized labour will

[46]For example, Frank Scott, *New Horizons for Socialism* (Ottawa: Woodsworth House Publishers, 1951) and David Lewis, *A Socialist Takes Stock* (Ottawa: Woodsworth House Publishers, 1955).

[47]Leo Zakuta, "A Protest Movement Becalmed," PhD thesis, University of Toronto, 1961, Part IX, p. 12.

[48]Quoted by Dorothy G. Steeves, *The Compassionate Rebel* (Vancouver: Boag Foundation, 1960), p. 210.

[49]Zakuta, *A Protest Movement Becalmed* (Toronto, 1964), p. 94.

[50]Armstrong, "The Development of Trade Union Political Activity in the CCF," p. 87.

[51]Sept. 19, 1956.

welcome the Winnipeg Declaration. . . . With the tag 'Socialism-Will-Cure-Everything' off its back, the CCF should be . . . much more acceptable to union voters."

On February 4, 1956, a conference of fifty-two CCF trade unionists, convened by the national TUC, met at London, Ontario, to discuss the approach which would be taken by CCFers at the merger convention in April. There was a sharp division of opinion between those who favoured a fight for immediate endorsement of the CCF and those who supported the administration's more complex strategy.[52] The endorsationists argued that endorsement would be supported by a "comfortable" majority at the merger convention. They argued that any policy which stopped short of endorsement would represent a CCF retreat at a time when an advance was possible. It was true that the new congress would establish a political education department, but the type of political education which it would carry on might not be of much use to the CCF. "Endorsation is essential to give purpose and direction to any program of political education or action."

The endorsationists pointed to the experience of CCL-PAC. The official endorsement of the CCF by the Congress had been important in overcoming initial opposition to political action: CCFers "could always answer that they were merely advocating Congress policy." Many unionists, though they were not enthusiastic about Congress policy, were at least "not willing to go flat in the face of it" by supporting parties other than the CCF; and many, though unconverted at the outset, were gradually absorbed into political activity in support of the CCF. "In short, endorsation has been the base from which it has been possible to make significant (even if slow) progress in building up support for the CCF" [in the CCL]. Endorsement would be equally useful in converting TLC unionists. Without endorsement, the new political education department would have "no firm ground to stand on," and "powerful interests in the Congress which do not want realistic political education" might try to prevent the department from assisting affiliates' political action in support of the CCF. Instead of going forward, the CFFers would be thrown on the defensive.

[52]The following pages are based on these documents: (1) Statement on PAC Policy to Members of PAC and CCL Executive Committee Members from Lloyd Fell, Jan. 19, 1956, CLC-PEC files. (2) CCL-PAC Minutes, Feb. 3, 1956, *ibid.* (3) Background Information Prepared by the National TUC (to serve as introduction to the discussion at the London Conference), NDP files. (4) Address of Lloyd Fell to the PAC Conference, April 23, 1956, CLC-PEC files. Most of the quotations are from "Background Information."

The administration and its supporters opposed a fight for endorsement on two grounds: that it would be poor strategy, and that in any case the time had come for a new approach to the whole question of political action.

1. *Strategy.* That an endorsement resolution would be adopted by the merger convention was not an absolute certainty—if such a resolution were defeated, that would be a calamity for the CCF. The opponents of endorsement argued "that it would carry only by a narrow majority . . . at best and only if there is an intensive campaign before and during the convention." The CCF would be a "major divisive issue" at an otherwise harmonious convention. The merger itself would be endangered; some affiliates might secede. The press would say that the "CCF was prepared to sacrifice the very principle of unity in its bull-headed determination to force its will on the convention." More important, the unconverted within the TLC would be alienated. There were many who were undecided; these could be converted over a period of time. But "a blustering campaign for endorsation" might "drive many of them over to the other side." Such a campaign would also alienate the TLC members of the new CLC's executive—the very people who would be expected to implement an endorsement resolution. "If we ram an endorsation resolution down their throats these officers will be more than human if they do not do everything in their very substantial power to make sure that no real effect is given to it in practice."

The correct strategy would dictate support of a policy "that provides the maximum of satisfaction with the minimum of friction." Such a policy would protect "everything of value that we have so far achieved . . . and at the same time provide a basis for expanding those achievements." CCL unions would be free to continue supporting the CCF. TLC unions would be free to continue their non-partisan policy. The CLC itself would not endorse any party; at the same time, however, it would not merely "authorize" but "urge" the pro-CCF unions to continue their political action programs, and offer them the assistance of an official congress department in doing so. The PEC would be not a creature of the Executive Council but directly representative of affiliated organizations. This would prevent unsympathetic council members from hampering its work; such members would "have to contend with a democratically based committee which has official recognition in the Congress." The period between the first and second conventions of the CLC would "be used to promote a more satisfactory policy."

2. *A new approach.* The CCF was not making progress. A completely

new approach must be found. The merger convention provided an opportunity for initiating a process aimed at producing a new movement —either a new party or a reformed CCF—with which "economic organizations" would be directly linked through affiliation rather than indirectly linked through endorsement. A major weakness of the CCF was the absence of a direct, organic relationship with the trade union movement, a relationship similar to that which existed in Britain. "The very fact that [workers] endorse the CCF implies that they are not part of the CCF. No one would ask them to endorse the union or church to which they belong; they are already part of those organizations." Labour support could be increased in quantity and in quality only if rank and file unionists were given "a feeling that they and their unions are part of the CCF, with a right to participate in its affairs, and a duty to help build it." For this, endorsement would not be sufficient; affiliation was necessary. "It may be that the time is now ripe to make a new start in realizing the original objective of the CCF."

The merger convention should therefore instruct the Congress executive to initiate discussions on "co-ordination of action in the legislative and political field" with the CCF and farmers' organizations. "The ultimate objective would be the integration of the economic and political movements either by affiliation . . . to the CCF or by the formation of a new federation." The "traditionally timid" farmers' organizations would probably not be won over for a long time, but that was no reason for labour to delay. Labour might be ready as early as 1958. "The important point now is to lay a foundation for gradually bringing the trade union movement and if possible the farm movement into close and active association with the political movement."

The administration proposed two draft resolutions (one on political policy, the second on discussions with the CCF and farm organizations) which embodied its approach. The conference was assured that the two resolutions "can pass the merger convention without open opposition," and that the TLC members of the CLC executive, though many of them preferred that the new Congress abstain from political action, would "go along with the resolutions as a reasonable compromise. Thus, the really important work that follows the convention will not have to be carried on in a bitter . . . atmosphere of resentment."

The conference approved the two resolutions, making only one important amendment acknowledging the CCF's friendliness to labour. On April 22, a conference of delegates to the merger convention who were sympathetic to the CCF approved the resolutions. They were then

presented to the full convention by the combined CCL-TLC leadership
and adopted without opposition.[53]

[53]Text of the two resolutions as adopted by the convention (Proceedings, p. 49):
"1. *Political Education and Action*
Whereas labour in Canada has always recognized that it must play its full part
in the political life of the nation, and with the unity of the two major Congresses,
it has an even more important part to play in the future in giving voice to the
urgent needs of the people of Canada; and
Whereas in the past there have been two different approaches in political activity;
on the one hand, there has been a non-partisan policy and on the other hand a
policy of active support for the Co-operative Commonwealth Federation and it
is acknowledged that the CCF has fought consistently for labour's legislative
programme inside and outside of the parliament of Canada and the provincial
legislatures; and
Whereas notwithstanding these differences of approach, however, there has been
a basic unity of purpose, and both Congresses in their own way have contributed
in great measure to the improvement of conditions in Canada, and both have
stood firmly for the democratic principle of government, repudiating absolutely
all efforts by communists or fascists to use the labour movement as a means of
advancing their own political ends; and
Whereas the overriding need now is to go forward in a spirit of unity to achieve
the basic objectives we hold in common while at the same time ensuring to
affiliated organizations maximum freedom of action as to the specific methods
they will use in pursuing those objectives;
Therefore be it resolved that, with this end in view this Convention
(1) Directs that there be established within the Congress a Political Education
Committee, consisting of representatives of affiliated unions and federations, to
formulate programmes of political education; and that the Political Education
Department carry out the programmes as formulated and give all possible assistance to individual affiliates in carrying out programmes of political education
or action;
(2) Urges all affiliated unions and federations (*a*) to take the utmost interest in
political affairs, (*b*) to continue such forms of political action or education as
they may have carried on in the past and (*c*) to undertake such further activities
as may in the future appear to be appropriate for achieving the basic objectives of
the Congress.
2. *Co-operation in the Legislative and Political Field*
Whereas both The Trades and Labor Congress of Canada and The Canadian
Congress of Labour have traditionally taken an active interest in legislative or
political affairs and have been in the vanguard in seeking legislation and other
government policies that will benefit the majority of Canada; and
Whereas there are other organizations that have taken the same broad humani-
tarian approach to political and legislative problems in Canada, including the
great farm organizations which represent the other main body of basic producers
and other free trade unions; and
Whereas these organizations are more likely to be successful in achieving their
basic legislative objectives and political aims if they work together for that purpose;
and
Whereas the unification of Canada's two main labour congresses affords a great
new opportunity for achieving such co-operative action and for examining the
whole political structure within Canada;
Therefore be it resolved that the Political Education Committee under the guidance

Claude Jodoin was elected president of the new Canadian Labour Congress. Donald MacDonald of the CCL was elected secretary treasurer; and Gordon Cushing of the TLC was elected first vice-president.[54] Thus, of the three top officers of the CLC, one (MacDonald) was a CCFer, and one (Cushing) was non-partisan. The balance was held by Jodoin, a non-partisan committed to some sort of co-operation with the CCF. In a CPA report on Jodoin's election, CCFer Morden Lazarus wrote: "Today he is politically independent, suited to the new policies of the CLC. . . . But if the CLC should decide to cast its political lot, Claude Jodoin would not be averse."[55]

5. THE TLC

The agreement of the TLC leadership to leave political policy to the regular conventions of the new congress represented a tacit acceptance of the inevitability of eventual CLC support for the CCF. That CCF strength in the CCL combined with CCF strength in the TLC would be sufficient to swing the merged congress behind the CCF within the next few years was just as clear to the TLC leaders as to the CCL-CCF leaders.

In 1962 Percy Bengough confirmed[56] that the agreement to let political action "find its own level" in the merged congress was in effect an agreement that the congress's political policy would develop towards some kind of partnership with the CCF. According to R. K. Gervin (who left the labour movement before the merger convention) a minority of the TLC executive—himself, Carl Berg, and James Whitebone—opposed the rapid progress towards merger, in part precisely because of its probable political consequences. In a merged congress some sort of alliance with the CCF would be the logical thing to expect. Gervin, Berg, and

---

of the incoming Executive Council, be authorized to initiate discussions with free trade unions not affiliated with the Congress, with the principal farm organizations in Canada, with the co-operative movement, and with the Co-operative Commonwealth Federation or other political parties pledged to support the legislative programme of the Canadian Labour Congress, excluding communist and fascist dominated parties, and to explore and develop co-ordination of action in the legislative and political field."

[54]Executive posts were parcelled out by agreement between the two Congresses before the convention; the convention's task was merely to give formal sanction to the agreement. Of the thirteen regional vice presidents, seven were from the TLC and six from the CCL. Of the former, one was a CCFer (Donovan Swailes), and the remainder were non-partisan.

[55]*UAW-199 Local Union News*, May 1956.

[56]In an interview, Sept. 24, 1962.

Whitebone wanted "solid reassurance" that this would be prevented, but the majority of the executive did not appear to be concerned about the problem.[57]

After agreeing to let political action "find its own level" the TLC leadership made further concessions: they agreed to set up a Political Education Department with a CCF director; they agreed that the Department would assist affiliated organizations which desired to support the CCF; and, most important of all, they agreed that the Congress would discuss with the CCF the establishment of a new "people's political movement." The only concession made by the CCL was its agreement that the merger convention itself would not endorse the CCF— that for the first two years of its life the new Congress would be officially non-partisan. The resolutions adopted by the merger convention represented a "compromise" only for the short run; for the long run, they represented a virtual abandonment of the TLC's traditional non-partisan policy. As was remarked by Stuart Jamieson, "to the extent that the CLC . . . and its affiliated organizations actually do adhere to the resolutions . . . they would have little or no alternative but to support the CCF."[58]

Why did the TLC leaders surrender so easily? Why did they not offer real opposition to the movement for support of the CCF? Why did they not demand "solid reassurance"? The essence of the TLC's political policy was not opposition to the CCF and a preference for other political parties, but a reluctance to engage in any sort of political activity, a belief that trade unions should not get "mixed up" in politics. This is the classical position of weak labour movements composed primarily of craftsmen. It is only when great masses of industrial workers are organized that the labour movement becomes active in politics. In Great Britain, the Labour party was built on the "new unionism"; in the United States and Canada large-scale political action was initiated by the CIO unions. In all three countries, the new, aggressive industrial unions led the way; the old craft unions followed, more or less reluctantly.

Unlike the AFL, the TLC was not opposed to the idea of a labour party. The TLC was in its youth committed to independent labour political action; labour parties were set up under its sponsorship; those parties were among the precursors of the CCF. The leaders of the TLC in the forties and fifties could recall their own involvement in politics

[57]Gervin interview, Oct. 2, 1962. The TLC leadership's tacit acceptance of eventual support for the CCF was also confirmed in interviews with Harry S. Crowe, Jan. 3, 1962; Home, March 28, 1962; Millard, Jan. 9, 1963.
[58]*Industrial Relations in Canada* (Ithaca, 1957), p. 98.

before and after the First World War. Furthermore, the TLC never assumed a rigid ideological position of opposition to socialism. Socialists were active and influential in its independent labour parties. The TLC convention of 1933 which rejected endorsement of the new CCF also declared itself in favour of co-operative ownership of the means of production. The convention of 1943 proposed a program of post-war reconstruction virtually identical with that of the CCF. Professions of faith in "free enterprise" were common in the AFL; they were practically non-existent in the TLC.

The TLC's political policy was not, like that of the AFL, a *positive* policy of support for capitalism *against* socialism. Gompers Canadianized is not an atheist, but an agnostic—not an anti-socialist, but a non-socialist susceptible to socialist influence; not an opponent of labour and socialist parties, but an opponent of *union* involvement in their activities. The AFL's non-partisanship meant no preference for Republicans as against Democrats, or *vice versa*, but preference for *both* as against labour or socialist parties. The TLC's non-partisanship did not mean a preference for Liberals and/or Conservatives against socialists. It meant no preference for anyone; "no politics" *at all*.

There have never been in the TLC any suggestions that labour ought to support the Liberal or Conservative parties; nor has there been any such thing as support of political action combined with opposition to the CCF. Those who were for political action were for the CCF; those who were against the CCF were against political action. TLC leaders like R. K. Gervin, James Whitebone, A. F. MacArthur, who were Liberal or Conservative supporters, did not argue that labour should support one or the other of these parties. They agreed with the genuine non-partisans that labour should stay out of politics, that only by eschewing political activity could labour maintain friendly and co-operative relations with government. They insisted that they themselves supported the old parties only as individuals, not as labour leaders; that they were duty-bound to keep their political sympathies and their work in the labour movement in rigidly separate compartments.

In cultivating friendly relations with government, some TLC leaders naturally became involved in the political party which formed the government. It was difficult to be "friendly" with politicians without also becoming "friendly" to their parties. The party sympathies of such TLC leaders depended upon the party complexion of the governments with which they had to deal. The government of British Columbia was a Liberal-dominated coalition: R. K. Gervin was a Liberal. The governments of Ontario and New Brunswick were Conservative: A. F.

MacArthur and James Whitebone were Conservatives. From their "friends" in the government they got small favours for their unions and patronage appointments for themselves. Most TLC leaders did *not* become involved in political parties. Nevertheless, many of them, because they were "friendly" to a government, were considered to be supporters of the political party which controlled the government. Percy Bengough was believed by many to be a Liberal; but Percy Bengough denies it. He describes himself as a labour leader, pure and simple, without any attachment to any political party. R. K. Gervin confirms that Bengough was not in any sense a Liberal partisan. Rather, Bengough believed in working *with* the government of the day, not against it: "That was the way to make gains for labour; that was always the policy of the TLC."[59] Friendliness with Mackenzie King's government led the TLC to a very cautious and hesitant endorsement of the Liberal party in the federal election of 1945: but this step was taken under exceptional circumstances. It was unprecedented, and it was never repeated.

The TLC leaders can thus be divided into two categories: those who were non-partisan as individuals, and those who were partisan as individuals. Both groups agreed that the labour movement should "work with government, not against it." Both groups agreed that labour leaders could be permitted to involve themselves as individuals in political parties, but that they must make no attempt to tie their unions in any way to any political party. Whatever the politics of labour leaders as individuals, their organizations must be strictly non-partisan. The labour leader would keep his politics out of his union; in return, the union movement would select its leaders without regard to their politics and solely on the basis of their performance as unionists. A labour leader might even be a Communist, so long as he did not permit this to influence his behaviour as a unionist. It was on this basis that Pat Sullivan became second in command of the TLC in 1943; and it was on this basis that Percy Bengough and the majority of the TLC executive resisted the efforts of the AFL and Frank Hall's anti-Communist group within the TLC to expel Sullivan's union (the Canadian Seamen's Union) in 1948 and 1949.

The TLC's non-partisan policy was reinforced by its rivalry first with the ACCL, then with the CCL. TLC antagonism to "dual unions" was transferred to the political party which was supported by dual unions. Furthermore, the association of the CCL with the CCF meant that the TLC, by remaining non-partisan, could secure an advantage over the CCL in the sphere of relations with government. The rivalry between

[59]Gervin interview, Oct. 2, 1962.

the CCL and the TLC hampered political action in *both* Congresses; the CCL leadership were somewhat reluctant to intensify their support of the CCF for fear that in doing so they would give the TLC even more of an advantage over them so far as relations with the government were concerned.

When the CCL and TLC decided to merge, the question of which of the two would have the advantage in relations with government disappeared, for henceforth the two would be one. The relative advantage of the TLC in relations with government ceased to be an incentive for continuation of the TLC's non-partisan policy, and it also ceased to be a disincentive to intensified political action in the CCL. Of course, the merger also meant that antagonism to the CCL could no longer be transferred to the CCF—since the CCL no longer existed.

Another factor which reinforced the TLC's non-partisan policy was the example of the AFL. So long as AFL unions were politically inactive in the United States, it was extremely unlikely that they would become politically active in Canada; the Canadian sections of AFL unions were generally less autonomous than Canadian sections of CIO unions, and less likely to take action which might cause difficulties with the international. Once the AFL began to become more active in American politics on a non-partisan "reward friends and punish enemies" basis, the road was cleared for similar political action in Canada. But the TLC leaders, especially those sympathetic to the old parties, were reluctant to embark on this road. "Non-partisan political education"—the circulation of voting records with the suggestion that workers support "friends of labour"—would lead inevitably to support of the CCF.[60] The TLC leaders talked about "rewarding friends and punishing enemies," but they never took the trouble to point out the friends and the enemies. The TLC under Bengough was authorized in convention to set up an LLPE similar to that of the AFL; but no such organization was set up until after the election of Jodoin to the presidency, for Jodoin, unlike his

[60]In June 1955, the Hotel and Restaurant Employees and Bartenders International Union, Joint Executive Board, issued a Special Ontario Election Issue of its organ, the *Catering Unionist*. An article on the elections declared: "As one of the children of our parent body, the TLC, our . . . union . . . must not support any one individual party. If we allege [*sic*] with any one party, we would be in open conflict with the policy of the TLC. However, it remains our sacred right to try to elect the friends of labor and . . . defeat . . . the enemies of labor. . . . Elsewhere in this issue Bill Kitching of local 254 has written on some of our friends of labor who are aspiring for election. . . . All members are urged to vote for [them] . . . regardless of their political affiliations." The "friends of labor" were all CCF candidates, but the *Catering Unionist* did not identify them as such.

predecessors, regarded with equanimity the prospect that "non-partisan" political education would lead to support of the CCF.

Most TLC leaders did not resist the trend towards support of the CCF in the merged congress because (a) they were not ideologically opposed to socialism or to "class parties": many of them had themselves co-operated with socialists in independent labour parties before and after the First World War. They were in a sense returning to an earlier tradition. (b) There was some real disillusionment with the old parties, coupled with recognition of the fact that the CCF was indeed labour's best friend in politics. (c) The factors arising out of the rivalry of the two Congresses had ceased to play a significant role. (d) The TLC leaders were still of the opinion that political activity would hamper relations with government—but their desire for merger was much stronger than their fear that the merged congress would get into difficulties with government. (e) The TLC leaders saw the growing strength of the CCF in their own movement: the narrow margins by which the OPFL avoided endorsement of the CCF, the increasing CCF strength in the conventions of the TLC, the election of a president who was *at least* not unfriendly to the CCF.[61] The average TLC leader had no strong personal or ideological motives for opposing the CCF; his only vital interests were to preserve the position of his union and his personal power within it. A leader who attempted to organize opposition to the CCF in the merged congress would be endangering his own vital interests

[61]Late in 1958, John Porter conducted a survey of Canada's labour élite—the most important union leaders in the country, two hundred and seventy-five in number. Among the questions he asked was: "Which political party do you normally support?" The responses broke down as follows:

	TLC	CCL	Independent*
CCF	45%	93%	27%
Liberal	12	0	26
Conservative	9	0	16
Other	3	1	6
None	20	1	12
Not given	12	4	22

*UE, Mine Mill, Railway Brotherhoods, Teamsters, etc.

This illustrates clearly enough the overwhelming strength of the CCF in CCL leadership circles and the striking difference, in terms of degree of support for the CCF, between the CCL and the TLC. But it also shows that the CCF was favoured by a very large minority—just under half—of the TLC leaders, and that of the non-CCF majority less than half were Liberals and Conservatives. Moreover, according to Porter, all but one of the Liberals and the Conservatives were from eastern Canada, by which I presume he means Quebec and the Atlantic provinces. See *The Vertical Mosaic* (Toronto, 1965), p. 350.

for no good reason; he would be making enemies of the CCFers in the labour movement and possibly in his own union. The same "don't rock the boat" conservatism which led TLC leaders to oppose labour support for the CCF when the CCF was weak inside the TLC led them to abstain from opposition once the CCF had grown stronger, and especially once the TLC and CCL merged into a single Congress in which CCFers were the majority.

When he was interviewed in 1962 about his attitudes to the CCF and to political action, Percy Bengough was anything but dogmatic. He praised the achievements of the CCF government in Saskatchewan and volunteered the information that he had on some occasions in the past voted for CCF candidates. Political action comes in "cycles," he said, and history had brought it to the forefront once again. He himself had been active in the old Canadian Labour party in the twenties. The decision of the CLC to help found the New Democratic party did not surprise him—he had expected something of that nature to develop out of the merger; it was "coming," it was "in the wind." He did not object to it. In the past, "circumstances" were such as to rule out political action; "maybe circumstances have changed." In any case, this was now the policy of the labour movement, and as a loyal labour man he should go along with it. When he was asked whether the Liberals are better "friends of labour" than the Conservatives, Bengough replied with an unqualified negative and volunteered the information that tight party discipline made it impossible for Canadian labour to imitate the American procedure of rewarding "friends" regardless of party. To the question "what *can* labour do in Canadian politics?" Bengough had no definite answer; but the clear implication of his remarks was that labour should work through a party of its own—*if* such a party could succeed. The old labour parties had not succeeded. The CCF had not succeeded. He had grave doubts that the NDP would succeed—but he was willing to give it a chance.

The few TLC leaders who did *not* make peace with the trend to the CCF—men like Gervin and MacArthur—were not, like Bengough, genuinely non-partisan labour men; they were partisans of the old parties. As such they did have a personal stake in opposition to the CCF. A labour movement tied to the CCF would not have room at the top for old party supporters. R. K. Gervin explained that he left the labour movement because he "saw what was coming." His opposition was of no avail; he must either "go along" or "get out." He got out.[62]

[62]Interview, Oct. 2, 1962.

6. THE CLC 1956–1958

The CCF did not wait for the CLC to set up a political education committee. Fearing that the Congress officers might delay the formation of a committee, the CCF persuaded several key unions to name representatives without waiting for any move from the Congress itself. The CCF also asked a CLC vice-president, CCFer Donovan Swailes, to accept the chairmanship of the committee. Swailes accepted.[63]

In August the CLC Executive Council set up a PEC. It announced that Swailes had been appointed chairman and that the director of the Political Education Department would be Howard Conquergood of Steel, formerly education director for the CCL.[64] The *Toronto Daily Star*[65] interpreted Swailes' appointment as an indication that there would be a "closer alignment of the new CLC to the CCF." The appointment of Swailes and Conquergood was offset to some degree by the assignment of the Political Education Department to non-partisan Gordon Cushing as one of his responsibilities as first vice-president of the Congress. Of the members of the PEC itself, the great majority were CCFers.

The first meeting of the PEC (October 2–3, 1956) formulated a political education program for affiliated unions. In accordance with the policy adopted at the merger convention, the political education program was non-partisan: it involved general discussions of "how legislation is enacted and how governments function," "election issues and related Congress policies," and exhortations to vote "intelligently" for candidates supporting the legislative program of the CLC. Unionists who studied the PEC material could have no doubt whatever that the only "intelligent" vote was a vote for the CCF.

The chief activities of the Department were: (*a*) The publication at the end of each session of the House of Commons of a bulletin entitled *Parliament in Session*, outlining "party votes on all recorded votes of interest to labour." The bulletins emphasized that under the Canadian system of government, parliamentary votes were party votes; policies were made by parties rather than by individual legislators. The bulletins recorded the behaviour of the four parliamentary parties without comment, but no comment was necessary. The great superiority of the CCF in so far as friendliness to labour was concerned was made

[63]Ingle to Swailes, July 5, Swailes to Ingle, July 9, 1956, NDP files.
[64]CLC-PEC Minutes, Aug. 13–14, 1956, CLC-PEC files.
[65]Aug. 25, 1956.

quite clear by the bare record. (*b*) The distribution, in connection with the 1957 federal election, of two pamphlets, one summarizing the CLC's annual brief to the government and the resultant government action or lack of action (mainly the latter); and one entitled *Your Rights and Responsibilities on June 10th*, which set forth the provisions of the Elections Act and urged unionists to exercise their franchise. The CLC Executive Council issued an official election statement urging trade unionists to vote for candidates supporting the legislative program of the CLC, and ending with a covert reference to the CCF's third-party position: "A vote in support of these principles is an indication of support for them. The only vote lost is the one not cast."[66]

The PEC also assigned staff members on request to assist the newly merged Ontario and Saskatchewan federations of labour in their election efforts, the greater part of which were in direct support of the CCF. This was in line with the merger convention's decision that the PEC would encourage political action by affiliates whether or not this action was "non-partisan." The Ontario Federation of Labour, at its merger convention (March 27–29, 1957), had voted to support the CCF. It set up a PAC which gave the same type and degree of support to the CCF as had been given by the CCL's OFL-PAC in previous elections. Half the expenses of the CCF campaign in 1957 were assumed by the new federation's PAC.[67]

The Saskatchewan federation adopted a compromise policy similar to that of the CLC itself. The federation itself did not endorse the CCF; its campaign "was confined to getting out the vote and in a negative sort of way . . . pointing out labour issues and how labor should vote."[68] But the federation also set up a subcommittee of its PEC to co-ordinate and assist the efforts of former CCL affiliates (mainly Office Workers, Packinghouse, and Retail-Wholesale) which desired to support the CCF. None of the other new provincial federations had adopted definite political policies; consequently they did not participate in the 1957 election campaign.

In implementation of the 1956 convention resolution on "co-operation in the legislative and political fields," the PEC developed a program for the improvement of relations between the labour movement and the farm organizations. In the summer of 1956 the PEC co-operated with

[66]*CLC News*, May 1957.
[67]Report on Conduct of 1957 Federal Election, n.d., CLC-PEC files.
[68]Interim Report on Questionnaires Received—Labour's Participation in June 10 Federal Election, n.d., *ibid.*

several labour councils and locals in setting up labour exhibits at sixteen farm fairs in Ontario: "Much ground was gained in breaking down the misunderstanding and suspicions that existed between farmers and labour."[69] The CLC Farm Implement Committee and the Interprovincial Farm Union Council presented a joint brief on the problems of the farm implement industry to the federal government. This was the first occasion on which a labour organization and a farm organization co-operated in an approach to government. A Farmer-Labour Economic Council (later renamed the Farmers-Labour Coordinating Council) was set up, with James Patterson, President of the IPFUC, as chairman and Gordon Cushing as vice-chairman.[70] Cushing and Conquergood attended provincial farm union conventions. Plans were made for a series of conferences between farm, co-operative, and labour leaders to discuss "greater co-operation and understanding," to be held in the fall of 1957.[71]

The rationale of these activities was that there could be no "people's political movement" embracing farm and labour organizations and the CCF until the misunderstanding and lack of co-operation between farm and labour organizations in the economic sphere had been eliminated.[72] The Political Education Program described these activities as "only the initial steps in the long range program envisaged by the second . . . resolution. . . . [It] certainly envisages eventually a new political alignment in Canada. The success of such an undertaking will certainly depend in part upon the extent to which the cooperatives and farm organizations are prepared to participate. A great deal of preliminary work will have to be done."[73]

Early in 1957 the CCF and CLC leaders began a series of secret formal and informal discussions on the future relationship of the CCF to the labour movement. In February Stanley Knowles reported that the Congress officers "have reached the realization that they have got to give the CLC political leadership or pro-CCF action will be taken from the floor at the next CLC convention. The need for a broader base was basic to our discussion. It was all to the good."[74] That there would be little time for leisurely long-range thinking and planning, that the *status quo*

[69]Report of Political Education Department to First General Board Meeting of CLC, *Canadian Labour*, June 1957.
[70]A similar council had been set up on CCL initiative in 1954.
[71]*CLC Political Education Program* (Ottawa: CLC Political Education Department, 1956), p. 20.
[72]Interview with Cushing, Oct. 25, 1962.
[73]*Political Education Program*, p. 19.

on Congress policy could not be maintained much longer, was under-lined at the merger convention of the Ontario Federation of Labour, March 27–29, which adopted a resolution declaring its "full support" for the CCF.

The 1956 convention of the OPFL had again rejected an endorsement resolution by a tie vote. At the 1957 merger convention, there were 432 delegates from OFL unions and 287 from OPFL unions.[75] The com-bined strength of CCFers from both previous federations was therefore overwhelming. The vote on the resolution was not recorded, but a par-ticipant estimated that it was about 600 to 20 with very few absten-tions.[76] Since the OFL comprised about half the total membership of the CLC, its decision to support the CCF was of major significance, both in itself and as a guide for the CLC. The OFL's decision to support the CCF did not represent a rejection of the idea of a new movement including the CCF, labour organizations, and farm organizations. Exactly what *shape* the new movement would take and *when* it would be established; whether it would be a reformed CCF or a new federation; whether or not it would retain the name of the CCF—none of these things had been decided. But on one matter there was a high degree of agreement among CCF trade unionists: the structure of the party must be changed to allow for a massive affiliated union wing like that of the British Labour party.[77]

In October the second convention of the BCFL resolved by a five to one vote that "the CCF warrants the support of the workers in British

[74]Knowles to MacInnis, Feb. 9, 1957, Knowles' files.

[75]Armstrong, "The Development of Trade Union Political Activity in the CCF."

[76]Bryden to Thayer, Aug. 9, 1957, BC NDP files. The resolution declared "full support" rather than endorsement of the CCF because, in Bryden's words, "full support was less objectionable to some of the old AFL boys than 'endorsation,' since it apparently let them feel that they weren't having the old CCL policy rammed down their throats holus bolus. Moreover, it avoided a direct association with what some people regarded as the past failures of PAC in the CCL. . . . It caused some trouble among some of the rabid CCF supporters. . . . However we persuaded them that 'full support' is actually stronger than 'endorsation' since it implies that labour is not merely giving the CCF its blessing but plans to do some-thing about it."

[77]After the Ontario merger convention, the secretary treasurer of the OFL, Douglas Hamilton, canvassed the secretaries of the socialist parties of Britain, New Zealand, and nine European countries for information on their relationships with labour. He explained that the "whole future of the CLC and the CCF [is] a subject of great discussion." (Hamilton to Morgan Phillips, July 29, 1957, OFL-PEC files.) "We are concerned that we should . . . develop a relationship with the trade unions which is much more organic and effective than simple endorsation." Hamilton to Otto Probst, Austria, Sept. 16, 1957, *ibid.*

Columbia."[78] The BCFL's merger convention (November 15–18, 1956) had adopted an interim policy modelled on that of the CLC. The executive was instructed to establish "an effective political education program" which would not interfere with the existing policies of its affiliates, and also to set up a "broad committee" which would consult with farm and co-operative organizations and the CCF and report to the next convention, giving definite proposals for a permanent political action program.[79]

The BCFL merger convention did not directly support the CCF not only because of the necessity to placate TLC unionists, but because of a strong sentiment among some unionists for the formation of an independent labour party.[80] This independent labourism was a relic of the period during which the CCL in British Columbia had been Communist-dominated. In Ontario the CCL and the CCF had developed an extremely close relationship since the entry of the CIO in 1937. In British Columbia the process of informal integration began only with the overthrow of the Communist leadership in 1948–49. The development of close relations was, moreover, impeded by the presence in the British Columbia CCF of a significant left-wing minority which feared the unionists as "non-socialists." By 1956 the British Columbia labour movement and the CCF were closer than ever before, but there were still tensions, misunderstandings, and ideological differences which did not exist in Ontario; consequently, there was in British Columbia no extremely close and harmonious consultative relationship such as that which existed in Ontario; and the current of independent labourism which had appeared some years before had not yet run dry. There were still prominent unionists who felt that the CCF was not sufficiently hospitable to labour and that labour should therefore form a party of its own. This feeling was similar to that of many loyal CCF trade unionists that the party should give unions as such a greater share of power. It differed from the feeling of CCFers in that it was more intense and, of course, it envisaged the formation of an independent party of labour, which would "deal" as an equal with the CCF.

In March 1957 the BCFL executive set up the "broad committee" called for in the resolution of 1956. The committee invited the provincial CCF, Farmers' Union, and Co-operative Union to discuss the matter. The CCF accepted the invitation. The other two organizations declined on the ground that they were non-partisan. The special committee's

78*Vancouver News-Herald*, Oct. 30, 1957.
79PAC Report to the Second BCFL Convention, n.d., BCFL files.
80Thayer to Ingle, March 25, 1957, BC NDP files.

report to the BCFL's 1957 convention rejected the idea of independent labour political action. It recommended that consultations with the CCF and other organizations continue with a view to the "ultimate development in Canada of a . . . political organization similar . . . to the British Labour party, to enable an expanded basis of participation and representation," and that in the meantime labour support the CCF. The resolution adopted by the convention was in line with these recommendations: it declared "that the CCF warrants the support of the workers in B.C.," and instructed the PEC "to continue . . . to bring together representatives of . . . groups pledged to support the program of the BCFL." The merged British Columbia labour movement—in importance to the CCF second only to that of Ontario—thus joined with the Ontario movement in declaring its support of the CCF.

Top-level discussions within and between the national CCF and the CLC continued from January 1957 to February 1958. The meetings were not frequent, and progress was slow. The discussions were restricted to a few key figures in both organizations; outside of those directly involved, no one in the CCF or the CLC knew what was going on. Most CCFers expected that the 1958 convention of the CLC would endorse the CCF, and perhaps in addition recommend that discussions on future relations between labour and the party continue. On October 24 Donovan Swailes reported[81] that there was "practically unanimous agreement" in the CLC executive council that the CCF should be transformed into a party with a large affiliated union wing, that there should be room in the structure for farm and professional organizations, and that its relationship with the CLC should be similar to the relationship between the British Labour party and the TUC. At its meeting of February 26–28, 1958, the CLC executive council decided to prepare a resolution for submission to the next convention (April) instructing the executive to "establish a consultative committee with the CCF for the purpose of developing an effective political instrument patterned along the lines of the British Labour Party."[82]

In the election of March 31, 1958, the CCF suffered an electoral catastrophe. Its representation in parliament was reduced from twenty-five to eight; among the defeated candidates were the chief parliamentary leaders, including M. J. Coldwell and Stanley Knowles. Immediately after the election the CLC executive offered Knowles a nomination as CLC executive vice-president at the forthcoming convention; Knowles accepted.

[81]To Lewis, Hamilton, and Knowles, Oct. 25, 1957, NDP files.
[82]*Canadian Labour*, April 1958.

The CLC convention of April 21–25 adopted a resolution[83] calling for the establishment of a new "broadly based political movement which embraces the CCF, the labour movement, farm organizations, professional people and other liberally minded people." If not for the election defeat, the turn of events might have been different. According to Stanley Knowles, if the CCF had not suffered such a severe setback—if it had elected twenty or so members—the convention would not have called for a new party. It would have simply endorsed the CCF. Eamon Park and Joe Morris, however, insist that a resolution substantially the same as that adopted by the convention had been prepared before the election, and would have been introduced regardless of the election results. Park concedes that if the CCF had done very well in the elections—if it had elected forty or forty-five members—the decision to present the new party resolution might have been reconsidered.[84]

[83]"This Convention believes that the imperative need of the Canadian political scene today is the creation of an effective alternative political force based on the needs of workers, farmers and similar groups, financed and controlled by the people and their organizations.

"During the past quarter century the CCF has made a tremendous contribution to the welfare of the Canadian people, both in and out of Parliament. The organized Labour Movement fully recognizes that contribution and knows that, with its limited facilities, it continues to battle for the ideas of social justice, security and freedom, which are also the goals of this Congress.

"The time has come for a fundamental re-alignment of political forces in Canada. There is the need for a broadly based people's political movement, which embraces the CCF, the Labour Movement, farm organizations, professional people and other liberally-minded persons interested in basic social reform and reconstruction through our parliamentary system of government. Such a broadly based political instrument should provide that Labour and other peoples' organizations may, together with the CCF, participate directly in the establishment of such a movement, its organizational structure and basic philosophy and program, as well as in its financing and choice of candidates for public office.

"The experience of Labour and social democratic political parties elsewhere should be studied for whatever their history and structure might contribute, while recognizing that any effective political instrument in Canada must be Canadian in character and structure.

"In participating in and initiating the creation of a new political movement, Labour emphasizes that not only is there no wish to dominate such a development, but there is the fullest desire for the broadest possible participation of all individuals and groups genuinely interested in basic democratic social reform and the democratic planning necessary to such reform.

"This Convention, therefore, instructs the Executive Council to give urgent and immediate attention to this matter by initiating discussions with the CCF, interested farm organizations and other like-minded individuals and groups, to formulate a constitution and a program for such a political instrument of the Canadian people; and to report on such a plan, draft constitution and program to the next Convention of this Congress for action."
CLC Convention Proceedings (1958), p. 49.

[84]Interviews with Knowles, March 27, 1962, Park, Jan. 14, 1963, and Morris, March 20, 1963.

There is some evidence that, after the merger and especially after the election of June 10, 1957, the CCF leaders had become less enthusiastic about the idea of a new party, or, more precisely, they tended more and more to think in terms of what might be called the minimum program—retention of the CCF, with constitutional changes to facilitate large-scale affiliation of trade unions—as opposed to the maximum program—the construction of a new party by the CCF, labour, and other interested groups. This attitude may have been shared by those CCF trade unionists who had not been enthusiastic about the new party idea when it was first brought forward during the merger negotiations. It appears that at least some of the few CCF leaders who were involved in the discussions with the CLC before the 1958 elections were arguing that the 1958 CLC convention should follow the example of the OFL and BCFL by adopting a resolution of support for the CCF.

This approach was encouraged by the successes of the CCF in the election of 1957: the CCF elected twenty-five members—the largest group since 1945—and held the balance of power in the House. A few months after the election Stanley Knowles was arguing that the Conservative resurgence meant that

the Liberals are on the way out and the CCF can become Canada's second party. . . . We can and must sell the idea that we can replace the Liberals, especially with Labour, Farm and Co-op backing. I'd say the arguments for a new vehicle are less strong now than they were when the CLC was formed. It takes a long time to get a party to the place where it gets 10–11% of the popular vote. . . . Let [labour] ask us to make changes in our constitution if they wish—to approach the British pattern—but let's urge with all we've got that the new situation presents a realistic and valid opportunity to back the CCF and win.[85]

After the 1958 election, all but those directly involved in the CCF-CLC discussions expected that the CLC convention would endorse the CCF. The new party resolution came as a complete surprise to the vast majority of convention delegates. Among those who were surprised were such important officials as Douglas Hamilton (secretary treasurer of the OFL), who criticized the resolution on the floor of the convention. He and other delegates expressed resentment that the CCF was being dispensed with, and fear that its achievements would be lost while the new party was being established. Knowles had to assure the objecters that the resolution was not, as one of them had put it, "the beginning of the end of the CCF" but "a real beginning for the achieving of the things the CCF has fought for."[86] William Mahoney had to remind them that

[85]Knowles to Thayer, Aug. 18, 1957, BC NDP files.
[86]CLC Convention Proceedings (1958), p. 51.

the resolution was the product of the discussions with the CCF that had been called for by the 1956 resolution.

It is clear that the *final, definite* decision to proceed with the new party resolution was not made until after the election. It is also clear that the CCF leadership was at least not unanimously in favour of a new party resolution until the election defeat in March. The election defeat had the effect of removing all doubt in the minds of men like Knowles that what was needed was a new party now. Their hopes that Liberal decline meant CCF resurgence were shattered. Knowles told the convention that the CCF could choose one or the other of two futures: "It can go ahead as it is at present organized . . . making progress but making it slowly. Or it can become part of a much larger group such as is envisaged in this resolution, and instead of being a small party on the opposition side, it can look forward to being part of the movement that formed the first people's government of this country."

For the future, the most important result of the 1958 election was the weakening of the resistance of rank and file CCFers to changes in the structure of their movement. If the CCF had held its own in 1958, and if the CLC convention had called for a new party, the negative reaction of CCFers between 1958 and 1960—"Why a new party? Why not support the CCF as you never supported it before?"—would have been much stronger and much more widespread.

The 1958 convention expanded the executive committee from three to eight members; instead of a president, a secretary treasurer, and an executive vice-president, there were a president, a secretary-treasurer, two executive vice-presidents, and four general vice-presidents. Jodoin and MacDonald were re-elected. Cushing retired to become Assistant Deputy Minister of Labour and was replaced by Stanley Knowles and William Dodge, both veteran CCFers. The new posts of general vice-president were filled by George Burt of the UAW, William Mahoney of Steel, Frank Hall of the Brotherhood of Railway Clerks, and William Jenoves of the Bricklayers.[87]

The election of Knowles was especially significant. He was not a labour leader, but a CCF politician who had retained his membership in the ITU. There could be no more emphatic demonstration that the CLC's formal non-partisanship was a thing of the past and that the CLC and the CCF had now entered into a very close partnership. Knowles' election also meant that there would be a full-time officer of the CLC who would

[87]Hall and Jenoves had both been TLC non-partisans. Hall had been a Liberal and Jenoves a Conservative sympathizer. Both supported the 1956 and 1958 resolutions.

devote the great bulk of his time and energy to the implementation of the new party resolution.

There was no non-partisan opposition to the new party resolution at the 1958 convention. Since the 1956 convention, all TLC members of the CLC executive council had been persuaded either to support the political action policy which would be presented to the 1958 convention or at least not to oppose it. Thus, the potential leadership of a non-partisan opposition group was neutralized from the beginning. The only organized force on the political issue within the labour movement were the CCFers.

In view of Gordon Cushing's background, he might have been expected to oppose the developments of 1956 to 1958. The coincidence of his retirement at the same convention which passed the new party resolution and elected Knowles to the Congress executive gave rise to a widespread belief within the labour movement that Cushing had opposed a closer relationship with the CCF, and that his retirement was connected with his failure to prevent it. But interviews with Cushing, Knowles, MacDonald, Lewis, and Millard led to the conclusion that this assessment of Cushing's role is incorrect. Cushing's retirement to take the post of Assistant Deputy Minister of Labour—a post, incidentally, which was previously held by M. M. Maclean of the CCL— had been planned even before the defeat of the Liberal government in 1957. It had nothing to do with any difference of opinion on political policy between Cushing and the other executive officers. A difference of opinion did exist, but it was not significant enough to lead to a rupture. Cushing had not opposed the resolution of 1956. Like most other TLC leaders, he had accepted the fact that there would be discussions with the CCF leading to co-operation in the political field, and he had recognized that in a merged congress, the influence of the CCF supporters would be decisive: some kind of alliance at some time in the future was inevitable. Like other TLC leaders, he had since 1954 been nudged by the moderate Fabian strategy of the CCF into a virtual surrender, by easy, almost imperceptible stages, of his previous non-partisan position. As executive vice-president of the CLC and as the officer in charge of the political education department, he did not oppose the decision to seek a relationship with the CCF similar to that of British unions with the Labour party. As a Congress officer he participated in the formal discussions which led to that decision. One of his tasks as fraternal delegate to the TUC in 1957 was to study the relationship between British unionism and the Labour party.

Though he accepted and supported the developing political policy, Cushing was not a party to the *informal* discussions between CCF and

CLC leaders, including Jodoin, in which that policy was worked out. The policy was developed and initiated by others; Cushing accepted it in its successive stages. Knowles suggests that, although he "went along," "his heart wasn't really in it"; David Lewis suggests that his support of the new political policy was essentially "cerebral," a surface phenomenon, and that in his basic attitudes he remained a conservative, non-partisan craft unionist. All who were interviewed on the subject, including Cushing himself, agreed that though he accepted the idea of a partnership with the CCF he was much more gradualistic about it than the other key figures, more cautious, more inclined to consider it an ultimate rather than an immediate goal. Since this was Cushing's position, no rapid progress towards the achievement of the goal could be made while he was an officer of the Congress; he played a restraining role, he "held things back."

Whether or not Cushing spoke out against the decision to proceed with the new party resolution at the 1958 convention (he did not oppose it at the convention itself), there is little doubt that personally he did not agree with it. Cushing outlined his position in an interview: a successful CCF-farm-labour party could not be built until the basic prerequisites had been satisfied. These prerequisites were, first, the education of the masses of rank and file trade unionists to political interest and political activity; second, the establishment of a close co-operative relationship between labour and the farm organizations. These were the aims embodied in the political education program of the CLC from 1956 to 1958. They had not been achieved by 1958. The time for a new party had not come. Cushing was also opposed to the involvement of the CLC *itself* in partisan politics. If the relationship of the CLC to the new party was to be like that of the TUC to the Labour party, only affiliated unions would be involved in politics; the CLC, since it was the instrument of partisan and non-partisan unions and since its primary task was to represent labour to the government, would remain strictly separate, in personnel and in function, from the party. The two errors which were committed by the Congress were its excessively rapid advance towards a new party before the appropriate groundwork had been laid in political education and close relations with the farmers, and its involvement *as a Congress* in an inappropriately close relationship with the CCF. Both errors were associated with the election of Knowles to the Congress executive. This identified the Congress too closely with the party. After it, everything moved too quickly.

The CLC executive council decision of February 1958—that a consultative committee with the CCF would be set up to discuss the establishment of a party like the British Labour party—may have been acceptable to Cushing, since it did not require that the party be established *immediately*. The discussions could go on for a long time. After the election defeat in March and Knowles' acceptance of a CLC post, things moved too quickly for Cushing. It was definitely decided to proceed *immediately* to the actual construction of a new party; Knowles was in the Congress for that purpose; that he was in the Congress identified it too closely with the party. If Cushing had remained in the Congress, he might have gone along with these developments as he had gone along with previous developments. It was his retirement which made it possible to discover something about the quality of the support which is given to partisan political activity by a not unrepresentative "convert" from the camp of the non-partisans. They go along, they do not fight; but things move too quickly for them; they "hold things back."

6.   *The New Party*

1. INTRODUCTION

Immediately following the 1958 CLC convention, the CLC and CCF executives set up a "Joint Political Committee," with ten representatives from each organization, to implement the new party resolution. Stanley Knowles served as chairman, and Carl Hamilton, CCF national secretary, was named vice-chairman and secretary.

In July the national convention of the CCF hailed the new party resolution[1] as a "landmark in our country's history," authorized the executive to continue its discussions with the CLC, and instructed it to report the results of the discussions to the next convention. The Joint Committee, which renamed itself the National Committee for the New Party (NCNP), instituted a series of seminars, conferences, and forums throughout Canada, at which CCFers, unionists, and interested farmers and "liberally minded" persons were brought together to discuss a possible constitution and program for the new party. Similar discussions were held independently at all levels of the CCF and the labour movement.

[1]This following is the complete text of the resolution:

"This National Convention of the CCF reaffirms its belief that the future welfare of Canada and its people lies in the further development and early victory of a broadly-based people's political movement. As democratic socialists, we believe that such a movement must continue to be dedicated to the principles of democratic social planning and to the widest forms of social security and individual liberty. It must remain steadfast in its determination to introduce, where appropriate, public control and public ownership in place of the present monopolistic domination of our economy, and indeed, our whole society, by large private corporations.

"Such a movement must dedicate itself to the task of democratically rebuilding our society so that co-operation will replace greed, constructive development will replace exploitation of man by man and unity of farmer and worker, east and west, French-speaking and English-speaking, will replace disunity and deliberately contrived conflict. Its aims must be to build our society on moral foundations of social justice and human dignity.

"For these reasons this Convention welcomes the resolution adopted by the Canadian Labour Congress at its Convention in Winnipeg in April of this year, looking to the building of such a political movement together with the CCF and farm organizations, groups and individuals ready to join in common objectives.

In January 1960 the NCNP, having studied the results of the discussions, issued "study papers" outlining a proposed constitution and program; these "study papers" were to serve as "guides for discussion" during a second stage of conferences and seminars which would culminate with the formulation by the NCNP of final drafts of the constitution and program for presentation to the founding convention of the new party at Ottawa on July 31–August 4, 1961. The founding convention would consist of delegates from the CCF, union locals, and "new party clubs." The purpose of this long gestation period was not only to permit thorough rank and file consideration of the details of program and structure, but to arouse interest, support, and if possible enthusiasm for the new party idea among the CCF and union rank and file and in the general public. Another consideration may have been the desire of the CCF-CLC leadership to postpone the founding convention until Premier Douglas became available for the leadership of the new party.[2]

In April and August 1960, the CLC and CCF executives reported to their respective national conventions. Both conventions, by nearly unanimous votes, adopted resolutions finally committing the CLC and the CCF to participation in the establishment of a new party.

The CLC's new party resolution had invited "farm organizations, professional people, and other liberally-minded persons" to participate

---

At its merger convention in 1956, the Canadian Labour Congress adopted a political program which the CCF convention, held some months later, was able wholeheartedly to endorse, thus establishing once again the identity of the CCF program with the social objectives of labour in the same way as CCF policies have always been identical with those of farmers as well as other groups in our society. Indeed, since its inception the CCF has always appealed to organized labour and to organized agriculture to join in building a people's political movement, strong and representative of all sections of the Canadian people. The CLC resolution is thus a landmark in our country's history and presents a greater opportunity for progress in this direction than ever before.

"This Convention, therefore, authorizes the National Council and National Executive to enter into discussions with the Canadian Labour Congress, the Canadian and Catholic Confederation of Labour, interested farm organizations and other like-minded groups and individuals looking toward the achievement of the objectives set out and to present the results of such discussions to the next regular or to a special convention of the CCF for action. Further the Convention authorizes the National Council and Executive to initiate and conduct the fullest discussion on this matter within the party, and instructs that any draft Constitution for such proposed broader political party be submitted to the CCF members, through their clubs and associations, for study and recommendation, before being submitted to the Convention and that any other propositions concerning the above, which are to be put before such Convention, shall be circulated to CCF clubs and associations at least two months prior to the Convention."

[2]M. J. Coldwell had resigned as leader of the CCF after the election of 1958.

in the establishment of the new party. Approaches were made to the farm unions in Alberta, Saskatchewan, and Manitoba. All three responded with convention resolutions reaffirming their non-partisan policies.[3] Any other reaction would have been a great surprise; the decisions of the prairie farm union conventions merely "confirmed our previous fears that it would not be possible to get organized farm support."[4] The Canadian Federation of Agriculture and the eastern farm unions were not even approached, for "we knew in advance that their answer would be 'no' and therefore we thought it better not to risk the publicity which they might give to a negative answer."[5] The Ontario Farmers' Union was requested to make suggestions on agricultural policy to the NCNP, but refused to involve itself even to that extent in the affairs of the new party. The OFU's Gordon Hill explained[6] that "our executive members individually are quite sympathetic . . . but fear that any action taken by our organization would be interpreted by some farmers as endorsing the new party. . . . We must exercise extreme caution lest we provoke an unfavorable attitude in these individuals."

As matters stood, Canadian farmers would be represented at the new party's founding convention only indirectly, through CCF constituency associations composed of farmers; farm organizations as such would be unrepresented. Furthermore, since the great bulk of farmer members of the CCF were in Saskatchewan, farmers in other provinces would not even be indirectly represented. The NCNP was therefore inclined to continue its efforts to secure direct, formal representation of farmers by "soliciting individual farm local affiliations and . . . building up . . . an independent national farmers' political association."[7] However, by late 1959 these plans were abandoned in favour of the "new party club" project. Through new party clubs, individuals not members of the CCF or of the CLC could participate in the discussions of program and constitution and in the founding convention. Farmers outside of Saskatchewan were urged to set up such clubs.

Three important provincial elections took place while the preparations for the founding of the new party were going on. In one of them, the CCF government of Saskatchewan was returned to power (1960). In the other two elections, the Ontario and British Columbia federations of labour became more closely involved with the CCF than ever before.

[3]*Globe and Mail*, Dec. 16, 1958.
[4]NCNP Minutes, Report of Farm Subcommittee, Jan. 23, 1959, NDP files.
[5]Carl Hamilton to G. R. Fawcett, March 11, 1960, *ibid.*
[6]In a letter to Hamilton, Dec. 23, 1959, *ibid.*
[7]NCNP Minutes, Report of Farm Subcommittee, Jan. 23, 1959, *ibid.*

In the Ontario election of 1959, the OFL and the CCF pooled their resources and conducted a single integrated campaign supervised by a joint campaign committee. The chairman was Henry Weisbach, who was at the time an official of both the CLC and the Ontario CCF.[8] The CCF representatives on the joint committee also acted as a CCF committee to deal with purely CCF matters such as the endorsement of candidates. All money raised for the campaign was pooled in a single fund from which disbursements were made by the joint committee. The total spent was about $35,500. About $10,000 of this was provided by the Ontario CCF, and about $10,500 by the OFL-PAC. The remaining $15,000 was contributed through the CLC-CCF Joint Political Committee by several major unions. OFL and CLC officials were active in the campaign.[9]

At the end of 1959, twenty-two local unions with a membership of 19,594 were affiliated with the Ontario CCF. An additional sixty-six locals (fifty-nine of them in Steel) with a membership of 28,487 were paying per capita dues to the OFL-PAC and were thus "indirectly affiliated" with the CCF.[10] These eighty-eight locals which were directly or indirectly affiliated served as the base of the affiliated union wing which the NDP has been building in Ontario.[11]

In the British Columbia election of 1960 an unprecedented but remarkably close and efficient linkage of the CCF and BCFL organizations brought about significant gains for the CCF. The labour forces were spurred to energetic participation by the restrictive labour legislation which was being enacted by W. A. C. Bennett's Social Credit government.[12] The CCF vote rose from 28 to 35 per cent and the representation in the legislature from ten to sixteen. Twelve of the elected candidates were trade unionists. Nine seats were lost by less than 350 votes apiece.

The CCF campaign was conducted by a CCF-BCFL Joint Liaison Committee which had been set up early in 1958 to fulfil two functions: to work with the CLC-CCF Joint Political Committee to promote discussions of the new party in British Columbia and to bring about an interim "working partnership" for the purpose of fighting the provincial

[8]He was chairman of the Ontario CCF executive and CLC education director for Ontario.
[9]Report on Conduct of 1959 Provincial Election Campaign in Ontario, Aug. 6, 1959, OFL-PEC files.
[10]OFL-PEC Minutes, Nov. 1, 1959, OFL-PEC files.
[11]See below, p. 259.
[12]In 1952 Social Credit replaced the defunct coalition as the government and chief "obstacle to socialism" in British Columbia.

election. Financial resources were not pooled, but on the provincial and constituency levels there was tight co-ordination of CCF and labour efforts. The unions created "Constituency Associations of Labour" consisting of all interested unionists residing within a single constituency. Co-ordination with the CCF was thus greatly facilitated, since the CCF constituency associations could co-operate with bodies representing the unionists resident in the constituency rather than with local unions whose membership was scattered through several constituencies. Labour-CCF constituency conferences discussed candidates and local campaign plans. The recommendations of these conferences were then placed before regular CCF nominating conventions. The local campaigns themselves were co-ordinated efforts of the CCF and labour constituency associations, supervised by campaign committees representative of both groups.[13]

The close relationship between labour and the CCF which was achieved for the 1960 election was carried over into the British Columbia NDP.[14] Of the nineteen New Democrats elected to the House of Commons in June 1962, ten were from British Columbia.

2. THE RATIONALE OF THE NEW PARTY

The transformation of the CCF into the New Democratic party was an attempt both to strengthen the labour base of the party and to broaden its appeal to the "liberally minded" elements of the middle class. That achievement of the first of these goals might be an obstacle to achievement of the second—that a party even more closely identified with labour than the old CCF might be even less attractive to the middle class than the CCF—was not admitted by the creators of the new party. Their objective was to achieve both goals simultaneously; to create a party as closely identified with labour as the British Labour party, and at the same time to prevent it from becoming a purely labour party. The new party was to be a party of labour, of farmers, of the middle class; a great "people's movement" of the "democratic left," embracing all "liberally minded" people; a party with so broad an appeal that it would quickly displace the Liberals as official opposition. The CLC's new party resolution emphasized that labour had no desire

[13]Provincial Liaison Committee Memorandum, Dec. 6, 1958; Memo on PAC for Unions of the BCFL, April 1959; Interim Report of Provincial Liaison Committee, March 30, 1959, all in BCFL files.

[14]The offices of the BCFL and the British Columbia NDP are now in the same building.

to "dominate" the new party it was helping to create: "There is the fullest desire for the broadest possible participation of all individuals and groups genuinely interested in basic democratic social reform." The new party was not to be a labour party but "a political instrument of the Canadian people."

The leaders of the CCF had realized since its formation that eventually there would have to be a large affiliated union wing. No socialist party anywhere in the Western world could succeed without the financial and organizational support of the trade unions. The CCF was no exception. Since the Second World War the dependence of the CCF on the unions —for money, for party workers, for candidates, and for votes—had been growing steadily. The logical next step was to fulfil the original intention of the founders by bringing into being a massive affiliated-union section through which labour could participate directly in the affairs of the party, and which would provide the party with a stable and growing financial base. The CCF could not continue indefinitely to ask for more and more support from the unions and at the same time to preserve the almost exclusive control of the individual membership within the party. Throughout the forties and fifties there was dissatis-faction among CCF trade unionists with the role assigned to trade unions as such within the party. There was the feeling that the CCF wanted labour support, but not labour participation. By the time of the merger of the CCL and TLC, CCF trade unionists generally saw the party as "a political entity apart from the unions which . . . supports labour's legislative objectives."[15] It was this feeling which led to the demands for a political movement similar to the British Labour Party— a movement which would embrace within itself both the CCF and the trade unions. Such a movement need not necessarily be a completely new party superseding the CCF; it might be created through amendment of the CCF constitution in order to facilitate large-scale affiliation, and perhaps also through a change in the name of the party. As late as September 1957, many of those involved in the CCF-CLC discussions were thinking in these terms. The final decision, however, was that a reformed CCF would not be enough. There must be a completely new party. The CCF would not merely amend its constitution; it would participate with labour and other groups in the formulation of a new constitution for a new party, and would then itself go out of existence. The election defeat of March 1958 may have played no small part in this decision.

Why a *new* party? Why *not* a reformed CCF? The reasons which

[15]Swailes to Hamilton, Sept. 21, 1957, NDP files.

were given by the proponents of the new party can be summed up in the one word "image." The established image of the CCF among trade unionists, especially among TLC unionists who were not tied to it in any way, was that of a party friendly to labour, not a party in which labour as such played a direct part. As one delegate to a TLC convention put it, the CCF, "while they are well-meaning, cannot truly speak for labor. . . . You can't expect school-teachers, lawyers, doctors, or hardware merchants to speak for labor."[16] There were in the TLC and in the British Columbia CCF recurrent demands for an independent labour party. The CCF might change its constitution and welcome trade union affiliations; but this in itself would not be sufficient because it would not change the established image of the party as a party not closely enough identified with labour. What was needed was a *new* party—a party not burdened with the image of the old CCF—a party in the *formation* of which labour unions as such would play a direct and significant role.

The CCF was handicapped in its appeal to TLC unionists not only by the absence of formal union participation in its councils but by its very close informal association with the old CCL. TLC unionists were quite capable of describing the CCF at one moment as a party of doctors, lawyers, and hardware merchants, and at the next moment as the party of the rival CCL. The formation of a new party would smash both images simultaneously: the new party would suffer from neither the non-labour nor the CCL flavour of the old CCF.

Another element of the CCF image which restricted its appeal to unionists was its "doctrinaire socialism." The CCF might moderate its socialism, as it did throughout the forties and fifties; it might renounce the Regina Manifesto, as it did in 1956; but the image of "stale, doctrinaire socialism," an image repellent not only to non-CCFers within the labour movement but to many loyal CCF unionists, would remain. To reconstruct the CCF was therefore not enough: the substitution of a *new* party with a new, modern, moderate image would evoke the support of unionists who had not supported the CCF because they associated it with doctrinaire socialism and the depression. The very fact of "newness" would enable the new party to break through the electoral barrier which was, for the CCF, insuperable. "New Party—New Ideas—New People —New Democracy—Take Your Part—Make History in 1961—Support the New Party."

Although the decision to affiliate unions to a *new* party rather than a

[16]TLC Convention Proceedings (1955), pp. 207–8.

reformed CCF can be accounted for by the desire to increase the party's appeal to labour, the primary consideration appears to have been the desire to "broaden the base" of the party in the general public, to make an effective appeal to the masses of the white collar workers and the middle class. The CCF appeal to these segments of the population had failed for much the same reason that its appeal to the majority of workers had failed. If a new party was necessary to increase the labour vote, the same applied *a fortiori* to the middle-class vote. According to the OFL-PAC, the new party was "a means of making a broad appeal to people both in and out of organized labour who have shied away from the CCF"; in order to do this, it must abandon the fetish made of the word 'socialism.' "[17] Donald Macdonald declared: "If the founding convention of the new party brings together little more than the CCF and the politically active sections of the trade union movement, then it will not fulfill the vision which inspired the historic resolutions of 1958."[18] Carl Hamilton insisted that the new party "must be not just a labour party, not just a revamped CCF, but must have as broad a base as it is possible for us to develop."[19]

The NCNP reported that the majority of participants in the first stage of conferences and seminars agreed that the new party should abandon the "CCF" label and choose a name that would have "broad appeal." The three most favoured names were "Social Democratic," "Democratic Socialist," and "Democratic"; but many participants thought that terms like "labour," "progressive," "farmer," "socialist," and "social" should be avoided, so as not to frighten away groups to which such terms do not apply.[20] By the time of the founding convention, the name "New Party" was most favoured; but the convention itself adopted the name "New Democratic party."

Together with the emphasis on the broad base went an emphasis on the modern, pragmatic image which must be created in place of the "old-fashioned, stale, doctrinaire" image of the CCF. Premier Douglas emphasized that "it is not the problems of the thirties but those of the sixties that concern us. . . . We cannot unlock the future with the blood-rusted key of the nineteen thirties. . . . We must adjust our approach to deal with the problems of today." Capitalism, though partly reformed, is not by any means perfect; glaring inequality and social injustice still

[17]*OFL-PAC Political Education Handbook Number 1*, n.d., "New Party Problems," p. 3.

[18]*New Party Newsletter*, Jan. 1960.

[19]*Saskatchewan Commonwealth*, Aug. 17, 1960.

[20]Report on Seminars, Schools, and Forums of the New Party, n.d., NDP files.

exist. "Some form of democratic socialism" is still "the world's best hope." The new party will therefore not abandon the goals of democratic socialism, but it will be prepared to revise traditional socialist "techniques." The new party must not make a "fetish" of the past and worship old, outmoded techniques (public ownership) but look to the future, and be prepared to adopt new means ("planning") to the never-changing end of the good society, the co-operative commonwealth.[21]

The NCNP's discussion of "the type of image we want to project to the public" resulted in agreement that

the basic theme should be that the New party is NEW. . . . We will not convince many people that the party is really new if we continue to use the old . . . jargon which is meaningful to us but means very little to most people and often raises vague fears and doubts in their minds. . . . A few examples: "people's movement" or "people's party," . . . "socialism." People who use this word freely are by no means agreed as to its meaning and most others have been conditioned to respond to it unfavourably. The ideas we espouse are far more important than the word used to describe them, so why not concentrate on the ideas?[22]

Neither the constitution nor the program adopted by the New Democratic party at its founding convention made any mention of the terms "socialism" or "social democracy." But one of the first official acts of the party was to apply for membership in the Socialist International.[23] It is quite clear that it was the aura, the image, the reputation of the CCF that was being abandoned, rather than basic principles and programs. Except for the avoidance of the *word*, the NDP program was no less "socialist" than the CCF's Winnipeg Declaration of 1956. It took almost exactly the same position on public ownership. The Winnipeg Declaration favoured increases in public ownership to the extent necessary to prevent monopoly control of the economy and to facilitate economic planning. The NDP program called for expansion of "public and cooperative ownership for such purposes as the operation of utilities, the development of resources, the elimination of monopoly concentrations of power, and the operation of major enterprises immediately and directly affecting the entire nation."[24] The small leftist opposition within the CCF, and the old party politicians and newspapers, made much of the new party's alleged "watering-down" of the

[21]Address of T. C. Douglas to the second national seminar of the new party, Montreal, Dec. 3, 1960.
[22]NCNP Minutes, Report of Subcommittee on Promotion and Public Relations, Jan. 27–28, 1961, NDP files.
[23]Park interview, Jan. 14, 1963.
[24]*Federal Program of the New Democratic Party*, p. 4.

CCF's socialism: The editor of the *Ottawa Journal* raised his voice in song:

> Oh no! We never mention it;
> Its name is never heard.
> Our lips are now forbid to speak
> That once familiar word
> Socialism.[25]

But the CCF itself had not been consistently fond of the word. The CCF in 1932, like the NDP in 1961, decided against using the word "socialist" in its name. In 1943 David Lewis wrote: "The [Regina] Manifesto . . . does not often use the word. . . . It . . . evoked associations with the Nazis and the Communists. . . . This is the reason why the word 'socialist' was avoided in the name of the party. . . . But socialism is avowedly the objective of the CCF."[26] Socialism—not the socialism of the thirties but the liberalized socialism of the fifties and sixties—is just as avowedly the objective of the NDP. The second convention of the NDP held in August 1963 reintroduced the controversial word to the party's official documents. The convention adopted a statement of principles endorsing "the principles of democratic socialism applied to our time and situation."[27]

The NDP's appeal to the "liberally minded," like its avoidance of the word "socialism," was not new. The CCF had always insisted that the Liberal party was liberal in name only, that "true" liberals should support the CCF. In 1956 F. A. Brewin wrote: "The Liberal Party which banishes to the Senate any of its more active members who display liberal tendencies has long since abandoned Liberalism. . . . The CCF has become in Canada the effective inheritor of the liberal tradition. . . . Let . . . us . . . make it clear to all who believe in the liberal tradition . . . that the CCF is their party."[28] What was new was the conviction that liberals who resisted the CCF appeal would be attracted to a new party in the formation of which they were invited to participate.

The effort to attract "liberally minded individuals" took organizational form in the "new party clubs," which attained a membership of approximately 8500 in about 300 clubs by the time of the founding convention.[29] The express purpose of the clubs was to "support the movement to form a new national party which will unite all democratic

[25]Feb. 4, 1960.
[26]In untitled manuscript, n.d., NDP files.
[27]*Winnipeg Free Press*, Aug. 7, 1963.
[28]*CCF News* (Ont.), Nov. 1956.
[29]*New Party Newsletter*, July 1961. Of the new party club membership, about 5000 were in Ontario and about 2000 in Quebec.

Canadians of the political left." A minimum of six people could form a club and apply for formal recognition by the National Committee for the New Party. The clubs participated in the "study, discussion and promotion of the new party project" and were invited to make proposals on constitution and program to the NCNP. They were given the right to representation at the founding convention on the same basis as the 40,000 or so members of the CCF constituency associations, that is, one delegate for each fifty members or major fraction thereof for the first two hundred members and, thereafter, one delegate for each additional hundred members or major fraction thereof, with a minimum of one delegate.[30] Of the total of 1801 delegates at the founding convention, 318 were from new party clubs. The clubs went out of existence at the founding convention, at which time their members presumably became members of the constituency associations of the New Democratic party.

In order to emphasize its desire for the participation of the "liberally minded" as equal partners with the CCF and CLC in the formation of the new party, the NCNP in January 1961 co-opted seven persons to serve as representatives of the new party clubs at the top level of the new party movement. Later three additional new party club representatives were appointed; the NCNP thus consisted of equal numbers of CLC, CCF, and new party club representatives. Four of the ten new members were prominent farm and co-op leaders and were appointed to represent farmers. The remaining six were appointed to represent "the broad new wing of the New Party Movement." They consisted of one high school teacher, two professors, a United Church minister, a journalist, and a doctor.[31]

Among the activists of the new party clubs were some "liberally minded individuals" who made a point of emphasizing that they were not "socialists." This produced some discussion of the exact meaning of the term "socialism," and it also raised, for the first time explicitly, the question of whether the new party was to be a "socialist" party. The

---

[30]A Guide for the Establishment of New Party Clubs, n.d., NDP files. The purpose of the new party clubs was to enable farmers and "liberally minded" people who were not members of either the CCF or the CLC to participate in the formation of the new party: "It is not intended to divert members of the CCF or of Labour Unions from working towards the new party through the machinery of their own organizations." However, a good many clubs, especially in Quebec, were organized within union locals which were themselves unwilling or unable to participate in the new party project. Outside of this sizable minority of unionists, the bulk of the new party clubs' membership consisted of farmers and professional people.

[31]New Party Newsletter, Feb. 1961.

consensus was that the new party was to be a party of *all* the democratic left—not exclusively a party of socialists—and that explicit renunciation of "socialism" by individual members was tolerable *if* the renunciation were accompanied by an appropriate definition of "socialism" as extreme left-wing socialism. Walter Young—one of the new party club representatives on the NCNP—defined "socialism" as "that political philosophy which is based on the idea of class struggle and state ownership of the means of production." He admitted that "many in the CCF" rejected socialism thus defined,[32] but he insisted, nevertheless, that "the CCF was too far out on the left for many. . . . Its basis was too narrow, its policies somewhat doctrinaire." "Liberally minded" Canadians who were dissatisfied with the Liberal and Conservative parties yet could not support the CCF were looking for a new party representing "the *whole* of the democratic left, not merely the socialist element—for in the narrow sense of this word, the ['liberally minded' person] is not a socialist. . . . Within its broad framework there *should* be a place for the rabid left-wing socialist, for the timid liberal, and the free thinking trade unionist."[33]

The official "Theory of the New Party Movement," as outlined by R. D. Sparham, the NCNP's director of new party clubs, was that the two major parties had become

exactly alike in political complexion—both middle of the road parties with a bias to the right. It therefore becomes necessary to organize a new party capable of appealing to the left wing of each of the two conservative parties as well as to the CCF party if a meaningful two party system is to be restored. The CCF acting upon this reasoning . . . agreed to give up its institution for democratic socialists only and to help to form the new party with as many other helpers as could be found.[34]

When Prime Minister Diefenbaker declared that the issue of the 1962 election would be "free enterprise versus socialism," Tommy Douglas accepted the challenge, defining socialism as economic planning for the benefit of the people rather than "every man for himself, as the elephant said while dancing among the chickens." The main slogan of the NDP in election campaigns has been "democratic economic planning." During

[32]He could have cited M. J. Coldwell, who, at the CCF Convention of 1950 declared that the CCF has never "preached nor practised the class war," and praised the socialists of western Europe for having "repudiated . . . Marxian class war" and accepted "the basic position of the British and Scandinavian socialist movements." CCF Convention Proceedings (1950), p. 23.

[33]W. D. Young, "The New Party—A Party of All the Democratic Left," n.d., mimeographed, NDP files.

[34]R. Desmond Sparham, "New Party Clubs and the Theory of the New Party Movement," n.d., mimeographed, *ibid.*

the 1963 campaign, when Douglas was asked in a television interview
to comment on a certain NDP candidate's declaration that he was not
a "socialist," Douglas responded that "socialism" could be defined in
many ways. The ideals and objectives of the NDP were the same as
those of the democratic socialist parties of Western Europe. The inter-
viewer said the candidate had specifically repudiated the "ideals of the
CCF." In that case, Douglas responded, that candidate had no place
in the NDP.[35] The candidate was Dr. Harding E. Bishop. Dr. Bishop
was the only delegate to the NDP's 1963 convention who protested
against the convention's endorsement of "the principles of democratic
socialism." He said this was a definite change from the "original intention" of the NDP. Of the 775 delegates, only four voted against adoption
of the statement.[36]

The prevailing tone of discussions of this matter within the party is
that the NDP is, like the CCF, a democratic socialist party, but one
which strives to make non-socialist left-wing "liberals" more welcome,
more comfortable, and therefore more numerous in its ranks than the
CCF did. The true meaning of the phrase "a party of all the democratic
left" is to be found in Douglas' address to the CCF National Council's
"reappraisal" meeting of 1956. In that address, Douglas pointed out
that a CCF success could not be achieved by "avowed socialists" alone;
that the objective of the CCF must be to build a *mass* movement in
which the "avowed socialists" would be the "dynamic core," but which
would include "hundreds of thousands of people who will accept the
objectives that we have without necessarily understanding the political
philosophy or ideology." These are Young's "timid liberals" and "free
thinking trade unionists."

3. CCF REACTIONS

To the overwhelming majority of CCF members the new party idea was
entirely new, and not entirely welcome. During the new party's three-
year gestation period, the idea of a new party had to be "sold" not only
to traditionally non-partisan elements of the labour movement, but to the
majority of CCF members who had no close ties with the labour movement. In February 1959 Donovan Swailes reported that "much more
interest [was] being shown by the trade union movement than by the
CCF groups. To some extent the CCF groups are fearful that something

[35]Pierre Berton Hour, CTV, March 27, 1963.
[36]*Winnipeg Free Press*, Aug. 7, 1963.

is going to slip from their fingers, they want to hang on to the name and to keep full control."[37] As the OFL-PAC put it, "there has been more questioning [of the new party idea] in CCF ranks where the membership was less prepared for a new remedy to what was becoming a chronic ailment—failure to win elections."[38] One might say that many CCFers had become accustomed to losing elections; one might add that for many CCFers there were things more important than electoral victory, such as preserving the identity of their movement and its pristine purity. The greater amount of "questioning" in CCF ranks is not surprising. The unions, after all, were not being asked to give up the organizational style to which they had become accustomed, in which they had a vested interest, and into which they had poured their enthusiasm. The CCF was being asked to give up its identity, its very name, and to resign itself to becoming just one element, perhaps even a minority, in a composite party including "non-socialists" from the unions and the ranks of the "liberally minded." And to the CCFers' question: "why?" the response was "you have failed." The first and not unnatural reaction of many CCFers to the CLC's new party resolution was expressed on the CLC's convention floor by Delegate Gardner:

It seems to me that this resolution indicates that since the CCF did not succeed in . . . taking power, we should try some new highfalutin name and some new banners and some new slogans, thinking that . . . would get something else elected. I say to you, Mr. Chairman, that one of the reasons why the CCF could not get elected . . . is because Labour did not support the CCF, and particularly the majority of the so-called leaders of Labour did not support the CCF.[39]

In short, why form a new party—why not support the CCF as you never supported it before? The feelings of CCF activists who were asked to "co-operate" with formerly unco-operative unionists was well expressed by a leading Nova Scotia CCFer: "It seems to me that the principle we believe in and have fought for these many years is worth a little dignity, and not have to go crawling for help from people that should be with us."[40]

CCF "questioning" of the new party idea centred around two familiar themes: fear that the influx of new elements (unionists and "liberals") would be accompanied by a "watering-down" of the CCF's socialism, and fear that the new party would be "dominated" by its affiliated

[37]To Hamilton, Feb. 26, 1959, NDP files.
[38]*OLF-PAC Political Education Handbook Number 1*, n.d., "New Party Problems," p. 1.
[39]CLC Convention Proceedings (1958), p. 46.
[40]Florence Welton to Hamilton, March 26, 1960, NDP files.

unions. Those who concentrated on the latter theme were motivated by one or more of the following feelings: the desire to preserve the control of the individual membership over the party machinery; fear that a party closely associated with labour would be incapable of making an effective appeal to farmers and other middle-class people; doubt that labour would support a new party any more than it had supported the CCF[41]; and anti-labour sentiment, pure and simple. The name of James Hoffa was much in use among people harbouring such sentiment. A new party organizer reported that he had heard "our people talk with regret about 'losing the CCF to Hoffa types.' "[42] A retired British Columbia farmer wrote Carl Hamilton that he had decided to leave a few thousand dollars to the CCF in his will, but was now reconsidering his decision in the light of the fact that the CCF was being turned over to "Hoffaites." Some anti-labour, anti-administration individuals within the CCF acquired the habit of referring to David Lewis as "Hoffa's lawyer."

Opposition party reaction to the new party included the charges that it was dominated by labour, that it was dominated by the American superiors of Canadian labour leaders, that it was controlled by American labour racketeers. An exchange in the House of Commons illustrates the virulence of this type of attack:

Mr. Horner (Conservative, Acadia): I am afraid [Mr. Hazen Argue, leader of the CCF group] has sold the farmers down the river to the labour party which is controlled by unions in the U.S. . . .
Mr. Argue: . . . this party for which we have been working will not be a labour party, and the people who are most determined to see that it will not be a labour party are the trade union members themselves.
Another Conservative: Controlled by American labour racketeers.[43]

Readers of the *Calgary Herald*'s report on the New party seminar held there in December 1960 were perhaps given the distinct impression that the new party leaders were "protesting too much" about their innocence of contamination by "Hoffaites." "U.S. UNION INFLUENCE DENIED" was the headline. "It's utterly crazy— . . . fantastic and ridiculous," said Stanley Knowles to the enquiring *Herald* reporter. American unions exert no influence on the political activities of their Canadian branches.

41A rank-and-file member wrote: "[Labour has not supported] the CCF in spite of the fight we have put up for their cause. What guarantee have we that they will come over after the new party is formed? All sincere unionists should support our movement without all the conferences, organization, and especially the doubtful results at the polls of forming a new party." W. A. Jenkins to Hamilton, March 26, 1959, NDP files.
42Gerald Caplan to Hamilton, Sept. 5, 1959, NDP files.
43Reported in the *New Party Newsletter*, May 1960.

Knowles "cited the case of the Steelworkers Union which voted unanimously in favor of the new party after being advised against it by its international president."[44]

All that the new party spokesmen could do to meet this type of attack was to issue endless assurances that the party would not be labour-dominated and that Canadian unions are not controlled by their international headquarters. No effort was spared to avoid the slightest hint of American domination. CCF plans to invite Walter Reuther to address a new party banquet in Winnipeg were scuttled by Winnipeg unionists who "said he was the most wonderful man in the whole wide world but this new party must not be looked upon as a labour party."[45] The American Socialist Party–Social Democratic Federation was invited to send observers to the new party's founding convention. Irwin Suall of the SP-SDF suggested that "it would be very healthy" for an American trade union delegation to be present. Carl Hamilton replied that the AFL-CIO would not be asked to send observers because "we do not wish to do anything to lend credence to the charge that the new party is being influenced by international unions with headquarters in the United States."[46]

The most vocal of CCF critics of the new party idea was Douglas Fisher, MP for Port Arthur.[47] He had not opposed the new party in the early stages, but his experience in the Ontario election of 1959 changed his mind. Fisher wrote:

Of the $3,800 we raised only $380 came from unions, and two volunteers for a few days, though our candidate was a top trade unionist and we stressed labour issues. . . . Our regulars were immensely disappointed at the reticence, coolness, and in some cases antagonism of the unions and union members. . . . I have been told by the old reliables in Port Arthur that the local club will be forwarding a resolution to the provincial office requesting that new party pronouncements be postponed and reconsideration be given to the whole idea. . . . The general feeling is that there is no enthusiasm among union membership as a whole for the new party idea. . . . Further, that the tie-up insofar as it has gone has already put in jeopardy many who used to be for us. That is, the liberally minded people now doubt our integrity and cause. With no enthusiasm in the labour movement at the Lakehead for the

[44]*Calgary Herald*, Dec. 11, 1960. As far as American labour racketeers are concerned, James Hoffa advised Canadian Teamsters to steer clear of third parties. *Saskatchewan Commonwealth*, Oct. 12, 1960.

[42]Gerald Caplan to Hamilton, Sept. 5, 1959, NDP files.

[46]Irwin Suall to Hamilton, May 9, and Hamilton to Suall, May 18, 1961, NDP files.

[47]Other CCF MPs were critical of, or opposed to, the new party idea (Ames to Hamilton, Jan. 9, 1960, NDP files), but Fisher was the only one who spoke out publicly.

idea, what is the point of leadership pronouncements that we are going ahead? In this attitude, there may be something of the feeling that a marriage with the labour movement will only debauch our democratic socialism, but I do feel it is a more practical reaction than that. . . . I believe that if the new party idea is proceeded with further it will lead to the wiping out of our representation in the next federal election. Of course, we are so low now that the risk may be justified. . . . [Nevertheless, the "old reliables' "] perturbation and my own is so great that I feel it worth drawing to the attention of the executive.[48]

Fisher rose to criticize the new party idea in similar terms on the floor of the Ontario CCF's 1959 convention, and was later subjected to a certain amount of scolding by CCF leaders for his "irresponsible and thoughtless statements."[49] As a result of this scolding, and also as a result of increasing evidence of union enthusiasm for the new party project and the new party's startling victory in the Peterborough federal by-election of October 31, 1960,[50] Fisher moderated his criticisms. He was not opposing the new party, he explained, but merely expressing his doubts: "I would not hesitate to run under the New Party label [but] I doubt the long term ability of labour to change its tactics and role."[51] Speaking at the 1960 convention of the Manitoba CCF, Fisher explained that although he was now prepared to give the new party idea his "wholehearted support," he still had doubts about "the practical wisdom of being lined up with labour."

In the Steelworkers' publication *Information*, Fisher restated his position: "Labour unions are unpopular with the majority of Canadians." A party of which labour was an important part would be similarly unpopular. Moreover, there was no guarantee that the disadvantages of identification with labour would be compensated for by increased labour

48To Hamilton, June 18, 1959, NDP files.
49Coldwell to Hamilton, Oct. 28, 1959, NDP files.
50Peterborough is a mixed rural-urban constituency in Southern Ontario. (One quarter of the population lives in rural polls.) It had been one of the safest of "safe" Conservative seats. In the 1958 election the Conservative candidate received 19,032 votes, the Liberal 7,254 and the CCFer 1,887. In the 1960 by-election Walter Pitman, running with strong trade union backing under a "New party" rather than a "CCF" label, won with 13,208 votes as against the Conservative's 10,240 and the Liberals 5,393. Mr. Pitman joined the House of Commons as "New Party" member of a "joint CCF-New Party caucus." (*New Party Newsletter*, Oct.–Nov. 1960). He was later appointed to the NCNP as one of the representatives of the New party club movement. In the federal election of June 1962 he lost to the Conservative candidate by a small margin. See W. D. Young, "The Peterborough By-Election," *Dalhousie Review*, Winter, 1960–61, for an interpretation of the by-election as evidence of the superiority of the new moderate "image" of the new party to the "doctrinaire image" of the CCF.
51In a letter to GH, Feb. 3, 1961.

support, for most workers were, like other Canadians, politically apathetic, cautious, conservative, and lacking in class consciousness:

Look at Sault Ste. Marie. Here is an isolated city, dominated by one industry, and that industry completely unionized by the most politically conscious of all Canadian unions, the Steel workers. The response in support of the CCF has been pathetic. The same locals, the same leaders . . . will be there after the New Party starts. . . . Will there be a striking political transformation in the Sault?[52]

Those CCFers whose primary objection to the new party was based on fears that it would "water down" the CCF's socialism focused their criticism on the new party club movement. A member of the Prince Edward Island provincial executive wrote: "I am afraid the CCF ideals will not prevail in the new party—I hope I am wrong—I am afraid many of these new people have a lot to learn about a People's Party." Most of the criticism came from British Columbia and Alberta, the provinces in which the left wing of the CCF was particularly strong. In December 1959, shortly after the NCNP's decision to form new party clubs, Grace MacInnis, as secretary of the British Columbia CCF, informed the NCNP that in the view of British Columbia CCFers, the clubs were designed "just to get people in," without regard to ideology. The CCF had fought for "certain beliefs" too long and too hard to tolerate "a flood of newcomers for whom all this means nothing." The British Columbians felt that members of new party clubs should at least be required to subscribe to some sort of statement of principles indicating that they "share our views as to the sort of society that should be built in Canada." Othewise, the new party might turn out to be "in no important respect distinguishable from . . . the . . . capitalist parties." The British Columbia CCFers also felt that the basis of representation set by the NCNP for new party clubs at the founding convention was much too generous; some of them even feared that plans were being made "to scuttle the CCF before the founding convention and to give unwarranted strength to the new party clubs."[53]

Despite the strength of the left in British Columbia, the provincial party as a whole had entered into a very close relationship with the labour movement, and resistance to the new party idea as such was minimal. The objections of the party were largely confined to the new party club movement. Resistance to the new party idea as such was strongest in the three prairie provinces. In Saskatchewan the CCF was

[52]"Organized Labour in Canadian Politics," *Information*, Nov.-Dec. 1960.
[53]Letters by Muriel McInnes, Grace MacInnis, and Colin Cameron to Hamilton, 1959–61, NDP files.

primarily a farmers' movement whose relations with its labour minority
were troubled. In Manitoba the CCF, though its bastion was the city of
Winnipeg, had a strong and important agricultural wing. The Alberta
CCF, which had since the forties declined into a powerless sect with
minimal support from both farmers and workers, was controlled by
exponents of a brand of socialism so extreme that it made most British
Columbia "leftists" seem mildly liberal. The leaderships' relationship
with the CCF unionists in the province was neither close nor friendly.
Late in 1958, Carl Hamilton reported[54] that the prospects for CCF-
labour co-operation in Alberta were "pretty dim." The CCF leaders did
not "trust" the labour leaders; the labour leaders felt that the CCFers
were interested in the "problems of the Soviet Union," not the "realistic
political problems" of Alberta. The CCF in Alberta participated in the
new party project, but it did so reluctantly and with loud protests against
the "betrayal" of socialism. The Alberta CCF Convention of 1960
resolved to "repudiate . . . the idea of a mixed economy . . . and reaffirm
its conviction that public ownership is necessary."

Early in 1961, the Alberta executive launched a scathing attack on
the new party club movement:

[The] contracting parties to the formation of a new party were the CCF and
the CLC. . . . It was not . . . proposed that the . . . program and the constitution of the new party should be a matter of decision by a third group not
then existent and whose only commitment would be $1 plus a desire to see
the formation of a new party which was . . . in an undefined area "left of
centre."[55]

Though it had no right to do so, the NCNP had set up new party clubs
and the Alberta party had accepted the *fait accompli.*

[Now] we are joined by an ever growing crowd of people who themselves
are uncommitted to anything of a specific nature. When a member of the
NCNP, Reverend Mullins [an Alberta new party club representative], is
reported in the press as saying that a "chasm a mile wide" exists between the
CCF and the parties of the right and calls for the formation of a new party
to *fill this gap,* it must surely be agreed that the anticipated purpose . . . of
the new party clubs is to move the new party right up to the edge of the old
line parties. To call such a party a party of the "whole left" is to make a
joke of what "left" has always meant. CCF supporters whose interest is in
the building of an effective . . . new party are . . . concerned about this
attitude.

The basis of representation of new party clubs at the founding convention deprived the CCF of "even equal representation." Any group of six

---

[54]To Winch, Oct. 30, 1958, *ibid.*
[55]This ignores the CLC resolution's invitation to "other liberally minded
persons" to "participate directly in the establishment" of the new party.

people could form a club and be entitled to the same representation as a CCF constituency association. The founding convention would thus be "wide open to subversion by Liberals, Tories, Socreds and Communists coming in through new party clubs." The trade unions too were likely to be over-represented at the founding convention, but

> this problem is one . . . between an agreed . . . partnership and should not present any great difficulty. It can in no measure compare to the absurd proposal [for new party club representation]. Failure to consider these glaring inequalities would compel the Alberta section . . . to reluctantly reconsider its position in re to the new party. . . . We find it most difficult to believe that CCF national officers have given their approval to this parody of the trust still residing in them as *CCF* officers.[56]

The Alberta CCF's "Standing Committee on Constitution for the New Party" reported to the June 1961 provincial convention that the NCNP's draft program was "vague . . . meaningless"; it abandoned CCF principles by calling for the reform rather than the abolition of the free enterprise system; it repudiated the essential idea of socialism— that "the means of ownership and production" should be placed "in the hands of society as a whole." The convention resolved that the Alberta party "do not irrevocably commit itself at this time" to the formation of a provincial section of the new party. After the national founding convention and prior to the holding of a provincial founding convention, the Alberta CCF would hold a special one-day convention "devoted entirely to the consideration of the course to be pursued by the Alberta CCF."[57]

The spokesman of the Alberta unions participating in the new party project, Neil Reimer of OCAW, was so upset by the attitude of the CCFers that he asked the NCNP to deny the Alberta CCF representation at the founding convention: "In my view, the provincial CCF have disqualified themselves from attending the founding convention. . . . These people want to vote on the founding of a new party at the convention, and still reserve the right not to be part of it."[58] In the ensuing dispute, the NCNP, though it probably sympathized with Reimer, upheld the right of the Alberta CCF to representation. At the founding convention itself, the CCF members of the Alberta delegation were swamped by union and new party club delegates.[59]

[56]Nellie Peterson to Hamilton, Feb. 17, 1961, NDP files.
[57]Alberta CCF Convention Proceedings (1961), p. 19.
[58]In a letter to Donald Macdonald, June 26, 1961, CLC-PEC files.
[59]Seventy-one new party club delegates, twenty-two union delegates, thirty-eight CCF delegates.

After the founding convention, the Alberta CCF held its special one-day convention to determine the course it would follow. At that convention, the membership of the CCF were confronted with three proposals:

1. To maintain the Alberta CCF as a provincial party which would seek *affiliation* with the federal NDP. This was the course of action favoured by the provincial executive.
2. To disband the CCF completely, as was being done in other provinces.
3. To form a study group which would "advance the cause of socialism" within the Alberta NDP. This was a "compromise" adopted by the convention after it had rejected the executive's proposal. After the convention, Alberta CCFers set up a "study group" known as the "Woodsworth-Irvine Fellowship."

At the founding convention of the Alberta NDP, the CCFers were again greatly outnumbered.[60] Neil Reimer was elected president of the Alberta NDP. According to Reimer, relations between the CCFers and the new elements within the Alberta NDP continued to be strained: "The old CCF . . . now only form about 5 per cent of our membership and do not really endorse the NDP and their participation has been negligible."[61]

In September 1959, the *Winnipeg Free Press* reported that there was in the Manitoba CCF a "fair sized dissenting group" led by "men closely connected with the co-operative movement and actively working in agricultural circles," which would oppose the new party idea at the provincial convention of November 20–21. The proceedings of the convention reveal no such opposition. Stanley Knowles spoke on the new party and answered questions from delegates:

M. A. Gray: What is the opposition to the new party, and where is it?
Mr. Knowles: The opposition is spotty, due largely to lack of knowledge. In the trade union movement the feeling is either strongly in favour of the new party or is just luke-warm. In the CCF it runs from doubt and questioning to all out support.
Mr. Gray: What are you doing with the opposition?
Mr. Knowles: We are trying to carry on a program of education. . . .

A delegate: Does the CCF need to go along with labour?
Mr. Knowles: The CCF could go along without labour, but . . . with only the odd representative elected here and there. Would it not be much wiser to go along with other groups and win the power of government?

---

[60]One hundred and seventy-two union delegates, ninety-eight new party club delegates, eighty-five CCF delegates. Attendance at NDP Founding Convention, n.d., CLC-PEC files.
[61]In a letter to GH, June 25, 1963.

Ed Smee: . . . Too much pressure is being applied to impose the new party
on the CCF. Up to now the Manitoba CCF has agreed only to consider
the subject. Yet statements are made . . . that the new party is an accomplished fact in Manitoba.
Mr. Knowles: The new party will not become an accomplished fact until
. . . the founding convention. In the whole history of Canada it is impossible
to show where a more democratic procedure has been followed. The whole
question has been submitted for discussion from coast to coast. . . .
F. G. Tipping: . . . Every time there has been a revision, it has been a
revision to the right. In every case it has resulted in loss of support.
Mr. Knowles: A broadening of the base . . . does not mean a watering down
of policy. . . .
Mr. Manchur: Why cannot the labour people come into the CCF just as
it is now?
Mr. Knowles: We have been trying to get them . . . in for 25 years. Up to
now we've gone along with labour helping from the outside. Now . . . we
have a chance to get them inside. . . .

The convention adopted a resolution instructing the Provincial Council
and executive to "work closely with the Manitoba Federation of Labour
and others to build a stronger socialist movement in Manitoba in line
with the development of the proposed new party," and to promote
seminars and conferences on the new party.[62]

Open opposition to the efforts of the NCNP came not from the agricultural wing of the Manitoba CCF, but from a group of young urban
party activists described by Tommy Douglas as "a little group in Winnipeg South who are endeavouring to make things as awkward as
possible."[63] Their bastion of strength was the St. James constituency
association; their leaders were Al Mackling of St. James, provincial
chairman, and Howard Pawley, immediate past chairman. Mackling and
Pawley did not explicitly oppose the new party idea. They concentrated
their attacks on the proposed constitutional provisions for affiliate as
well as individual membership, and for representation of affiliates at
party conventions.

This was not a new issue. The CCF originally was intended to have a
large affiliated union wing. This did not come about, in part because the
unions were not "ripe," but also precisely because the CCF itself went
to great lengths to avoid labour domination. As Dean McHenry wrote
in 1949, "the CCF has been hard pressed in its desire to secure the
advantages of trade union affiliation . . . without accepting the bitter pill
of external domination."[64] To the unionist, the CCF desire for "the

[62]Manitoba CCF Convention Proceedings (1959), p. 41.
[63]In a letter to Knowles, Feb. 14, 1961, Knowles' files.
[64]Dean McHenry, *The Third Force in Canada* (Berkeley, 1950), p. 49.

advantages" without "the bitter pill" appeared as the desire to have the cake without paying for it: the CCF will take the unions' money and men, but it will not give them in return a say in policy determination and the selection of candidates. The CCF became, from the unions' point of view, a party *for* but not *of* labour. It was precisely this defect which the new party was intended to remedy. In the words of Eamon Park:

The method of [union] involvement in politics will change from "support" or "endorsation" to participation. *Through his union affiliation* [the unionist] will participate in . . . decisions on policy . . . in the choice of candidate . . . in the choice of leader. . . . The concept of the new party will raise the unionist from the level of recruited door-knocker or envelope stuffer . . . on behalf of the candidate chosen, with whatever good intentions, by a left wing elite, to that of a thoroughgoing participant.[65]

The new party idea contained a labour demand, addressed to the rank and file of the CCF: *quid pro quo*:

In essence, what Labor said is this: "We want to help, but in order to help effectively, we want a place in the political set-up. . . ." For years I have heard CCF'ers ask: "When is the labor movement going to come in and help us . . . ?" Now that the hoped for has happened, there seems to be dismay in some quarters. . . . It is indeed disturbing that a few of our people have misinterpreted Labor's offer to read "the better to eat you, my dear."[66]

The scheme of affiliation suggested in the NCNP's study paper on constitution and again in the draft constitution was not meant to permit "swamping" of constituency representatives by representatives of affiliated unions. It was, in the words of David Lewis, an attempt to establish a "proper balance" between the two; "to make sure that the individual member is not overwhelmed by representation from affiliates but, what is equally important, . . . [to] give affiliates . . . opportunities for participation and authority which will make affiliation meaningful to the members of the affiliated organization."[67] There would be no British-style "bloc vote." The voting system at conventions would be "one delegate, one vote." The British National Executive Committee structure was also rejected. Members of executive organs of the party would be elected as individuals by the whole convention; there would be no representation of affiliated organizations as such on executive bodies.

---

[65]"The New Choice for Canadian Voters," *Information*, Nov.-Dec. 1960.

[66]George Fawcett, "Labor and the New Party," *Canadian Democrat*, April-May 1960.

[67]Address of David Lewis to the second National Seminar of the New Party, Montreal, Dec. 3, 1960, mimeographed, NDP files.

Representation at conventions would be allocated between constituencies and affiliated unions as follows:

[For federal constituencies] One delegate for each fifty members or major fraction thereof for the first 200 members and, thereafter, one delegate for each additional 100 members or major fraction thereof, with a minimum of one delegate.
[For affiliated locals] One delegate for each 1,000 members or major fraction thereof, with a minimum of one delegate.[68]

These provisions—which were adopted by the founding convention—do not represent a startling departure from the provisions of the CCF itself, though they are, of course, more generous to affiliated unions. What is new is not provision for affiliation—that existed in the CCF—but the determination that it cease to be a dead letter, the determination actually to build up a large affiliated-union section.

Mackling and Pawley were not impressed by the assurance that the individual membership would not be overwhelmed. They insisted that there was a real danger of domination by affiliated unions. They called for "constitutional changes to see that constituency organizations—not affiliate groups—are the most effective units in the new party."[69] Local unions should be permitted to affiliate to the party, but there should be no separate category of "affiliated members" with rights and duties different from those of individual members. Members of affiliated locals should be offered individual CCF memberships. Affiliated locals should not be entitled to direct representation at party conventions, but only to indirect representation through those unionists who actually became individual members of the party. These views were obviously unacceptable to the unions; if implemented, they would have reduced the rights which affiliated unions already held within the CCF. The Mackling-Pawley doctrine was in effect a repudiation of the essence of the new party idea—a *greater* role for unions *as such* within the party.

The Mackling-Pawley group were also critical of the "watering-down" of socialism which they feared the new party would perpetrate. They were opposed on the provincial council by a group led by Lloyd Stinson, former provincial leader, and consisting according to the *Free Press* "mainly of union men in the CCF."[70] At the provincial council meeting of February 6, 1960, a struggle between the two groups resulted in a

[68]National Committee for the New Party, *Study Paper on Constitution of the Proposed New Party for Canada* (Ottawa: Mutual Press Ltd., 1960), p. 10; National Committee for the New Party, *Draft Constitution* (Ottawa: Mutual Press Ltd., 1961), p. 11.
[69]*Winnipeg Free Press*, Nov. 22, 1960.
[70]*Ibid.*, Feb. 24, 1960.

unanimously adopted "compromise resolution," expressing "concern" about possible domination of the new party by affiliates, and support for the principle of "membership without group distinction as to fees, rights, and privileges."[71] Not satisfied with this achievement, Mackling and Pawley sent to the NCNP a "personal" letter attacking the draft constitution and released copies to the press. The *Free Press* responded with a front-page story revealing that "the Manitoba CCF is split down the middle on the question of labour union control of the new party."[72]

In May the provincial council rejected Mackling's proposal that there be a special provincial conference on the new party constitution and program prior to the 1960 CCF National Convention. Mackling protested that the council had been "packed" against him and threatened that "there could be a storm of protest publicly aired." He also protested the appointment by the NCNP of Lloyd Stinson as new party organizer for Manitoba without consultation with the provincial council.[73]

At the provincial CCF convention of 1960 the Mackling-Pawley group submitted several resolutions which were described by Knowles as "a shocking display of ignorant and incredibly narrow-minded self-interest. Manitoba will have to be purged!"[74] Among these resolutions were:

1. (St. James) Resolved that this Convention manifest its grave concern [that affiliated unions will dominate new party conventions] . . . and remind the . . . National Committee that equitable representation . . . can only be attained by membership in the constituency organization. . . .

2. (Lakeside) Whereas there is a reluctance upon the part of rural people to take this step, be it resolved that the Manitoba CCF affiliate with the new party at the federal level only.

12. (St. James) That we commend to our present leaders the philosophy of J. S. Woodsworth, who steadfastly advocated adherence to principle, because he recognized the wisdom of accepting temporary political defeat in contrast to compromising principle in order to win a hollow victory.

15. (Wolseley) That [retention of the proposed constitutional provisions for affiliated membership] is comparable to an ostrich with its head in the sand because we will not be catering to a majority of Canadians but only to a small minority . . . in the trade union movement.[75]

Mackling told the convention that he was not "anti-labour"; he "welcomed association with the trade union movement." He had every right

[71] Al Mackling and Howard Pawley to the NCNP, Feb. 17, 1960, NDP files.
[72] *Winnipeg Free Press*, Feb. 24, 1960.
[73] Mackling to Lewis, May 31, 1960, NDP files.
[74] In a letter to Hamilton, Nov. 15, 1960, NDP files.
[75] Resolution Submitted to the Manitoba CCF Provincial Convention, Nov. 18–20, 1960, *ibid.*

to criticize the proposed constitution; it was, after all, only a draft issued for purposes of discussion. The Mackling group proposed that formation of a provincial section of the NDP be delayed until one year after the national founding convention. The convention, by a three to one vote, rejected this proposal and resolved to endorse the new party and to hold a provincial founding convention immediately after the national founding convention. The convention also rejected a resolution urging the NCNP to ensure that at new party conventions the majority of delegates be from constituencies. Mackling's bid for re-election as provincial chairman was defeated, but he was elected to the provincial executive. Pawley was elected vice-president.[76]

In March 1961, the Manitoba executive discussed Alberta's objections to the new party clubs and passed, by a vote of eight to two, a resolution expressing "deep concern" that the new party clubs would be over-represented at the founding convention.[77]

In June the executive defeated a resolution moved by Mackling and Pawley expressing "disappointment" with the draft program of the new party. At the national founding convention, Pawley was silent, but Mackling was quite vocal in his opposition to the affiliation provisions of the constitution and to the "non-socialism" of the program. It was rumoured that he would bolt the party, but in the Manitoba provincial election of 1963 he ran as a New Democratic candidate.

The greatest impediment to the establishment of the new party was the reluctance of the Saskatchewan CCF to risk weakening its support among the farmers of that province by entering a new party more closely linked with labour. This reluctance was most strongly felt by Saskatchewan CCFers who were themselves farmers or farm spokesmen, and as such distrusted unions and feared that the new party federally would be labour-dominated.

On March 25, 1959, Carl Hamilton met with the CCF caucus in the Saskatchewan legislature to discuss the new party. He found that many were "very worried about the whole new party idea." The general consensus of opinion was that, while the new party might be necessary for the CCF nationally, and Saskatchewan would therefore not oppose it, it was bound to cause at least temporary difficulties for the provincial party. The caucus was especially concerned about the harm that "new party talk" might do to the CCF in the forthcoming provincial election, and suggested that such talk be "played down" until the election was over.[78]

[76]*Winnipeg Free Press*, Nov. 22, 1960.
[77]Manitoba CCF Provincial Executive Minutes, March 18, 1961, NDP files.
[78]Hamilton to Argue, Knowles, and Lewis, April 2, 1959, *ibid.*

In the fall of 1959, in Winnipeg, the NCNP held the first of two national seminars on the new party. The delegates from the Saskatchewan CCF were so unenthusiastic that David Lewis felt compelled to explain their behaviour to the officers of the CLC. He acknowledged that the comments of the Saskatchewan delegates were "disturbing [and] showed a complete lack of understanding"; but he pointed out that the CCF in Saskatchewan was primarily a farmers' movement, that it had "little to gain within its borders" from the projected changes in the party, and that it was very concerned about the potential negative impact of these changes on the farm vote in the coming provincial election. "When one understands . . . these . . . very important factors which . . . govern the thinking of Saskatchewan CCF people, their doubts and anxieties become more comprehensible." Lewis assured the Congress officers that the Saskatchewan CCFers, despite their anxiety, would not create "any difficulty . . . certainly not after they have completed their election."

The Saskatchewan CCF and the NCNP reached agreement that there would be minimal attention to the new party project in Saskatchewan until after the election. It was also agreed that the CCF government, if re-elected, would be a *CCF* government until the next election. In this manner the Saskatchewan CCF was enabled to minimize the effect of Liberal and Conservative arguments that a vote for the CCF would be "wasted," a vote for a party that was going out of existence.

The provincial election of June 1960 returned the CCF government to power. Discussions of the new party within the CCF and the unions and between them could now be undertaken without qualms as to the electoral effects. The 1960 CCF provincial convention endorsed the new party idea, but not without debate. One delegate rose to oppose the new party on the ground that there was "a tremendous feeling against labour in the province," and Premier Douglas had to deliver an "impassioned appeal" to the farmer delegates "to unite behind the new party."[79]

When the Saskatchewan provincial council was asked to "release" Tommy Douglas from his provincial responsibilities so that he might be available for the leadership of the new party, sixteen of the fifty-two council votes were cast against release. The *Globe and Mail* reported that "farmers' distrust of a party in which organized labor plays a major, if not dominant role" accounted for the dissenting votes.[80] The Sas-

[79]C. E. Bell, "Labour Pains in Canada's Newest Party," *Saturday Night*, Sept. 17, 1960.
[80]June 3, 1961. David Lewis is convinced that "if this motive played a part it was a very small one. . . . The reason for the anti-vote was the simple one that they hated to lose Mr. Douglas. . . . They felt that they would lose the government without him." In a letter to GH, Aug. 16, 1966.

katchewan delegation to the founding convention was the only one in which CCFers greatly outnumbered trade unionists and new party club members.[81]

In Saskatchewan, the CCF did not go out of existence as a provincial party. Instead of holding a provincial founding convention of the NDP, as in other provinces, it was decided that the 26th annual convention of the CCF, Saskatchewan Section, be recognized as the first convention of the NDP, Saskatchewan Section.[82] The name of the party was changed to "The CCF, Saskatchewan Section of the NDP." Of the 592 delegates the vast majority were CCFers.[83] On the eve of the convention W. E. Smishek, the secretary of the SFL, reported that "a lot of patience and tedious work" had been required to carry through the transformation, and that "a great deal of reluctance about the NDP" remained in the Saskatchewan CCF, particularly among farmers.[84]

The 1960 national convention of the CCF endorsed the work of the NCNP and sealed the CCF's commitment to participate in the establishment of the new party. The vote was 500 to 5. But "there was no display of enthusiasm . . . and one has to assume a large element of silent acquiescence."[85]

The basis of representation of the three participating groups at the new party's founding convention had become a subject of heated controversy within the CCF. Many CCFers feared that CCF delegates would be overwhelmed by union and new party club delegates. Douglas and others[86] suggested that a maximum number of delegates be set, half to be selected by the CCF and half by the unions:

I can tell you right now that if you get some complicated formula which ends up by having 1200 trade unionists and about 500 CCF delegates you can put the new party in the morgue soon after it is born. There are people who have worked for the CCF for twenty-five years. They will be hurt and offended if they get the impression that the CCF has been tricked into a founding convention at which they can be outnumbered and outvoted.[87]

The NCNP itself was anxious to assure a "reasonable balance" among the three groups at the founding convention, so that no one of them

[81]Two hundred and sixty-seven CCF delegates, twenty-three union delegates, three new party club delegates.
[82]William Smishek to Home, Oct. 27, 1961, CLC-PEC files.
[83]Five hundred and fourteen CCF delegates, sixty-two union delegates, five new party club delegates. "Attendance at NDP Founding Conventions," n.d., *ibid.*
[84]To Home, Oct. 27, 1961, *ibid.*
[85]Hamilton to Caplan, Sept. 1, 1960, NDP files.
[86]Including Woodrow Lloyd, in a letter to Hamilton, Feb. 25, 1960, *ibid.*
[87]Douglas to Argue, Feb. 24, 1960, *ibid.*

should appear to be dominant.[88] On the basis of estimates of the number of union locals, new party clubs, and CCF constituencies likely to be represented, the NCNP prepared a basis of representation which was expected to produce a reasonable balance. The basis turned out to be the same as that provided in the draft constitution for regular conventions of the party:

For union locals—one delegate for each 1000 members or major fraction thereof with a minimum of one delegate.
For CCF constituencies and new party clubs—one delegate for each 50 members or major fraction thereof for the first 200 members and one delegate for each additional 100 members thereafter, with a minimum of one delegate.[89]

The *New Party Newsletter* then estimated that this should mean about 900 union delegates, 700 CCF delegates, and 400 or 500 club delegates. This did not satisfy everyone in the CCF. There were protests from the West, especially about the representation of new party clubs.[90] The actual representation at the founding convention was: unions, 631; CCF, 710; clubs, 318; others, 142; giving a total of 1801.[91]

The most dramatic aspect of the convention was the contest between Hazen Argue (who had been elected CCF leader at the 1960 convention) and Tommy Douglas for the national leadership. Douglas was far more popular and had far greater prestige than Argue, and was supported by both the Lewis-Knowles-Hamilton CCF "administration" and the CLC leadership. His victory was inevitable.[92] Nevertheless Argue, with the support of some members of the federal caucus (including Douglas

[88]Hamilton to Murdo Martin, Feb. 9, 1961, *ibid.*
[89]*New Party Newsletter*, Feb. 1961.
[90]Only one protest came from the unions: the secretary of the Fort William-Port Arthur Labor Council PEC thought that union locals should be represented on the same basis as CCF constituencies. Hamilton to Knowles, March 21, 1961, NDP files.
[91]Others are from NCNP, provincial committees for the new party, CCF MPs and MLAs, CCF provincial councils, CCF national council, provincial federations of labor, and from labour councils. A provincial breakdown of representatives, excluding the "others," was given in Fred Schindler, "The Development of the New Democratic Party" (MA thesis, University of Toronto, 1961), p. 100:

	Ont.	Sask.	BC	PQ	Alta.	Man.	NS	NB	Nfld.	PEI
Unions	411	23	62	56	22	27	14	7	7	2
CCF	164	267	96	57	39	51	16	9	3	9
Clubs	132	3	10	54	71	13	11	9	14	1
	707	293	168	167	131	91	41	25	24	12

[92]Argue's actual vote was approximately 380.

Fisher), had carried on a strenuous campaign, in the course of which his relations with the "administration"—already tense because of his opposition to Douglas—became embittered to the point of open rupture. Argue himself did not campaign on the issues of "labour domination" and "betrayal of socialism"; on the contrary, he appealed for labour support and he made no explicit appeal to leftist sentiment. He himself was anything but a leftist. However, the fact that he was the candidate opposed by the CCF "administration" and the "labour bosses" attracted a fair number of supporters from the left wing of the CCF. Their vote for Argue was a protest vote—against the liberalization of the party's image, against "labour domination," and, in a sense, against the new party idea itself.

4. UNION REACTIONS

The response to the new party idea within the politically conscious unions was more favourable, much less complicated by doubts and fears, than the response of the CCFers. The contrast between the CCF and CLC conventions of 1960 is instructive. The CLC vote in favour of the new party was as overwhelming as the CCF's had been,[93] but the CCF atmosphere had been one of "silent acquiescence" while the CLC atmosphere was one of enthusiasm and excitement. "The delegates rose to their feet, threw confetti in the air, and broke into the old union anthem Solidarity Forever."[94]

An indication of the degree of union support was the success of the New Party Founding Fund, a CLC drive to raise "$250,000 or more" to cover the costs of the founding convention and "launch the new party on the strongest possible footing." The drive was organized by a national trade union committee with William Mahoney of Steel as chairman and Morden Lazarus of the OFL as director. From January 1, 1961, to the date of the founding convention, approximately $175,000 was raised across Canada. Another index of union support was the "SOS Drive" launched by the OFL-PAC. This was a campaign to secure "statements of support" for the new party from Ontario union locals. Three hundred and seventy locals with approximately 177,000 members—one quarter of OFL locals, consisting of more than half of the OFL membership—adopted "statements of support."[95]

[93]The CLC vote was approximately 1660 to 40.
[94]New Party Newsletter, May 1960.
[95]PAC Report to OFL Executive Board, Sept. 15, 1961, OFL-PEC files.

The great majority of those who cheered at the 1960 CLC convention, those who contributed to the New Party Founding Fund, those who adopted the statements of support, were of course members of the politically conscious industrial unions, the former CCL unions which had supported the CCF. There is no mystery about the reason for their enthusiasm. The new party was a result of *their* dissatisfaction with the CCF and their demands for change. Unlike the CCF membership, they did not have to be "sold." But many of their "brothers" in the old apolitical craft unions, the former TLC unions, did have to be "sold."

There was no question of any attempt by elements of the old TLC to prevent the CLC from participating in the formation of the new party. This battle—hardly deserving of the name—had already been lost. The top leadership of the TLC unions had been persuaded either to support or not to oppose the establishment of the new party. The CLC's policy had been firmly decided by March 1958 at the latest; it could not be reversed. Only a small handful of craft unionists spoke against it at the CLC's 1960 convention. The question was no longer whether the TLC unions would oppose the formation of a new party, but whether they would *themselves assist* in its formation. It was no longer a question of persuading the craft unions to permit their *congress* to take political action, but of persuading them to take political action themselves. Some progress has been made in this direction, but the degree of craft union support for the NDP will probably never be comparable to that of the industrial unions.

Unfriendliness to the new party was most evident in some of the building trades. The only union which officially dissociated itself from the Congress' political policy was the International Brotherhood of Electrical Workers (IBEW), one of the largest building trades organizations. At the CLC convention of 1960, IBEW delegate Angus MacDonald said, "Our delegates cannot support this [new party] resolution. The IBEW will have to go on record at this time as adopting a position of neutrality on the formation of a new political party. We are going to leave the floor of this convention until the question has been put."[96] One local of the IBEW, local 353 in Toronto, disaffiliated from the OFL because of the latter's political policy.[97] In British Columbia, IBEW locals 213 and 244 were listed by E. P. O'Neal, the secretary of BCFL, among five BCFL locals which "actively opposed the BCFL's role" in the provincial election of 1960.[98]

[96]*New Party Newsletter*, May 1960 and CLC Convention Proceedings (1960), p. 38.

[97]*Hamilton Spectator*, Jan. 9, 1961.

[98]E. P. O'Neal, Report on the 1960 Provincial Election, n.d., BCFL files. For further evidence of the IBEW attitude, see below pp. 238 and 240.

In some areas, building trades opposition threatened to disrupt labour councils. In Belleville, Ontario, for example, the Carpenters' union withdrew from the labour council in protest at its support of the new party and the Plumbers threatened to withdraw, with the result that the president of the council decided to "go slow on political action until the time is ripe."[99]

In October 1960 the Ontario Building and Construction Trades Council defeated an endorsement resolution by a vote of 44–36.[100] The closeness of the vote was, however, a sign of progress. CLC Vice-President Dodge wrote that even discussion of endorsement, to say nothing of the close vote, would have been out of the question in previous years. "Tremendous progress has unquestionably been made in bringing the building trades around to a progressive position on political action."[101]

In Manitoba, coolness towards the new party by former TLC unionists on the Manitoba Federation of Labour executive had the effect of impeding full labour-CCF co-operation during the new party's gestation period. The MFL convention of 1958 instructed the executive to initiate a program of discussions on the new party in Manitoba unions. The resolution was implemented, but not at all energetically, because the secretary treasurer, Peter McSheffrey (of the Musicians' union), and the vice-president, Lawrence Taylor (of the Pulp and Sulphite union), were unreconstructed non-partisans.

At the National New Party Seminar held in Winnipeg, the Manitoba federation failed to report on the progress of new party discussions. Instead of sending a report, McSheffrey sent a letter stating that "because of the divided opinion of the Federations' membership no useful purpose could be served by attending the National Seminar."[102]

At the 1960 MFL convention, new party supporters (led by the MFL president, Jimmy James, the MFL vice-president, Sam Goodman, and Grant McLeod, president of the Winnipeg Labour Council) decisively rebuked the non-partisans. Vice-president Taylor "was booed when he declared that his pulp and sulphite union 'will not affiliate with a new party, Khruschev's party or any other party.' " The convention adopted

[99]Henry Nokes to Home, Aug. 18, 1959, CLC-PEC files.

[100]*Winnipeg Free Press*, Oct. 17, 1960.

[101]William Dodge to Frank Quaife, Nov. 2, 1960, CLC-PEC files.

[102]Report of Delegates of the Winnipeg Labour Council at the Winnipeg National Seminar, n.d., CLC-PEC files. McSheffrey opined that "the union membership is not going to be told how to vote . . . the Winnipeg 1958 convention had all the earmarks of a railroading job." In 1959 Taylor's Pine Falls Labour Council threatened to disaffiliate from the MFL if it continued its partisanship. *Winnipeg Tribune*, Oct. 17, 1960.

a resolution urging affiliates to support the new party by a vote of 188 to 12.[103]

The New Brunswick Federation of Labour was the only federation which adopted a political policy directly contrary to that of the CLC. CCF organization in New Brunswick had always been virtually non-existent. The labour movement of the province was dominated by the TLC craft unions, whose local leaders developed close ties with provincial Liberal and Conservative politicians. The president of the TLC federation, James A. Whitebone, was a partisan Conservative. The defeat of the Liberal government in 1952 was ascribed in part to strong TLC support for the Conservatives.[104]

The tiny CCL movement in the province, though it formally complied with CCL political policy, was also dominated by non-CCFers. At the CCL federation's 1952 convention a resolution withdrawing the federation from CCL-PAC was narrowly defeated.

When the two provincial federations merged, James Whitebone was elected president of the new NBFL. The attitude of the NBFL to the new party project was extremely unco-operative. Its 1959 convention resolved "that the NBFL will . . . take a nonpartisan part in politics and will not obligate its affiliates . . . to any political party."[105]

James Whitebone had been a member of the minority group within the TLC national executive which had tried to prevent the TLC's tacit surrender on the political issue during the merger discussions. The other members of this group—men like Gervin of British Columbia, Berg of Alberta, MacArthur of Ontario—soon lost their positions of prominence in the labour movement. Whitebone was an exception. The weakness of the CCF in his area enabled him to continue to oppose political action yet retain his position of strength. Though he could not do anything about Congress policy, he was strong enough to defy it on his own ground.

In July 1960 the NCNP reported that "the resolution on the book of the NBFL, as interpreted by the Executive, has prevented new party discussions."[106] The convention which adopted that resolution also removed Whitebone from the presidency, but this did not alter the political situation in favour of the new party. Whitebone's successor was Angus McLeod, a Liberal. In the provincial election of 1960, McLeod ran as a Liberal candidate. His nominator was the NBFL's secretary-

103*Winnipeg Tribune*, Oct. 17, 1960.
104Fell to D. C. MacDonald, Nov. 21, 1952, NDP files.
105*CLC Political Education Information* (Booklet no. 5, March 1960), p. 10.
106Report of Developments re New Party across Canada, July 7, 1960, NDP files.

treasurer, James Leonard.[107] A CCF leader commented: "In view of the present position of the two top officers of the NBFL, it is rather difficult to foresee any genuine support for the new party from the labour organization in New Brunswick in the immediate future."[108] The CCF itself lost a good part of whatever leadership it had to the Liberals in the provincial election of 1960. Four Liberal candidates were former CCFers, including one past-president of the provincial CCF.

Given the policy of the NBFL, what little effort there was to promote the new party in the province had to be undertaken by CLC staff in co-operation with officials of three friendly unions—NUPE, CBRT, and UPWA. (The president of the New Brunswick CCF, Ed McAllister, was a CBRT official.) Some progress was made. The labour councils of Moncton, St. John, and Fredericton were persuaded to contribute to the New Party Founding Fund. Of local union contributions, the great majority were from CLC directly chartered, UPWA, and CBRT locals; only one former TLC local (Bakery Workers) contributed. A labour delegation of seven was sent to the founding convention. Following the founding convention the Moncton Labour Council endorsed the new party after a heated debate between CBRT and craft union delegates. The vote was 17 to 13.[109]

The CLC did not passively accept the rebelliousness of its New Brunswick subsidiary. Some consideration was given to a suggestion that the CLC take the federation under "administration" despite the danger that "such action may well be used as propaganda implying that the Congress is the boss and its affiliates must toe the line with regard to political action."[110] In lieu of more drastic action, the CLC tried to organize opposition to the executive's policy at the NBFL's 1961 convention. A resolution urging locals to affiliate to the NDP met with strong opposition and never came to a vote. The resolution which was finally adopted read as follows:

Whereas the principles and policies as enunciated by the New Democratic Party coincide in almost every respect with those laid down and supported in the past by this Federation, Be it therefore resolved that this New Brunswick Federation of Labour adopt the policy of the Canadian Labour Congress and endorse the principles and policies of the New Democratic Party without direct affiliation.[111]

---

[107]*Saint John Times-Globe*, June 9, 1960. The Liberals defeated the Conservative government, but McLeod was not elected.

[108]Eldon Richardson to Hamilton, June 25, 1960, NDP files.

[109]Henry Harm to Home, May 9, and to William Dodge, Oct. 3, 1961, CLC-PEC files.

[110]Harm to Dodge, Oct. 3, 1961, *ibid.*

[111]NBFL Proceedings, 1961, p. 93.

James Whitebone, who had returned to the presidency, interpreted the resolution ("with a smirk on his face") to mean that the federation "is of the same opinion that it has been for many years—we will not be taking part in politics and I want this understood by all concerned."[112] The convention voted "for the policies of the new party—not for the new party. The policies of the new party are almost identical to those [of] . . . the Federation . . . and I fail to see how the Federation could not endorse its own policies."[113]

In 1962 the CLC convention removed Whitebone from his position as CLC vice-president for the Atlantic Region, electing in his stead John F. Simonds (of the Bakery Workers), vice-chairman of the New Brunswick NDP.[114] In 1964 Whitebone retired as president of the NBFL. Since then the federation's 1961 resolution has been interpreted as supporting the New Democratic party, not just its policies. Officers of the federation were active in support of the NDP in the federal election of 1965 and a provincial PEC was formed in the autumn of 1966.[115]

The former TLC union which was most responsive to new party overtures was the International Association of Machinists (IAM). Even before the merger of the CCL and TLC, CCFers had built up significant pockets of strength in this union, the most important being the Malton aircraft workers' lodges. The Canadian vice-president of the IAM, George Schollie, had been a member of the moderate group of TLC leaders, the group that surrendered its opposition to political action during the merger negotiations. After the merger, Schollie served on the CLC–PEC and "went along" with Congress policy, but without enthusiasm. In 1961 Schollie retired and was succeeded by Mike Rygus, a strong supporter of political action.[116]

According to the *Canadian IAM Newsletter* (Dec. 1961), Machinists' lodges "were very active in helping establish the NDP." Twenty-seven of the union's 163 lodges contributed a total of $4,566 to the New Party Founding Fund. This was the largest contribution from former TLC unions. At the founding convention, the IAM delegation of eighteen (representing sixteen locals) was the largest delegation from former TLC unions. The ILGWU had the second largest delegation (fifteen). No other former TLC union had more than five delegates.

Of the total of 530 union delegates on the founding convention's

[112]Tom Jones to Dodge, Sept. 5, 1961, CLC-PEC files.
[113]*Saint John Telegraph Journal*, Aug. 31, 1961.
[114]*Canadian Labour*, June 1962.
[115]Interview with Clifford Scotton, Jan. 30, 1967.
[116]Interview with Home, May 15, 1962.

delegate list, 427 were from former CCL unions (over 300 of these from Steel, Auto, Packinghouse, and Woodworkers), and 93 from former TLC unions.[117] The breakdown of the CLC delegation to the founding convention reflects fairly accurately the relative strength of the NDP in the several wings of the Canadian labour movement: very strong in the big four—Steel, Auto, Packinghouse, and Woodworkers; strong in other former CCL unions and a few former TLC unions; weak or non-existent in most non-CCL unions.[118]

[117]The remaining ten delegates were from locals directly chartered by the CLC.
[118]Attendance at the founding convention by union is given as follows in Fred Schindler's "The Development of the New Democratic Party," p. 100:

CCL unions	delegates	locals	TLC and other unions	delegates	locals
1. UAW	60	57	1. Bakery Workers	4	3
2. Brewery Workers	6	6	2. Barbers	3	3
3. ACWA	14	14	3. Bookbinders	1	1
4. Communications Workers	1	1	4. Bricklayers	1	1
5. IUE	6	3	5. Carpenters	8	2
6. Glass & Ceramic	7	7	6. Cement Workers	1	1
7. OCAW	18	17	7. Chemical Workers	5	5
8. UPWA	69	67	8. ILGWU	15	8
9. Retail-Wholesale	17	14	9. Grain Millers	2	2
10. Steelworkers	165	147	10. Laborers	3	1
11. Textile Workers	24	24	11. Hotel & Restaurant Workers	1	1
12. IWA	30	15	12. Locomotive Firemen	1	1
13. CBRT	8	8	13. IAM	18	16
14. NUPSE	1	1	14. Meat Cutters	2	2
15. BC Shipyards	1	1	15. Sheet Metal Workers	2	1
	—		16. Molders	2	1
	427		17. Office Employees	2	2
			18. Pattern Makers	1	1
			19. Plumbers	5	3
			20. Pulp & Sulphite Workers	5	5
			21. Street Railway Employees	4	2
			22. Teamsters	1	1
			23. Tobacco Workers	4	4
			24. ITU	1	3
			25. Upholsterers	1	1
				93	

CCL	427
TLC and others	93
Directly chartered	10
Total delegates	530

7.   Obstacles to Political Action

1. THE INTERNATIONAL PROBLEM

Many international unions formerly affiliated to the AFL and TLC have clauses in their constitutions which prohibit participation in partisan politics, financial support of a particular political party, or even discussion of partisan politics in local meetings. These prohibitions do not prevent American locals from participation in the AFL–CIO's formally non-partisan Committee on Political Education (COPE), but they do prevent Canadian locals from supporting or affiliating with the NDP.

Constitutional restrictions are not the only form of American pressure affecting the political policies of Canadian unions, nor are craft unions the only ones subject to such pressure. Even the mightiest and most autonomous of industrial unions, Steel, has had to contend with the problem of American opposition to political action. It is important, however, to note that American influence has not always been negative; in some cases the international connection has encouraged rather than discouraged political action. In 1952 Steel and the UAW agreed to take on the burden of the CCF's National Organization Fund. The different methods which were used by Steel and Auto in meeting their commitments to the NOF cast light on the subtle pressures, in part favourable and in part unfavourable to political action, which arise from the international connection of Canadian trade unions.

The international leadership of the UAW consisted of "ex-socialists" personally friendly to the CCF. Emil Mazey, the secretary treasurer, was still a socialist, and a proponent of a third party for labour in the United States. The Reuther group had been allied with the CCF in the battle against the Thomas-Addes regime, and the international union had, in its political action policy, been influenced to a certain extent by the CCF.[1] The international's intense interest in political action was itself a spur to UAW political action in Canada. The Canadian UAW therefore encountered no obstacles at the international level to complete and direct support of the CCF. Its commitment to the National Organization Fund was met in the form of direct cash contributions to the party.

[1]See above, pp. 56, 113–18.

Although the Canadian section of the Steel union had always been the CCF's most reliable and vigorous supporter in the labour movement, the union's international leaders were, as David Lewis wrote Reuther,[2] "not 'raving radicals,' to put it mildly. They certainly don't have any real sympathy with the various political forces and movements which you and your Secretary Treasurer support out of conviction. This is the reason why Charlie's [Millard] assistance does not always come in a direct way." When Steel searched for a method of meeting its commitment to the National Organization Fund in 1952, "it became clear . . . that because of marked lack of sympathy toward a socialist movement at the international level, it would be difficult to get the money."[3] Instead of obtaining a direct contribution for the CCF, Millard appointed two PAC representatives and turned them over to the CCF to act as CCF organizers responsible to the provincial CCF but drawing their salaries from the union. Thus, even in the case of the most autonomous of Canadian unions (except, of course, for purely Canadian unions like CBRT) a lack of sympathy to the CCF in the American head office acted as a brake on support for the CCF in Canada. As D. C. Mac-Donald wrote Millard, "Steel has provided greater assistance than any other union. That such has been done in spite of the problem of getting action at the International level is proof, as you say, that where there's a will, there's a way."[4] In the case of unions less autonomous than Steel and Auto—and most unions in Canada are less autonomous, especially the craft unions and the smaller industrial unions—the attitude of the international would be even more important.

The traditional non-political policy of the AFL had always been an obstacle to TLC political action, not only because of potential and actual international pressure, but because of spontaneous Canadian imitation of American ways. In the case of the CIO, the main effect of the international connection was to force Canadian political action into the same *forms* as it assumed in the United States. This may be one of the main reasons why the original intent to affiliate unions directly to the CCF was given up. Direct affiliation to a political party was unacceptable in the United States, but indirect support through political action committees was not. Political action in Canada therefore took the form of PAC support for the CCF. Any other form of support would cause difficulties with the international.

When the CIO became active in politics, the obstacle to political action *per se* was removed for the Canadian sections of CIO unions;

2June 26, 1950, NDP files.
3D. C. MacDonald to Frank Snowsell, April 18, 1952, *ibid.*
4Jan. 26, 1952, *ibid.*

but the form which their political action might take was restricted to PAC. In the case of unions like Steel, which were very friendly to the CCF, this had the effect of setting limits to the support which they were able to give the CCF. But in the case of unions like the UAW, which were less active politically or less friendly to the CCF than their American parents, it had the effect of spurring them to political action which they might not have taken if they had been independent. It would probably be correct to say that most CIO unions outside the Millard group and UMW-26 agreed to involve themselves in CCL-PAC in part because of the American example, and that some of them would have been less *active* in CCL-PAC if not for the intense involvement of their American parents in CIO-PAC. An example is the Communication Workers' union. During the federal election of 1949 it did not participate in the CCL's PAC campaign. Shortly afterward Henry Weisbach reported that since "their international is quite active in PAC work . . . the situation is very likely to change. Communication has now gone forward to Brother William Dunn, the . . . PAC director of CWA-CIO, re the situation in the Canadian locals."[5]

During the new party's foundation period many former TLC locals claimed that they were unable to contribute to the New Party Founding Fund or participate in the founding convention because of restrictions imposed upon them by their international constitutions. For many of these locals, this was merely a convenient excuse for non-participation. Others, however, sincerely desired to participate, and in some of these the constitutional restrictions were evaded by the formation of new party clubs.

In the spring of 1959 Claude Jodoin discussed the constitutional problem with George Meany and William Schnitzler of the AFL-CIO.[6] The Americans seem to have told Jodoin that the AFL-CIO itself could do nothing and that the problem would have to be solved by direct contact with the officers of the international unions concerned. The international officers could help by simply ignoring Canadian offences against the constitution,[7] by interpreting the constitutional provisions in such a way as to permit Canadian locals to support the NDP, or by facilitating

[5]Weisbach, Report on Meetings Attended in Saskatchewan, May 17, 1950, CLC-PEC files. Note also the attempts of the CCL-PAC in 1944 to exert pressure on the Communist-dominated UE and IWA through the IWA and CIO international leaders, above, p. 100.

[6]Jodoin to Dodge, May 11, 1959, CLC-PEC files.

[7]This was John L. Lewis' reaction to the 1938 affiliation of UMW-26 to the CCF, which was illegal under the UMW constitution. Interview with Donald Macdonald, April 30, 1962.

the amendment of the constitution in international convention. By the fall of 1962, a number of international constitutions had been amended, including those of the IAM, the Retail Clerks International Association, the Brotherhood of Locomotive Firemen and Enginemen, the Pulp and Sulphite union, and the International Chemical Workers' Union.[8]

Three unions which refused to amend their constitutions were the Carpenters' union, the Brotherhood of Railway Clerks,[9] and the Laborers' union. At the 1962 convention of the CLC, Gerald Gallagher, president of local 183 of the Laborers' union and an NDP candidate in the 1962 federal election, complained that his local "had been instructed by the international to stay out of politics and that he had been subjected to heavy pressure. Mr. Gallagher . . . said his local members had repeatedly urged affiliation of the local with the NDP 'and to heck with U.S. dictation.' " The convention adopted a resolution introduced by a Carpenters' local instructing the CLC executive to "discuss with the international unions the question of amending union constitutions to give Canadian unions political freedom."[10]

The constitutional obstacle is not absolutely insurmountable. One Carpenters' local and one Laborers' local are unconstitutionally affiliated to the NDP; their international officers have not taken action against them. Nevertheless, very few locals can be expected to say "the heck with the constitution" or "the heck with U.S. dictation." So long as constitutional restrictions are retained, craft union support for the NDP will be inhibited.

An amendment to an international constitution does not necessarily mean that the Canadian locals are given full political freedom. In some cases the constitutional restriction may be removed only to be replaced with equally prohibitive informal pressure against political action. In other cases the constitutional amendment may moderate rather than completely remove the restrictions on political action. The constitution of the RCIA, for example, was amended to read: "The International Executive Board shall be empowered to give special consideration to Canadian bodies, upon written request. Such special consideration shall not be inconsistent with the purposes of this Constitution."[11]

RCIA locals are not permitted to become directly involved in politics. Those of their members who wish to take political action may form voluntary "Active Ballot Clubs" for that purpose. The active ballot

[8]*CCF News* (BC), Sept. 28, 1960; *Canadian Labour*, Nov. 1962.
[9]*Toronto Daily Star*, Sept. 30, 1960.
[10]*Globe and Mail*, April 10, 1962.
[11]*CLC Political Education Information* (Booklet no. 5, March 1960), p. 27.

clubs, though sponsored by the RCIA, function separately and apart from it. Union dues are not used for political purposes; the dues of the club are completely separate, are not deducted on check off, and are set by the club itself. The secretary of the local serves as secretary of the club in order to protect the club's funds, but there is no further connection between the local and the club. Club activities are co-ordinated by the International Active Ballot clubs, a body headed by the international president but formally independent of the international union. The RCIA's constitutional amendment was not used to exempt Canadians from this active ballot club procedure, but to permit the Canadian RCIA to set up its own active ballot clubs and to permit the latter to affiliate to a particular party. An "Active Ballot Clubs of Canada" was chartered by the International Active Ballot Clubs and authorized to operate as a separate unit with the RCIA's Canadian co-ordinator as director. The director was required to submit a weekly report on his activities. Canadian clubs were to operate "in all respects in conformity with the principles and policies of the CLC. . . ."[12] This meant that they were bound to support the NDP and permitted to affiliate to it. In April 1962, one RCIA active ballot club with ten members was affiliated to the NDP.[13]

Constitutional restrictions and informal control are not the only American influences on Canadian unions' political policies. The Canadian tendency to imitate American ways is still an important factor. It probably played a part in the decision to duplicate the American active ballot clubs in Canadian RCIA locals. At least one labour council PEC officially calls itself a COPE in order "to conform with the American practice."[14]

The American influence continues to be double-edged. In some unions it has the effect of inhibiting political action; in others it encourages political action. The IBEW is an example of the latter. In the United States it is active in COPE; its international constitution does not restrict political action. In Canada the IBEW has been firmly opposed to political action. In October 1962, *Canadian Labour* reported that the international convention of the IBEW had "rectified" the position taken by the Canadians at the CLC's 1960 Convention by passing a constitutional amendment "aimed at the organization of political activity in every local union." According to George Home,[15] the IBEW's interna-

12David Wade to RCIA locals, May 1, 1961, CLC-PEC files.
13This affiliation must have lapsed sometime before December 1965, according to "Local Unions Affiliated to the NDP," as of Dec. 31, 1965, *ibid.*
14David Archer to Lazarus, April 23, 1959, *ibid.*
15Interview, March 20, 1963.

tional president Freeman has "rebuked" the Canadian leadership for its negative attitude to the new party.

2. THE POLITICAL CULTURE PROBLEM

Early in 1962 the CLC-PEC sent a questionnaire to all CLC locals asking what action they had taken on the matter of affiliation to the NDP. Of the 289 locals which had responded by April 1962, 34 had not yet considered the matter, 12 had discussed it but had not arrived at a decision, 98 had voted for affiliation, and 145 against. The comments of the locals rejecting affiliation consisted either in citations of constitutional prohibitions of political activity or declarations that affiliation would constitute an offense against the individual liberty of the membership:

The feeling was that each member should have the choice of affiliation individually.

Our local is . . . contacting all our members on an individual basis to join the NDP.

It is the feeling . . . of our membership that they would rather use their political privileges as individuals, not as a group.

Unions should not tie in with any political party, but be free to vote as they choose, according to their democratic right.

Affiliating with a political body . . . would work against freedom of vote.

The officers of the local urged any members who were desirous of affiliation to support the NDP on an individual basis.

These comments are expressions of liberal political philosophy; they are based upon a conception that politics is a matter for individuals rather than for groups. Society is seen as an agglomeration of individuals; the existence of social and economic groups may be acknowledged, but in the same way as the existence of sex is acknowledged. Neither is "nice." The political process is seen not so much as one in which *groups* with differing interests confront one another and arrive at a compromise, but as a process in which individuals *suppress* their group interests. The individual in politics is not a Ukrainian, or a farmer, or a suburbanite, but a Canadian: he does not ask himself "what is good for my group?" but "what is good for Canada?" The result of the political process is not a compromise hammered out by contending groups, but a "general will" produced by individuals communing with their own consciences and rationally discussing the "issues." No group interest or group pressure should come between individuals, between the individual and the State, or between the individual and his conscience. A political party is an association of individuals with a common answer to the question "what is best for Canada?" not an organization of people having similar group interests. The liberal frowns on "class parties." *Group* action in politics is illegitimate because it opposes the interest of a part to that of the whole and because it interferes with the free choice of individual members of the group.

This liberal, individualist, anti-group, anti-class approach is not so strong in Canada as it is in the United States; but it is stronger in Canada than in Britain. Liberal, Conservative, and Social Credit attacks on the CCF-NDP as a "class party," and on labour political action as an infringement of the unionists' individual rights have always struck a responsive chord among many Canadian unionists, especially in TLC unions with an established tradition of non-partisanship. The slogan on the masthead of the *Western Construction Tradesman*, organ of the building trades unions in the four western provinces, is: "To Every Member the Religious and Political Beliefs of His Choice."

The NDP has tried to deal with such attacks by revising the image of the CCF, by abandoning the old emphasis on the idea of a *farmer-labour* party and stressing the newer idea which appeared in the CCF in the fifties, the idea of a party for all "liberally minded Canadians." The image of the NDP, however, contains a contradiction: while there is less reference to classes and class interests in the party's electioneering, there is a new—formal and direct rather than informal and indirect—relationship with a particular class, the working class.

The result has been a renewed emphasis in old party propaganda on the "class" character of the socialist party, and on the "undemocratic" nature of union affiliation to a political party. What right—the question is asked—do the "labour bosses" have to pressure their rank and file to support a "particular" party? What right do they have to divert union dues for partisan political purposes, to affiliate unions whose membership is not unanimously in favour of the NDP to that party?

These questions are also asked by the non-partisans in the labour movement. The officers of an IBEW local in British Columbia declared: "We are completely opposed to having one party dictate how we shall vote and tapping our pocket books. . . . We believe wholeheartedly that the ballot and religion are matters of private choice and conscience. We will not surrender these hard-won rights . . . to the CCF or any other . . . party."[16]

[16]Statement by L. J. Crampton of IBEW Local 344 and Jack Ross, IBEW International Representative, Sept. 9, 1960, BCFL files.

The unique method of political action chosen by the RCIA appears to be a concession to the strength of liberal individualist ideology among its members as well as to the international constitution and the American influence. The Canadian director has assured his membership that he is cognizant of the attacks

in the press and by management . . . [on] the affiliation of trade unions to the new party and the use of trade union funds . . . for political purposes. Such accusations cannot and will not be hurled at the Active Ballot Clubs of Canada. . . . Only those members who wish to . . . support the principles and policies of the CLC in political matters will be asked to become members of the Active Ballot Clubs. Not one cent of your local union's funds . . . will be used for political purposes.[17]

The CLC, like the CCL before it, reacts to individualist attacks first with assurances that labour political action is not intended to interfere with the free exercise of the ballot. No one is "telling the membership how to vote"; the rights of the dissenter in a union affiliated to the NDP are protected by provisions for "contracting in" or "contracting out" (the choice is left to the union); and second, with the charge that business supports the old parties with even less regard for individual liberty:

As is traditional in a free and democratic union movement, not a penny of the member's dues will be spent on political action without his consent. How different this is to the unfortunate shareholder in a big corporation. Out of his money huge slush funds are voted to the old parties by small meetings in the executive suites of corporation offices and the shareholder often isn't even told! . . . This has not happened, cannot happen and will not happen when labour gets into politics.[18]

In 1927 the Conservative government of Great Britain made "contracting in" mandatory for unions affiliated with the Labour party. Perhaps it is the greater strength of liberal individualism in Canada which accounts for the far more drastic action of the Social Credit government in British Columbia. By the terms of its "Bill 42," enacted in 1961, unions are prohibited from using union dues for political purposes. British Columbia unions which desire to contribute to the NDP or pay affiliation dues to it may now do so only with funds specially raised for the purpose.[19]

[17]Wade to RCIA locals, May 1, 1961.
[18]*New Party Newsletter*, April 1960.
[19]Prince Edward Island has enacted similar legislation.

3. RELATIONS WITH GOVERNMENT

The NCNP let it be known early in the new party's foundation period that

a central organization like the Canadian Labour Congress, which itself is made up almost entirely of affiliated organizations, will not be affiliated to the new party as a Congress. Individual trade unions will each make their own democratic decision whether to affiliate to the party or not. If they decide in favour, they will be affiliated to the CLC for economic purposes and to the party for political purposes. It is important to keep the two functions separate. The Congress and the new party will undoubtedly have a very friendly relationship with each other, but in all probability there will be no formal ties between them. This is the situation in Great Britain and other democratic countries.[20]

In Britain, the formal separation of the TUC and the Labour party is justified on two grounds. First, the Congress is the instrument not only of unions affiliated with the Labour party, but of unions which are unaffiliated. Among these are organizations of civil servants which must, for reasons both legal and practical, rigorously abstain from political activity. Under these circumstances, affiliation of the Congress to the Labour party is clearly inappropriate. Second, one of the main functions of the Congress itself is to deal with the government of the day; its relations with a Conservative government would be needlessly hampered if it were formally affiliated to the Labour party. The same situation exists in Canada and dictates the same sort of relationship between the "legislative mouthpiece" and the "political arm" of labour.

The fact that it was the CLC which had called for the formation of a new party and was one of the three groups which were actually bringing it into existence meant that the CLC, during the new party's formation period, was unable to project the correct image of its relations with the party. The press spoke of a "CLC-CCF merger"; the election of Stanley Knowles as a CLC vice-president heightened the impression that the new party was to be some sort of amalgam of the socialist party and the labour congress itself. When the Congress tried to clarify the situation, the result was further confusion. The press interpreted Claude Jodoin's statement (at the Winnipeg seminar) that the CLC itself would not affiliate to the new party as a repudiation of the new party idea.

During the period of the new party's formation the CLC as such was

[20]CLC-CCF Joint National Committee, *A New Political Party for Canada: A Discussion Outline* (Ottawa: CLC-CCF Joint National Committee, Nov., 1958), pp. 16–17.

directly involved to an abnormally great degree in political activity. This was necessary for the formation of the party, but it was not intended to continue beyond the early stages and it has not.[21] While the NDP was being formed, the most prominent and most newsworthy feature of the CLC's activities was its participation in the formation of the party. Now that the NDP is an accomplished fact, the CLC is returning to its proper role as an organization devoted primarily to strictly trade union functions, like the CCL before it and the TUC in Britain.

In Canada and in Britain there is some tension between the labour movement's role as a pressure group and its role as sponsor of a political party. The effectiveness of pressure groups as such seems to be limited if they are associated with a particular political party, and heightened if they are non-partisan and free to "reverse alliances." This was always the main argument used by the TLC unions in justification of their political policy, and the CCL unions, though they were not nearly so impressed by it, were far from unaffected. Even in Britain, where the Labour party is a long-established alternative government, there are unionists who are concerned enough about the effect of their political activity on their relations with the government to advocate abstention from political activity:

One should not overrate the importance of the man or the seriousness of his intent, but at the Labour [party] Conference of 1953 the then Chairman of the General Council of the TUC advocated in an interview that the trade unions should withdraw from the Labour party and the TUC should divest itself of its present political activities. A principal advantage, he claimed, would be that thereby the TUC would be less embarrassed in its dealings with a Tory Government. . . .[22]

One of the immediate results of the CLC's new party resolution was a turmoil within the civil servants' associations, a turmoil significant enough to evoke a reassuring statement from Claude Jodoin on May 2, 1958: "There are within the CLC a number of affiliated unions consisting exclusively of government employees. The Congress recognizes that these unions must maintain . . . a position of strict neutrality. It was not anticipated that this position would be changed by the Congress decision nor would the Congress want to have this happen." Such assurances failed to satisfy some civil servants' associations. The Alberta Civil Servants' Association strenuously opposed endorsement of the new party by the Alberta Federation of Labour at the latter's 1959 convention, and reacted to the endorsement by disaffiliating from the federation

[21]*CLC Political Education Information* (Booklet no. 4, Oct. 1959), p. 137.
[22]Samuel Beer, *British Politics in the Collectivist Age* (New York, 1965), p. 14.

and the CLC.[23] Other civil servants' associations which disaffiliated from the CLC because of its involvement in partisan politics were the Newfoundland Government Employees' Association and the National Unemployment Insurance Commission Employees' Association.

The issue of government relations was regularly cited—though not so often as the issue of "individual liberty" and the provisions of international constitutions—by unconverted non-partisans throughout the labour movement. President Herb Barker of the Hamilton Municipal Employees' Association declared: "On city council we have to deal with people in all parties. We have found good friends both among Liberals and Conservatives. They have never let politics interfere with their dealings with us and we feel we should do the same." He announced that his local was disaffiliating from the OFL.[24] The *Western Construction Tradesman* (Nov. 1961) insisted that "our members are dependent for their livelihood on all political parties who form governments in the various provinces." At the 1960 Convention of the UMW District 26, an exchange between two delegates nicely encapsuled the arguments on both sides of the government relations issue:

Delegate MacDonald: . . . You are going to the government to keep Caledonia [mine] open and you are here pledging yourself to the CCF. Delegate Grant: If we had the right party, Caledonia wouldn't close.[25]

There is no doubt that for some unions the need to avoid antagonizing old party officeholders is so pressing that partisan political action on any significant scale may be impossible. William Mahoney felt[26] that Frank Hall's Brotherhood of Railway Clerks and the other non-operating railway unions fell into this category. So too would public employees' unions, young unions still in the early stages of organization, and the unions of Joey Smallwood's Newfoundland.

Newfoundland became Canada's tenth province in 1949. Since then

---

[23]*Toronto Daily Star*, Nov. 9, 1959.

[24]*Hamilton Spectator*, Jan. 9, 1961. The Hamilton local is a local of NUPE, a former TLC affiliate. The national union left the matter of political action "entirely to its locals." The former CCL union in the same jurisdictional area, NUPSE, endorsed the new party and encouraged its locals to affiliate. The Hamilton local's attitude was not representative of the general feeling in NUPE. Several NUPE locals adopted the OFL's Statement of Support; six NUPE and eleven NUPSE locals were affiliated to the NDP as of April 1962. In 1965 the two unions merged to form the Canadian Union of Public Employees (CUPE).

[25]UMW-26 Convention Proceedings (1960), p. 18. The convention adopted the following resolution: ". . . Whatever name the new party is [sic] if it follows the pattern set by the CCF . . . we pledge ourselves to it. . . ."

[26]Interview, Jan. 9, 1963.

it has been ruled with an iron hand by Liberal Premier "Joey" Small-wood, who had been in his youth a socialist who organized unions and contributed articles to the *New Leader*.[27] Until 1949 Smallwood's rela-tions with the provincial labour leaders had been quite friendly. A prolonged and bitter strike of the IWA changed the situation overnight. Smallwood's reaction to the strike was to use RCMP forces (stationed in Newfoundland for service as provincial police) as strike-breakers, and to enact extremely restrictive labour laws which, among other things, outlawed the IWA in Newfoundland. The legislation was condemned by the Liberal and Conservative press[28] in Canada and by the ILO.[29]

For Smallwood, any union and any union leader supporting the IWA became an enemy. The CLC and the Newfoundland Federation of Labour supported the IWA. The 1958 convention of the NFL had not been able to reach a decision on political action. The 1959 Convention reacted (July 20–24) to Smallwood's treatment of the IWA by adopting the following resolutions:

Whereas the policy of the Federation throughout its history . . . has been one of political neutrality, and whereas a continuance of this policy under normal circumstances might well be in its best interests, the fact still remains that organized labour is being attacked viciously. . . . Therefore be it resolved that this federation give its full support to the political action policy . . . of the CLC.[30]

The NFL, with the assistance of the CLC, set up a Newfoundland Democratic party (incorporating the CCF's skeleton organization in Newfoundland) to contest the provincial election of August 1959. The

[27]Before Confederation he assured M. J. Coldwell that Newfoundland would be excellent vote-hunting territory for the CCF. Coldwell interview, March 28, 1962.

[28]But not by Liberal politicians in other provinces. At a Liberal Study Con-ference at Queen's University in September, 1960, William Mahoney rejected suggestions that labour would be "better served" by the Liberals than by the socialists. Mahoney told the Conference that labour could not support a party which officially tolerated the Smallwood legislation. Instead of repudiating Small-wood, said Mahoney, "we had the disgusting spectacle of an influential spokesman of the [federal] party . . . Mr. J. W. Pickersgill [MP for Bonavista-Twillingsgate, Newfoundland], praising this petty tyrant Smallwood as a great Canadian." Pickersgill, in the audience, rose to reaffirm his support of Smallwood's action. But Mr. Paul Martin "anxiously reassured Mr. Mahoney in private that he and many other Liberals disassociate themselves from Mr. Pickersgill's position." In a cohesive party, the only permissible deviation from the party line, which in this case dictated "no comment," is anxious private reassurance. As a result Liberals in every part of Canada had their images tarnished a bit. *Canadian Labour*, Oct. 1960.

[29]*Ibid.*, Nov. 1962.

[30]*CLC Political Education Information* (Booklet no. 5, March 1960), p. 10.

CCF had never before contested a provincial election in Newfoundland. In 1959 the Newfoundland Democratic party polled over 10 per cent of the vote and came second in seven ridings.[31]

The NFL had declared war on Smallwood. Smallwood reacted by intimating that labour leaders who supported the IWA, the NFL, and the CLC could not expect any tolerant interpretation of the new labour legislation in cases involving their own unions. He terminated official relations between the government and the NFL, and denounced its president, Larry Daley (a Teamster), as an "agent of Hoffa."[32]

One immediate result of Smallwood's intimidation tactics was the disaffiliation from the CLC and the NFL of the Newfoundland Government Employees' Association. Another was the birth in the provincial labour movement as a whole of what might be termed a "copperhead" movement, pressing for the restoration of friendly relations with the government. In 1960 the copperheads temporarily gained control of the NFL.

The expulsion of the Teamsters from the CLC in June 1960, made necessary the resignation of Larry Daley as NFL president. He was replaced on June 2, 1960, by the secretary treasurer, Steve Neary. Neary had been a Democratic candidate in the provincial election, but in his new position he became a copperhead overnight. He arranged a meeting with Smallwood "to talk peace and to discuss amendments to labour laws. . . . Obviously pleased with the new state of affairs, the government obliged by accepting many labour-proposed changes."[33] Neary then repudiated the previous NFL convention's decision on political action. The federation would return to its traditional political neutrality: "Now that we are on friendly terms with the government we should stay that way."[34]

On June 16 Neary received a wire from Claude Jodoin "ordering him to hold an executive meeting and suggesting that the new policy be dropped." On the same day Neary resigned as president (but not as secretary treasurer). His resignation, he said, was a protest against the "interference" of Jodoin, aided and abetted by one of the federation's four vice-presidents, CCFer Esau Thoms. Neary warned that if "the policy which I refuse to follow" were carried out, the result would be the "liquidation of the Newfoundland Federation of Labour."[35]

Neary's resignation was only a gesture. He referred the election of a new president to the four vice-presidents, three of whom voted to re-elect

[31]St. John's Daily News, Aug. 21, 1959.
[32]St. John's Evening Telegram, July 11, 1960.
[33]Ibid.   [34]Ibid., June 9, 1960.   [35]Ibid., June 17, 1960.

him. The dissenter was Esau Thoms. The reinstated president announced that at the next NFL convention—July 11—he would recommend that the federation disassociate itself from the Newfoundland Democratic party.[36]

The convention met, with CLC Vice-President William Dodge and Smallwood's Minister of Labour, Charles Ballam, as interested observers. Ballam was disappointed. Dodge and H. Landon Ladd of the IWA urged the delegates to uphold CLC policy; the delegates responded by defeating Neary and his three vice-presidents, electing Thoms to the presidency and four Thoms supporters to the remaining executive posts, and declaring support of the Newfoundland Democratic party and of the CLC's political policy.[37]

Smallwood lowered the flag of truce and the state of war was resumed. The NFL was not "liquidated," but from July 1960 the government of Newfoundland refused to recognize the NFL as the representative of Newfoundland labour or to receive any communication from it. Smallwood encouraged Newfoundland unions to approach him directly rather than work through the federation. The CLC journal reported that many unions "succumbed to Smallwood's blandishments. . . . the function and authority of the Federation continues to be eroded." The Federation endorsed the NDP, but only a handful of the province's unionists affiliated. Smallwood had warned that unions which support the NDP "are trying to take over the government, and will be treated as enemies."[38]

4. "SUCCESS PSYCHOLOGY"

Aside from Claude Jodoin, the best-known labour leader at the time of the founding of the NDP was Frank Hall, Canadian executive assistant to the grand president of the Brotherhood of Railway Clerks, and a general vice-president of the CLC. Before the merger of the labour congresses, Hall's public image was that of a practical business unionist. He was a firm supporter of the non-partisan policy of the TLC, and though he himself was never in any way active in politics, he was known to have strong Liberal sympathies and close and friendly relations with prominent Liberal politicians.

[36]*Newfoundland Herald*, July 3, 1960.
[37]*St. John's Evening Telegram*, July 15, 1960. Neary later became a Liberal member of the Newfoundland legislature.
[38]Ed Finn, Jr., "Newfoundland Curbs Unions," *Canadian Labour*, Nov. 1962.

During the merger negotiations, Hall was a member of the moderate group of TLC leaders. At the merger convention he was the only TLC executive member who spoke on the political resolution. He praised the resolution as a wise compromise: "The resolution . . . disposes in a very adept way of a problem which might very well have disturbed the equanimity of this newly founded body. . . . This is a question on which there is plenty of room for discussion and difference of opinion, and it is not a question to be decided . . . at the ultimate in this Convention." Hall implied, somewhat subtly, that the ultimate decision would be in favour of the CCF. He compared the CCL and TLC to a young married couple who disagree about politics. If they argue about politics during the first few months of their marriage, they will end up seeking "a divorce on the grounds of incompatibility." If they avoid arguments in the early stages, "maybe in four or five years they are both of them voting CCF; and in fifty years they will be celebrating their golden wedding anniversary."

Hall also implied, much less subtly, that his own political position was no longer non-partisan:

It has been said that the question of how a man or woman should vote is one of individual conviction and individual conscience. To me, that is, however, today, only partly a sound idea. . . . Sam Gompers . . . brought forward the idea that we should vote for our friends and defeat our enemies. . . . But it is increasingly difficult, after you have elected these people, to tell who are your friends. After they get in there, they are not your friends any longer. I say to you, Brother President, my conscience is in a state of torment at this particular time. We had a strike on the railways in 1950. . . . Members of the [Liberal] Government voted in division against the constituencies from which they came, railway constituencies. I say that is a situation that has to be corrected, and I say, if there is to be freedom of conscience on the part of the voters, there must also be freedom of conscience on the part of the members of Parliament who must be free to speak for their constituencies.[39]

The proceedings of the 1958 CLC convention contain no comment by Hall on the new party resolution. The Canadian Press reported that he would be a leading opponent of the new party movement. But Frank Hall became a member of the National Committee for the New Party. He was not an active member, attended few meetings, and generally remained in the background of the new party development. He made no public statements in favour of the party.

[39]CLC Convention Proceedings (1956), p. 52.

On May 13, 1959, the Toronto *Globe and Mail* carried a story headlined "Hall against CLC-Backed Labor Party." At the international convention of the BRC he "for the first time publicly placed himself on record against the CLC's efforts to create a new . . . party." A Canadian delegate had proposed a constitutional amendment to permit Canadian lodges to participate in partisan politics. The Canadian delegates had defeated the proposal by a vote of sixty-three to fifteen with nine abstentions, and this decision had been upheld by the full convention. Among those speaking against the amendment was Frank Hall. He "suggested labor would lose more than it would gain by associating with a specific political party at this time. . . . He had no great enthusiasm for the projected party, not because he lacked sympathy with the efforts of working people and intellectuals to form their own party, but because such a party had no political future for years."

What happened? Perhaps Hall *was* feeling new qualms about his commitment to political action. Or perhaps his stand at the BRC convention was dictated by the internal situation in his Canadian union, or in the international. Whatever the reasons, the *Globe and Mail* was wrong; Hall had opposed amendment of the BRC constitution, not the establishment of the new party. After the convention, he neither did nor said anything which could be construed as opposition to the new party. He remained a member of the NCNP. At the 1960 CLC convention, he refused an invitation from the small non-partisan opposition to act as their spokesman.[40] He was present as a NCNP delegate to the new party's founding convention: he said nothing but he was there, on the platform.

From that time onward there was not so much as a whisper from Hall—in public—on any political question. He was so silent that in October 1962 *Canada Month*, a national right-wing magazine, in an article entitled "Frank Hall—Canada's Grand Old Railway Fighter," could insist that he was an opponent of the new party. He was quoted as saying:

"Representatives of organized labor should keep their skirts clean of politics. They have to do business with all governments, whatever their political complexion may be." . . . Even if Hall did want to see the unions joined to a political party he would not choose the socialists. He says: "I am a free enterprise man. . . . I don't see anything better than the basic economic system we have now."

But in March 1961 Douglas Fisher had had "unimpeachable word that

[40]Knowles interview, March 27, 1962; Mahoney interview, Jan. 9, 1963.

Frank Hall . . . has come over, forsaking his Liberal ties."[41] And half a year before the *Canada Month* article appeared, Hall quietly wrote to all BRC lodges in the Winnipeg area, asking them to support an NDP candidate and hinting that the BRC constitution would soon be amended[42]:

> As you know the Constitution of our Brotherhood forbids association of the lodges with any political party. This is no doubt a subject which will be dealt with at the Brotherhood's convention to be held next year. However, Brother Stanley Knowles is as you know a candidate for one of the Winnipeg constituencies and the purposes of this letter is to solicit support for him. . . . I hope that those of you who may be in his constituency will do everything they can to support his candidature.[43]

The authenticity of the *Canada Month* quotation is obviously extremely doubtful.

Knowledgeable people in the NDP and in the labour movement had two explanations for Hall's conversion to political action: his disillusionment with Liberal "friends of labour" and his strong belief in solidarity within the labour movement. According to David Lewis, Hall became disillusioned with the Liberals after the Second World War. The Liberal government, supported by "friends" of railway labour on the Liberal backbenches, twice enacted legislation forbidding impending railway strikes. Hall's disillusionment was encouraged by Lewis, who had as a labour lawyer become friendly with him. Hall began to notice that "the only ones who did anything for labour were socialists." By the time of the merger negotiations, his views on political action had, as he hinted at the merger convention, undergone a drastic transformation. He was personally in favour of political action in the merged congress. He supported the new party proposal, and Lewis is "convinced" that he voted for the NDP in the 1962 federal election.[44]

According to George Home and William Mahoney, Hall supported Congress policy because it was Congress policy. The majority decided to take political action, and it was the duty of the CLC officer either to "go along" with the majority's decision or to resign.[45]

There is no doubt that the labour movement's strong emphasis on solidarity has played an important part—both in the old CCL and in the new CLC—in neutralizing non-partisan opposition to Congress

[41]From a letter to GH, March 13, 1961.
[42]According to Knowles (interview, March 27, 1962), Hall had promised to seek an amendment, but in August 1966 the BRC constitution was still unamended.
[43]April 18, 1962, CLC-PEC files.
[44]Lewis interview, Jan. 15, 1963.
[45]Interviews with Home, March 28, 1962, and Mahoney, Jan. 9, 1963.

political policy. At a Political Education Conference in Vancouver in 1960, George Home declared:

This is an accepted fact in Canada, that there is going to be a new party. The two . . . groups . . . have made their decision and therefore any section of our movement that attempts to speak out against this decision is speaking out against national policy. There is no compulsion. No union or group of unions have to go along, but I think they should have the respect and the decency to recognize national policy.[46]

This was the approach taken by CLC representatives with incorrigible non-partisans and old party supporters in the craft unions: "We know we can't convert you personally—but the Congress has a policy; while you and your union need not actively *support* the NDP, you should 'go along' with Congress policy; you should do nothing to undermine it." "Congress policy" was one of the main reasons given by Percy Bengough for his favourable attitude to the NDP.[47] Probably the fact that the majority of the merged congress were in favour of political action played some part in Hall's abandonment of non-partisanship. Both his belief in solidarity and his "practicality" would have prevented him from opposing political action.

Though Hall supported the NDP, his support was minimal. He studiously abstained from close involvement in political action. If his support had been withdrawn and replaced by mere neutrality, no one outside the top leadership of the CLC and NDP would have perceived the change. Two explanations are suggested: William Mahoney argues[48] that the railway unions for which Hall speaks are so dependent on the federal government in the area of collective bargaining that extreme caution is necessary in the area of political action. If Hall or his union were in the forefront of political action, the efficiency of the union as an economic organization would be seriously impaired.

David Lewis and Jack Weldon (a New Democratic economist who does work for Hall's organization) believe that the main reason for Hall's caution was his scepticism about the NDP's electoral prospects. In Weldon's words, Hall "is interested in a *successful* NDP," that is, in an NDP which appears to have a real chance of becoming a major party. Both Weldon and Lewis suggest that Hall would not become publicly active in support of the NDP until it elects forty or so MPs.[49]

What Lewis and other socialist intellectuals call labour's "success

[46]Minutes of Political Education Conference, Vancouver, Oct. 23, 1960, BCFL files.
[47]Interviews with Home, March 20, 1963, and Bengough, Sept. 24, 1962.
[48]Interview, Jan. 9, 1963.
[49]Interviews with Weldon, April 18, 1962, and Lewis, Jan. 15, 1963.

psychology" has always been a brake on political action in the Canadian labour movement. It was a factor in the TLC's abandonment of political action after the First World War, and in its reluctance to support the CCF in later years. Percy Bengough's present favourable attitude to the NDP is qualified primarily by doubt about its prospects. Even the CCL became politically active only *after* the CCF had begun its rapid ascent in the early forties; the CCF's slow decline after the Second World War finally led to labour demands for a new party which would attract new support and become a major party. Unionists are "practical," even CCF unionists. In the absence of CCF victories, the CCF unionist is reluctant to increase his investment in the party, and the non-CCF unionist is unwilling to make the initial investment. Labour support is dependent on party victories. Party victories are dependent on labour support. Labour's "success psychology" helps to keep the party unsuccessful.

Throughout Canada, former TLC unions are withholding active support from the NDP, marking time, waiting to see "how it will do"—how many *other* unions will support it and how many votes it will get: The international leadership of the Distillery Workers' union (DRWAW), for example, has enunciated a policy of "watchful waiting with regard to the NDP." For the present, no Canadian local will be permitted to affiliate. "The key to the degree of future . . . participation in the NDP . . . would be the number of trade unions participating actively in its affairs."[50] The *British Columbia Typographical Bulletin* (July 1961) described the position of the ITU as "wait and see." And the director of OFL-PAC asked the NDP federal secretary to send him a list of affiliated locals, since unaffiliated locals "want to be assured that the drive for affiliation is meeting with some success" before they themselves take the step.[51]

Frank Hall's attitude to the NDP is no doubt representative of that of the bulk of the former TLC leaders and not a few of the former CCL leaders. They either do not oppose it or give it minimal support. They are waiting for success.

[50]*DRWAW Journal*, Nov. 1961.
[51]Lazarus to Hamilton, Nov. 14, 1961, NDP files.

8. *The Future of Labour in Politics*

1. UNION-PARTY RELATIONS

The relationship between unions supporting the NDP and the NDP organization itself will probably continue to be quite similar to that which existed between the CCL unions and the CCF. Many of the problems involved in that relationship will continue to exist. The "egghead" constituency activists and the "practical" unionists will find it difficult to work together.[1] Despite the increased influence of labour in the party as a whole, there will be localities in which the unions will feel deprived of their appropriate share of influence, and in these localities there may be talk of "independent labour" candidates. Among the non-labour elements of the party, the suspicion of unions and the fear of trade union "domination" will probably not disappear.

The close articulation of union and party organizations will give rise to certain difficult situations. Even in the past, the fact that the leadership and membership groups of CCF organizations and union organizations in many cases overlapped or interlocked resulted in occasional friction within and between the two organizations.[2] This problem, like the problem of tension between unionists and non-unionists, is not one which can be solved once and for all; it is something that must be "lived with." Since labour is present in greater numbers in the new party structure, the problem is likely to be somewhat more serious than it was in

[1]In the federal election of 1962, the BCFL's policy was to funnel election workers to NDP constituency organizations rather than set up separate PEC election organizations. After the election the BCFL sent a memorandum to unionists who were active in the campaign, enquiring whether "the constituency associations [were] able to absorb and effectively use people from the trade unions? . . . If not, what suggestions do you have? Should we . . . work at a constituency level and try to build a strong constituency organization or should we try to build an organization *within our membership* that would be available to work under the direction of trade unionists?" (Jim McNevin to all Unionists who Attended Meetings re Recent Federal Campaign, July 5, 1962, BCFL files.) George Home believes that the differing "psychologies" of unionists and non-unionists will always tend to prevent complete integration of party and union election work. Union political activists are *union* political activists. They would much sooner do political work within the union organization than be sent out to work with the "old ladies" in the constituency association. Interview, May 30, 1962.
[2]See above, pp. 142–3.

the CCF; but there is a silver lining. George Home points out that the top leadership positions in the labour movement are now held by relatively young people, who are not likely to relinquish their positions for years to come. There is no "room at the top." Home hopes that some of the still younger generation of secondary leaders, who will eventually become frustrated with the lack of upward mobility within the union movement, will be diverted from rebellion by the opportunities for advancement available within the NDP. Instead of threatening the established union leaders, they will assume leadership roles within the party.[3] The younger generation of labour leaders will thus provide a reservoir of activists and candidates for the NDP; and the NDP will provide a safety valve for discontent within the union movement. The minimal turnover at the top will not cause dissatisfaction down below, for the youngsters will be kept warm and contented in political activity until they are ready to be co-opted into union leadership positions. Viewed from this very special angle, labour political activity may be a mechanism which helps to ensure an orderly circulation of élites within the labour movement.

Union-party relations will differ from those of the past most significantly in that many more local unions will be directly affiliated to the NDP than were ever affiliated to the CCF. This may or may not have the intended consequence of increasing the NDP's share of the labour vote by habituating loyal unionists to think of the NDP as *their* party, but it will certainly mean a larger and more stable financial base for the party. 250,000 affiliated members paying 60 cents per capita will provide a guaranteed annual income of $150,000. This is a far cry from the CCF's annual budget of thirty or forty thousand dollars. Affiliation will also mean that representatives of unions will, *as such*, play a much more significant role in the provincial and federal conventions of the NDP than was ever the case in the CCF. Of the 775 delegates to the 1963 federal convention, 188—about a quarter—represented affiliated locals and central labour bodies.[4] At the 1965 convention, 228 of the 825 delegates represented labour organizations.

The NDP's affiliated-union section will probably remain, for some

[3]Interview with Home, May 30, 1962.

[4]Affiliated locals—147 delegates; central labour bodies—41 delegates. Central labour councils and provincial federations are not eligible for affiliation, but may be "recognized" by the federal council and granted representation at federal conventions on the following basis: one delegate from each "recognized" central local body, two delegates from each "recognized" central national or provincial body. NDP Convention Proceedings, 1963, p. 47. (Article 5, section 5 of the NDP federal constitution).

time to come, primarily an affiliated *industrial* union section. By August 16, 1966, 678 locals with 241,977 members (about 20 per of the membership of the CLC) were affiliated to the ten provincial parties. 591 locals with 220,986 members were from former CCL unions. Only 50 locals with 16,435 members were from unions formerly affiliated to the TLC or independent. Thus, over 90 per cent of the affiliated-union section of the NDP is of CCL origin. The predominance of the Steel, Auto, Packinghouse, and Woodworkers unions is particularly striking: these four unions provide about 74 per cent (177,028) of the unionists affiliated to the NDP. Steel and Auto alone provide about 56 per cent (142,465).[5]

Of Canada's thirty-five major unions—those with memberships of ten thousand or more—there are seven which have affiliated more than a third of their membership to the NDP. These are: Auto 89 per cent, Packinghouse 72 per cent, Steel 66 per cent, Retail-Wholesale 53 per cent, Rubber Workers 53 per cent, Textile Workers 40 per cent, Woodworkers 37 per cent.[6] All seven are former CCL unions. The percentages for the other major CCL unions are: ACWA 19 per cent, CBRT 15 per cent, IUE 10 per cent, OCAW 6 per cent. Only one major TLC union—the Plumbers' union—has affiliated a significant portion (20 per cent) of its membership to the NDP. Only two others—the IAM and the Chemical Workers (6 per cent each) have affiliated more than 5 per cent of their members.

The percentage of a union's membership which is affiliated to the NDP is only one index of the degree of that union's support of the NDP. Other indices are political education activity, election work, cash donations, votes. The fact that Steel, for example, has affiliated (proportionately) four times as many members as the CBRT does not necessarily mean that it is four times more active in support of the NDP than the CBRT. There are a myriad of structural, situational, and accidental factors which may account for the low degree of affiliation in one union compared to another.[7] Nevertheless, broadly speaking, the affiliation situation reflects the general political situation in the sense that support of the NDP comes almost entirely from the industrial unions and in very large part from the Steel and Auto unions.

[5]Local Unions Affiliated to the NDP as of August 16, 1966, CLC-PEC files.
[6]All percentages are approximate.
[7]E.g., if the union is highly centralized and consists of a small number of huge locals, a pro-NDP leadership will relatively easily secure affiliation of a high proportion of the locals. If the union is very decentralized and consists of a large number of small locals, it will be much more difficult to obtain a large number of affiliations.

TABLE I

LOCALS AFFILIATED TO THE NDP AS OF AUGUST 31, 1966

Union	No. of locals affiliated, August 1966	Total no. of locals, 1965	No. of members affiliated August 1966	Total membership 1965
Former CCL Unions				
UAW	33	69	69,184	77,515
Brewery Workers	8	58	1,817	7,000
CBRT & GW	26	207	5,733	32,148
ACWA	11	41	2,947	16,500
Communication Workers	1	10	478	3,168
IUE	6	59	1,136	10,000
Glass and Ceramic Workers	6	30	1,919	5,860
OCAW	6	65	761	12,964
UPWA	135	179	18,254	25,000
RWDSU	18	54	9,431	17,000
URWA	20	59	7,867	13,950
USWA	247	496	73,281	110,000
TWUA	59	85	8,671	19,000
IWA	11	54	16,309	43,553
UMW-26 (ind.)	4	25	3,198	7,979
	591		220,986	
Former TLC and other unions				
Bakery & Confectionery	2	26	1,085	8,370
Bookbinders	1	18	600	3,309
Brick and Clay	1	3	182	298
Bricklayers	1	52	750	5,712
Bro. Railway Carmen	3	94	375	17,429
Carpenters	1	230	71	63,960
Cement, Lime & Gypsum	1	34	133	4,522
Chemical Workers	5	94	949	15,100
Fire Fighters	2	132	62	12,680
Grain Millers	1	8	700	1,032
Laborers & Hod Carriers	1	39	50	24,297
Locomotive Firemen & Enginemen	3	96	159	6,918
IAM	11	155	2,674	41,243
Meat Cutters	2	34	857	9,471
Moulders	2	35	942	6,837
OPEIU	3	53	388	6,956
Painters & Decorators	1	61	250	7,944
Plumbers & Pipe Fitters	2	73	4,000	19,603
Pulp & Sulphite	1	116	650	36,942
IATSE	1	54	27	2,838
Amalgamated Transit	1	32	170	12,010
ITU	1	59	50	7,307
Upholsterers	2	12	813	4,156
Teamsters (ind)	1	41	498	42,382
	50		16,435	

TABLE I (concluded)

Union	No. of locals affiliated August 1966	Total no. of locals, 1965	No. of members affiliated August 1966	Total membership 1965
CUPE (merger of NUPSE-CCL and NUPE-TLC)	22	522	3,170	84,847
Directly chartered locals	15	162	1,386	19,100
	678		241,977	

SOURCE: CLC-PEC files, and Department of Labour, Canada, *Labour Organizations in Canada* (Ottawa, 1965).

TABLE II

BREAKDOWN BY PROVINCE OF LOCALS AFFILIATED TO NDP, AUGUST 31, 1966

Province	No. of locals affiliated	Affiliated membership
British Columbia	29	20,021
Alberta	42	6,314
Saskatchewan	42	3,558
Manitoba	32	6,274
Ontario	445	187,111
Quebec	46	9,632
New Brunswick	14	1,156
Nova Scotia	26	7,600
PEI	2	326
Newfoundland	1	15
	679*	242,007*

*Includes affiliation of Jewish Labour Bund with 30 members.

TABLE III

PERFORMANCE OF THE CCF AND NDP IN FEDERAL ELECTIONS, 1935–1965

	1935			1940		
	Popular vote		Seats won	Popular vote		Seats won
	n	%		n	%	
British Columbia	97,015	34	3	103,181	28	1
Ontario	127,927	8	0	61,166	4	0
Saskatchewan	73,505	21	2	106,267	29	5
Canada	391,185	8.9	7	393,230	8.8	8

TABLE III (concluded)

	1945			1949		
	Popular vote		Seats won	Popular vote		Seats won
	n	%		*n*	%	
British Columbia	125,945	29	4	145,442	31	3
Ontario	260,502	14	0	306,551	15	1
Saskatchewan	167,233	44	18	152,399	41	5
Canada	816,259	15.6	28	782,410	13.4	13

	1953			1957		
	Popular vote		Seats won	Popular vote		Seats won
	n	%		*n*	%	
British Columbia	125,487	27	7	131,873	22	7
Ontario	212,224	11	1	274,069	12	3
Saskatchewan	156,406	44	11	140,293	36	10
Canada	636,310	11.3	23	707,659	10.7	25

	1958			1962		
	Popular vote		Seats won	Popular vote		Seats won
	n	%		*n*	%	
British Columbia	153,432	24.8	4	212,997	31	10
Ontario	252,943	10.1	3	456,275	17	6
Saskatchewan	112,800	28.3	1	93,374	22	0
Canada	680,814	9.4	8	1,037,531	13.5	19

	1963			1965		
	Popular vote		Seats won	Popular vote		Seats won
	n	%		*n*	%	
British Columbia	218,015	30.6	9	239,086	32.9	9
Ontario	442,485	16	6	594,267	21.7	9
Saskatchewan	74,889	18.4	0	104,619	26	0
Canada	1,037,950	13.2	17	1,381,047	17.9	21

SOURCE: 1935–57, from Howard Scarrow, *Canada Votes*; 1958–65, from *Political Education Information*, no. 13 (Sept. 1966), pp. 55–8.

The political education committees of the CLC and its affiliates continue to be the most important vehicle of labour support for the NDP. A union may make significant contributions to the NDP through PEC, whether or not a significant portion of that union's membership is actually affiliated to the party. George Home estimates that the Canadian labour movement contributed about $400,000 (about $150,000 from national and international unions, about $150,000 from local bodies, and about $100,000 in "contributions in kind") to the NDP's 1965 election campaign.[8] There is no doubt that a substantial portion of this support came from unionists unaffiliated to the NDP. Affiliation itself can be viewed as one of the products of PEC activity, for one of the main tasks of PEC is to persuade unions to affiliate; another is to persuade affiliated members to become individual members of the party.[9]

2. A "LABOUR PARTY"?

The first three tests of the electoral strength of the NDP—the federal elections of June 1962, April 1963, and November 1965—indicated that the NDP had lost a significant portion of the CCF's support among Saskatchewan farmers, and that this loss had only just been compensated for by increased support from industrial Ontario and British Columbia. The performance of the NDP in those three elections was significantly better than that of the CCF in terms of popular vote, but not in terms of seats in the House of Commons.

The most striking difference between the CCF and the NDP parliamentary groups was the absence of Saskatchewan representatives in the latter. Until 1957 one-third to two-thirds of the federal caucus was

[8]Home interview, Jan. 3, 1967.

[9]Ideally, affiliate membership should be a halfway house between non-membership and full membership in the party. The Ontario NDP has attempted to encourage the involvement of affiliated members in the work of the party by providing that members of affiliated locals may attend and vote at constituency meetings and nominating conventions on a basis of full equality with individual members, except in the case of election of constituency delegates to provincial and federal conventions. (Resolution on participation by affiliated members, Constitution of the New Democratic Party of Ontario, 1963, pp. 21–3). The Ontario party has thus abolished much of the distinction between individual and affiliated membership on the constituency level. Any affiliated member who desires may enjoy almost all the rights of individual membership at a cut rate. The idea is to entice affiliated members into constituency meetings, to involve them in constituency activities, and when they are "ripe," to sell them individual memberships. Other provincial parties, adhering to CCF tradition, permit only *representation* of affiliated locals at nominating conventions.

elected in Saskatchewan (in 1953, eleven out of twenty-three; in 1957 ten out of twenty-five). In 1958, the year of the Diefenbaker landslide, only one CCFer was elected in Saskatchewan. He was Hazen Argue, who later defected to the Liberal party in order to get away from "labour domination." In 1962, 1963, and 1965 Saskatchewan did not elect a single New Democrat. Almost every single member of the 1962, 1963, and 1965 parliamentary groups was a representative either of an urban or of an extractive-industry constituency.[10]

The decline of the socialist party in Saskatchewan cannot be ascribed solely to dissatisfaction with the change from CCF to NDP, because the decline began before that change. In 1953 the CCF got 44 per cent of the vote in Saskatchewan; in 1958, only 28 per cent.[11] The main reasons for the decline appear to be, first and foremost, the Diefenbaker revolution in the Conservative party, which transformed it from the party mainly of Ontario business to the party mainly of the prairie farmer, and second, the long incumbency and consequent aging of the CCF provincial regime. The effect of the transformation of the CCF into the NDP was to *accelerate* the decline of the party in Saskatchewan. Whatever Hazen Argue's "true" motives were, his public explanation of his defection is significant as a reflection of the attitude of an increasing number of Saskatchewan farmers to the NDP: "The NDP now has become the tool of a small labour clique and is effectively under their domination and control. . . . Control of the NDP . . . rests with three men—the leaders of the UPWA, the USWA, and the UAW. [He advised farmers to avoid the NDP] like the plague."[12]

The purpose of the change from CCF to NDP was to increase labour's involvement and support and to "broaden the base" of the party in the general public. The trouble is that these purposes may not be easily compatible. While the NDP was being formed in Canada, there was increasing discussion in Britain of the disadvantages of the close association of the Labour party with the unions in view of the numerical decline of the working class and the rise of the new white-collar middle class:

The closeness of the unions and the Labour Party in the public mind have injured the latter in the last few years. . . . The . . . party suffers in the

---

[10]In 1965 the rural riding of Springfield, Manitoba, elected a New Democrat, Ed Schreyer.

[11]An even more startling statistic: the percentage of the national CCF-NDP vote contributed by Saskatchewan has declined from about 24 per cent in 1953 to about 16 per cent in 1958 to a mere 7 per cent in 1965.

[12]*Montreal Star*, Feb. 20, 1962.

public's eye from being tied too closely to the trade unions—both directly in its decision making and indirectly through being associated with some of the more unpopular facets of trade unionism. . . . Looking ahead, a loosening of the present links seems inevitable. . . . the party still depends, to a larger degree than is healthy in a country with a fast growing bourgeoisie, on the manual workers' vote.[13]

If it is true that in Britain, with its heavily unionized, class-conscious, and politically disciplined working class, the powerful socialist party is harmed by its close links with the unions, what must one say of Canada, where the white-collar class is growing just as rapidly, the working class is relatively smaller and less class-conscious, only one third of it consists of unionists, and only one quarter of these vote for a minor socialist party?[14] The formation of the NDP would appear to be a serious mistake. On the other hand, this analysis ignores one iron fact: a party of the left in any developed country in the West must of necessity depend for funds on the labour movement and must be at least partly controlled by trade unions. A socialist party may be harmed, when unions are unpopular, by its close association with them in the public mind. But without them it cannot exist, it has no basis for existence. The solution to the problem, in Britain and in Canada, lies not in the loosening of union-party links, but in the improvement of the image of the unions. As David Marquand points out in relation to the British problem:

The future of the Left in this country will depend less on what the Labour Party does than on what the unions do. The Labour Party's links with the unions are, at present, its greatest strength and at the same time its greatest weakness. It is sometimes said that the moral is that the Labour Party should abandon its working class image. That is nonsense, for it cannot do so without destroying itself altogether. What can happen, however, is for the unions to change their own image independently of the Labour Party. . . . The fact is that the unions need the support of the new "white collar" public just as much as the Labour Party does.[15]

Increased union support and increased middle-class support will become compatible goals for the NDP if and when the *unions* learn how to project a good image among the middle classes in general and the white-collar workers in particular. In the meantime, the NDP is doing all it can to minimize the harmful effects of its association with labour. It is

[13]George Cyriax, "Labour and the Unions," *Political Quarterly,* XXXI (July–Sept. 1960), pp. 325–32.
[14]According to the Gallup poll, 23 per cent of union members *and* the eligible members of their households voted for the NDP (as against 8 per cent of members of all other households) in the 1962 federal election. *Winnipeg Free Press,* May 1, 1963.
[15]"Has 'Lib-Lab' a Future?" *Encounter,* April 1962, p. 65.

trying to create an image not of a "labour party" but of a classless party of all "liberally minded Canadians," of "all the democratic left."

Though the NDP has substantially improved the electoral performance of the CCF in Ontario and British Columbia, the hope that it would rapidly become a major party has not been realized. During the party's formative period, its leaders hoped that it would win forty or fifty seats in its first federal election and go on from there to become the official opposition.[16] The groups of nineteen, seventeen, and twenty-one elected in 1962, 1963, and 1965 fall far short of this goal. It seems unlikely that the NDP will be able to achieve the purpose for which it was created: the rescue of the socialist party from its position as a minor party. As Duverger points out, "all Anglo-Saxon socialist parties [have had] to organize themselves on a trade union basis [because] it alone could put at their disposal sufficient strength for the 'take-off' "[17] to major party status. In 1943, it appeared for a moment that the CCF would reach Duverger's "take-off" point *without* being organized on a trade-union basis. That appearance was misleading. By the late fifties, the leading CCF unionists had convinced first themselves and then the non-unionist CCF leaders that the party could not take off unless it were reorganized on a trade union basis. The party has been reorganized. The take-off is yet to come.

One important obstacle to the take-off may be labour's own "success psychology." The CCF's deceptive pseudo-take-off in 1942–43 *preceded* the CCL's endorsement of the party. Who can say whether or not the take-off was an indispensable prerequisite for the endorsement? Today many labour leaders seem to be waiting for another take-off before they commit their unions to participation in the NDP. Union support is necessary for the take-off; but the take-off is a prerequisite for support from these unions. Their leaders want to back a winner; they want some assurance of large profits before they make their investment.

It would be unfair, however, to blame labour leaders for the NDP's failure to become a major party. The reasons for that failure are to be found elsewhere—in the past, especially in the 1940s. Even if the Canadian labour élite were unanimously and enthusiastically supporting the NDP, it would not be doing very much better, in terms of votes, than it is without such support. Voting habits are not easily changed. The NDP seems to have the near-permanent allegiance of something like 15 per cent of the electorate; the remaining 85 or so per cent seem to be rather solidly attached to the other parties. The failure of the New

[16]Memo on the New Party and the Next Election, n.d., NDP files.
[17]Maurice Duverger, *Political Parties* (London, 1955), p. 227.

party experiment indicates that nothing the socialist party *itself* does can greatly increase its strength. Unless there is a startling new development, some sort of crisis, *outside* the socialist party—a crisis severe enough to shake up Canadian voting habits, a crisis like the First World War which provided the Progressive party with its take-off, or the Second World War which provided the CCF with its pseudo-take-off— the NDP will probably not achieve major party status. Rather, it will consolidate and probably moderately strengthen its present position as a significant minor party. If an external crisis does come, and if the NDP is capable of appealing to the new mood which will be generated by the crisis, the events of the forties *may* be repeated: the party will score a few startling successes, success will breed further success, apathetic labour leaders will smell victory, craft union affiliations will quadruple, Frank Hall's successors will make speeches, money and men will pour into the party, the voters will lose their fear of "wasting" their votes—and then, perhaps, an NDP official opposition.

If there is no external crisis and no take-off, the socialist party may go through another reorganization within the next decade or two. The CCF's big disappointment came in 1945. By 1956 its leaders, especially the unionists among them, were tired of failure and looking for a "new vehicle." If the NDP does no more than tread water, there may sooner or later be talk of another "new vehicle." There is another possibility. The socialist politicians and their friends in the unions may become resigned to minor party status. It is better than nothing. For consolation, the socialists need only look southward.

Index

ACCL, *see* All-Canadian Congress of Labour

ACWA, *see* Amalgamated Clothing Workers of America

Addes, George, 109n, 114, 115

Affiliation: fails with ACCL and TLC 64–5; campaign for with CCL locals in Ontario, 70–5, in Nova Scotia, 71–3, and in Canada 74–7, leading to CCL endorsement of CCF, 70–80; collapse of this program, 80–4; CCF-TUCs and clubs established to propagate idea of, 107; rejected by UAW, 108; in BC, 118–19; fear in CCF of union domination, 140–50; "indirect," 154–7; and new party 203, 219–21, 239; and policy of international unions, 235–8; difficult in liberal society, 239–41, and with government employees' unions, 242–4; inhibited by "success psychology," 247–52; with NDP by province (1966), 254–9

AFL, *see* American Federation of Labor

AFL-CIO, 56, 213, 234, 236

Alberta: voting in 1962 federal election, 42n, 43n; early labour party in, 60; CCF in, 75, 80n, and its reaction to new party, 215–8, 223, 243–4; NDP in, 218, 257

Alberta Civil Servants' Association, 243–4

Alberta Federation of Labour, 243–4

Alford, R., quoted 41n–3n

All-Canadian Congress of Labour (ACCL), 182; founded, 63; relations with CCF, 63–6; merged to form CCL, 66, 68

Alles, A. N., 112

Alsbury, Stewart, 130, 131

Alsbury, Tom, 163

Amalgamated Clothing Workers of America (ACWA), 68, 86, 88, 92, 133n, 134n, 233n, 255, 256

Amalgamated Transit union, 256

American Federation of Labor (AFL): attitude to socialism and political action, 56, 58–63, 163n, 164, 181–3, 234–5; Committee on Political Education (COPE), 56, 234, 238

Ames, C. C., 131n

Andras, Andy, 92, 98

Archer, Doris, quoted, 27n

Argue, Hazen, 142, 158, 212, 226–7, 260

Armstrong, Myrtle M., quoted, 26n, 146–50, 162n, 171n, 189n

Bakery and Confectionary Workers' International Union of America, 231, 232, 233n, 256

Ballam, Charles, 247

Barbers' union, 233n

Barker, Herb, 244

Baron, Sam, 134

Beer, Samuel, quoted, 243

Bell, Daniel, quoted, 24n, 26–7, 28

Bengough, Percy, 103–4, 163–7, 179, 182, 183, 185, 251, 252

Bennett, R. B., 19–20, 21–2, 23, 31, 33

Bennett, W. A. C., 201

Berg, Carl, 167, 169, 179, 230

Bishop, Harding, E., 210

Bookbinders, International Brotherhood of, 233n, 256

Brannigan, Tom, 117

Brewery Workers, 134n, 233n, 256

Brewin, F. Andrew, 134, 149–50, 207

Brick and Clay union, 256

Bricklayers' union, 194, 233n, 256

British Columbia: early socialists in, 8, 26, 60–1; CCF in, 62, 80n, 81, 107, 118–31, 158–61, 189–91, 200–2, 204, 212, 214, 215, 257–8; Bill 42, 241; *see also* Co-operative Commonwealth Federation

Ross, Jack, 240
Rubber Workers, 92, 133n, 134n, 255
Rygus, Mike, 232

Salsberg, J. B., 79, 80, 86, 90n, 93, 97, 99n, 100, 102n
Saposs, David, quoted, 25
Saskatchewan, 42n, socialism in, 8, 9; CCF in, 62, 75, 80n, 81, 141–6, 257–60; reactions to new party in, 200, 215–16, 223–6
Saskatchewan Federation of Labour, 145–6, 187
Schindler, Fred, quoted, 226n, 233n
Schnitzler, William, 236
Schollie, George, 167, 232
Schreyer, Ed, 257
Schultz, Art, 65, 158
Scott, F. R., 174n; quoted, 31, 44
Sefton, Larry, 81n, 107
Shane, Bernard, 59
Sheet Metal Workers' International Association, 233n
Showler, B., 127, 128
Shipyard General Workers' Federation of BC, 85, 96, 100, 102, 118–19, 123n, 130, 233n
Shoe and Leather Workers' Organizing Committee, 72
Simonds, John F., 232
Simpson, James, 26, 58, 60
Smallwood, Joseph, 245–7
Smee, Ed, 219
Smishek, W. E., 225
Smith, Ralph, 60
Social Credit party, 46–7, 50, 99n, 201
Socialism: in North America, 3, 4, 7–9, 16–19, 22–3, 24–9; as ideology, 4–9, 16–17; Fabian, 9, 11, 24–6; Marxist, 24–9; and liberalism in US, 29–40, 54–6; and liberalism in Canada, 29–40; and US parties, 44–7; and parties in Canada, 44–57; attitudes to of TLC and AFL compared, 58–61; NDP's approach to, 206–10; see also Co-operative Commonwealth Federation, independent labourism
Socialist Labor party (US), 123
Socialist party (US), 26–7
Socialist Party—Social Democratic Federation, 35, 213
Sparham, R. D., 209

Spry, Graham, 67
Steelworkers of America, United (USWA), 67, 77, 78, 86, 87, 88, 92, 93, 94, 101, 102, 107, 115, 119, 122, 125n, 126, 127, 128, 129, 132, 133, 134, 143n, 148n, 149–50, 151, 154, 157, 158, 159, 161, 186, 194, 201, 213, 233, 234–6, 255, 256, 260
Stevens, H. H., 22
Stewart, William, 130
Stinson, Lloyd, 221
Street Railway Employees, 233n
Suall, Irwin, 213
Sullivan, J. A. "Pat," 102–6, 182
Swailes, Donovan, 138, 169, 179n, 186, 203, 210

Taft, Robert, 20, 22
Tallman, Eileen, 120–2, 126, 128
Taylor, Jack, 115, 158n
Taylor, Lawrence, 229
Teamsters, International Brotherhood of, 184n, 233n, 246, 256
Textile Workers Union of America, 133n, 233n, 255, 256
Textile Workers' Organizing Committee, 73, 147
Thayer, Harold, 163
Thomas, Norman, quoted, 39, 48
Thomas, R. J., 116, 117
Thoms, Esau, 246–7
Tipping, F. G., 219
TLC, see Trades and Labor Congress
Tobacco Workers' International Union, 233n
Toronto Daily Star, 105, 186
Toryism, as ideology, 4–9, 16–18, 21–2; "red," 22–3; in Canada, 10–23; in United States, 11–14, 18; see also Conservative party, Loyalists
Trades and Labor Congress: historical attitude to socialism and political action, 58–61, 180–1, 234–5, 243; and CCF, 58–9, 61–6, 69, 73, 76–7, 132, 162–71, 176–85, 195–7, 204, 252; and formation of CCL, 66; and Liberal government, 82, 102–6, 181–2; set up PAC, 104–5; in BC "government-labour committee," 125–8; politically active in Ontario, 132, in BC, 161; and merger with CCL, 155, 162–97; and